Language, Blacks and Gypsies:

*Languages Without a Written Tradition
and Their Role in Education*

Sylvia Erike (centre) with friends, Nira Yuval-Davis and Autar Brah

(Photograph courtesy of Nira Yuval-Davis)

LANGUAGE, BLACKS and GYPSIES

Languages Without a Written Tradition and Their Role in Education

edited by

Thomas Acton

&

Morgan Dalphinis

© The Contributors and Morgan Dalphinis 2022

All rights reserved.

Published by Morgan Dalphinis

Cover design by Reggie Freeman

Contents

Preface *Thomas Acton* _____ vii

1. LANGUAGES OF THE OPPRESSED
   Introduction _____ 3
   Standardisation and ethnic defence in emergent non-literate societies:
   The Gypsy and Caribbean cases *Ian Hancock* _____ 9
   Towards a typology of unwritten languages *Donald Kenrick* ___ 24

2. THE EMERGENCE OF LITERARY LANGUAGES
   Introduction _____ 35
   Historical, nationalistic and linguistic considerations in the formation
   of literary languages: past and current problems
   in the Balkan states *Victor A. Friedman* _____ 37
   On the writing of normative grammars for Caribbean Creole languages:
   The case of Guyanese Creole *Hubert Devonish* _____ 52
   The development of literary dialects of Romanes and the prospects
   for an international standard dialect
   Thomas Acton, Vangelis Marselos and Laszlo Szego _____ 59
   The development of literary Cypriot Greek:
   Has it any educational relevance? *Maria Roussou* _____ 71
   The United Bible Societies Romani scriptures programme
   Paul Ellingworth _____ 76

3. LANGUAGE IN SOCIETY
   Introduction _____ 83
   Language variation in Barbados *Ivy Devonish* _____ 85
   Phonological relationships within Caribbean English *J.C. Wells* ___ 106
   What is 'mother tongue'? Some problems posed by
   London Jamaican *Mark Sebba* _____ 109
   Jamaica speech: A language or a variety of language (dialect)?
   Dimela Yekwai _____ 122
   The status and prospects for Romanes in Germany
   Marion Papenbrok and Herbert Heuss _____ 125
   Shelta/Gammon in Dublin *Alice Binchy* _____ 128

4. EDUCATION AND LANGUAGE: STRATEGIES

Introduction _____ 135

Languages without a written tradition and the mother tongue movement: The Bengali/Sylheti and Cypriot/Greek debate *Hasina Nowaz and Maria Roussou* _____ 137

The status of Kachchi in Britain and India: Implications for language teaching *Safder Alladina* _____ 144

Language in communication and the teacher's role: The experience of the Caribbean Communications Project *J. Burke, Y. Collymore, H. Dale, P. Knight and E. Whittingham* _____ 152

Communication without writing: Pictorial art and the education of Gypsy children *Éva Pongrácz and Elemér Várnagy with T.A. Acton* _____ 160

Adult literacy and oral history *Jane Mace* _____ 165

5. EDUCATION AND LANGUAGE: PRACTICE AND POLITICS

Introduction _____ 171

Using Creole to teach reading in Carriacou *Ron Kephart* _____ 175

The use of Romanes in an Italian school *Jane Zatta* _____ 187

Adult literacy work with Sinti Gypsies in Bremen, West Germany *Ulrich Müller and György Szabo* _____ 212

Bilingual education among the Inga (Quechuan) people of South West Colombia *Stephen H. Levinsohn* _____ 216

The development of a multi-lingual educational policy in Sierra Leone *Freddie Jones* _____ 221

Caribbean Creole: The politics of resistance *G.L. Brandt* _____ 227

CONCLUSION: What is to be done? _____ 239

Notes on Contributors _____ 250

Preface

Thomas Acton

Sylvia Erike, whose picture appears as the frontispiece to this book, was born in 1953. Her mother was a German nurse and her father, whom she never saw, was a Nigerian student. She grew up in the down-at-heel Ladbroke Grove area of London, a Black girl with a White mother in a Black neighbourhood in a White society. 'I have no roots in this country, no roots at all,' she said.

As a teenager she found she had to learn Black English to be Black among other Black youth. She became an enthusiastic joiner, going to all the Black churches, all the Black pubs, all the leftwing political groups. She was an achiever: she went away to university then took a Master's degree and started on her PhD. Her clear analytical mind made her an inspirational speaker in the Black Women's and later, the Black Lesbian movement. She had also become an alcoholic. As her fears for her own identity overcame her, fears that all the organisations she had joined and ideologies whose discourse she so effortlessly mastered could not make her lovable for herself alone, she would go on terrible blinders, out of which she would have in agony and humiliation to pull herself back to work.

After taking her MA, she went to work for the Caribbean Communications Project, a Literacy and Educational Project in West London, and from there she went to Thames Polytechnic to work as a Research Assistant on a project on class, ethnic and gender relations. There she met Thomas Acton, and with him brought the Caribbean Communications Project and the National Gypsy Education Council together in 1982 to plan a conference on languages without a written tradition and their role in education. The first focus of the organisers was the oral languages of British Black and Gypsy populations, but soon other oppressed groups with mother-tongues submerged by powerful neighbours came into its scope. The conference was held at Thames Polytechnic in London at the end of August 1984.

Before then, however, in July 1983, Sylvia had died in a tragic accident. She was thirty years old. She was the first organiser and inspiration of the conference from which this book came.

It might be thought her alcoholism was a weakness that ought not now to be mentioned. But not to mention it would be to miss the point of her life. She lived the contradictions of being a Black woman in a racist society. Alcoholism was for her a disease which she fought, again and again, as she fought racism and sexism and linguistic prejudice. Out of truth about our own weaknesses, out of the need to challenge the myriad contradictory commonsense versions of reality which try to put us at ease with injustice and oppression, this book continues her struggle.

It has been some 18 years in the making, its papers subjected to continual leapfrogging revision, wearing out three different publishers. Fire, recession and sheer bad luck have dogged our footsteps, and many of the organisations who sponsored the original conference have fallen by the wayside, victims of the funding drought of the Thatcher and Major years.

The loyalty of our contributors, debating and criticising each others' work, sending revisions and updatings, has amazed the editors. When we started we all thought of ourselves as dissenting voices, some way out of the academic mainstream. Time has wrought its sobering work, however, and the list of authors now contains a number of well-known names, professors, heads of departments and senior professionals, as well as those who have continued in dedicated educational work with little wider recognition.

Some of the areas we identified in the early 1980s have become more mainstream concerns as we enter the third millennium. The internationalisation of the English language through the processes of colonisation, and cultural adaptation has become a specific topic within sociolinguistics (as in Pennycook 1994), which enables a contrasting focus on 'speech variations and dialects' (as in Verma 1998). It is as though the theoreticians of the standard have realised that, given certain scholarly rules, the study of the 'non-standard' only serves to throw into clear relief the standard-ness of the 'standard'. The study of Creoles and of Romani is also at last progressing beyond specialist scholarly publications to textbooks (Sebba 1997, Kyuchukov, Matras, Bakker et al. forthcoming.)

All of this perhaps makes it more vital than ever to point out that mere language awareness is not enough if we do not find and spread the skills to enable ordinary people in the homogenised Western societies to treat linguistic diversity not as a pain, but as the gift and a challenge that many smaller-scale societies uncomplicatedly find it. If grammar is to become politically important, then it is vital that educated people receive some grounding in a scientifically based descriptive linguistics before they are exposed to the moralising prejudices of traditional prescriptive grammar.

The ideal of multilingualism has made some progress in the policy of the European Union, and in some third world countries (Singh 1997, 1998) but in the United Kingdom it is still an isolated outcry in the wilderness. Hamers and Blanc (1989, pp. 192, 257) remain lonely voices in attacking the Swann Report's (1985) approach to bilingualism as a concept which is 'at best the sum of two monolingualisms'. Even one of our own contributors, Alladina, an enthusiast for multilingualism if ever there was one, had to entitle the popularisation of his work *Being Bilingual* (Alladina 1991). In our conclusion we shall present our own critique of Swann and its implementation; but we shall also argue that the self-proclaimed anti-racism of the Labour government elected in 1997 has not prevented a return to cultural deficit theories of the 'problems of ethnic minorities' in schools, and an institutional racism which complacently co-exists with its own repudiation.

Preface

If voices from the grassroots can add any strength to the faltering critique of the debilitating ignorance of the English ruling classes, then this book has its justification. We still live in a country where the question 'Why don't they all speak English?' can pose as a form of liberal anti-racism. If the white man still speaks with a forked tongue, it is perhaps because in his monolingualism, he does not realise how badly ambiguity and ambivalence usually sound in translation. It is left to the speakers of oppressed languages to expose double-talk.

Linguistic sophistication is not in itself, however, any guarantee of a multilingual approach. Although there is a growing literature on the 'mixed languages' formed in contact between Romani and various other European languages (Cortiade and Bakker 1991, Matras (ed.) 1995, 1998) for most of the authors the point of this is not to examine the vernaculars for their own sake, but as Cortiade and Bakker (1991) declare, to 'present stronger arguments for a scientific delimitation of the Romani language *propriae dicta*, as opposed to the Para-Romani idioms'. 'Para-Romani' is a term invented by Cortiade and Bakker to denote mixed languages such as the English Romani dialect described in this volume by Acton, Marselos and Szego. In an introduction to one of the most important overall collections on Romani linguistics, Matras and Bakker (1997, p.xvi) state bluntly: 'Two language groups are not considered in the present context of variation within Romani. First, the so-called Para-Romani languages or dialects ... The other group that is excluded from this discussion are the Indic languages of Gypsies outside Europe...'. This policy is also being followed in the proposed European Union-sponsored text book on the Romani language (Kyuchukov, Matras, Bakker et al. forthcoming), with the rather strange result that a book, printed in English in England on Romani will ignore the language called Romani in England, whose speakers outnumber those of other Romani dialects in England by ten to one.

Bakker is a leading Creolist; Cortiade is the architect of the morphophonemic orthography adopted by the Fourth World Romani Congress in 1990; Matras is by common consent one of the most brilliant young linguists ever to gather an international reputation. Even so they do not appear to have taken on board the critique that the delimitation of official languages is always and everywhere a product of the racist politics of the nation state, rather than a fact produced by linguistic science as such. To say this is not to belittle the project of creating a standard Romani literary language; but it has to depend upon the will and interests of its users, not upon destroying their vernaculars. We can see in the history of our own century how the interests of ordinary Welsh and Irish speakers, or, in a different way, those of Yiddish or Ladino have been betrayed by the politics of linguistic nationalists who have insisted on trying to play by the rules of a game already rigged against small languages. If anyone can, the Romani people ought to be able to avoid the traps of a politico-linguistic agenda dictated by super-literates who, out of misplaced idealism either fail, as Celtic nationalists have, to engage most of their own constituency, or else, as the Zionists have, abandon large parts of their own cultural heritage. We still believe that the vernacular of every child who comes to school must be respected as a valuable resource; and from that can come both a true understanding of the value of literary standards, and an endless enrichment of them.

Carrying out this multi-lingual approach, however, (even when it is disguised as merely a 'positive approach to bilingualism') may well, however, arouse opposition from traditional élites from the countries of origin of immigrants. Already there are language varieties, such as Patwa and Sylheti, which have been given a certain amount of status in Britain, but which are still devalued 'dialects' (in the negative sense of the word) in some of the lands where they originated.

Members of such elites may well argue that the contemporary value-free sociolinguistics of the developed metropolitan countries has had more effect in its advocacy of liberal tolerance of language varieties/'dialects' in the formerly colonised countries of the third world, than it will ever be allowed to do in the metropolitan countries, where the pressures to inculcate standard English and standard French, which are the languages of social domination, are as strong as ever. Support for Sylheti as a separate language in Britain, therefore can be attacked as a kind of neo-colonialist policy of divide and rule, contradicting the wishes for political unity in Bangladesh, which at present necessitate a view of Sylheti as being an oral variety to a written Bengali language.

We must respect such views, from whatever country they come. Of course it is not for us, from the easy security of the capitalist heartland, to take sides between the poor and oppressed non-standard-language speakers who are forced to become literate in another language if they want to get on, and regimes using nationalism and linguistic chauvinism as their ideological defence. Of course we have to be neutral if only because if we are not we risk imposing on any successor regime a new and different kind of neo-colonialism. We should never force mother-tongue teaching on any student (which must include not forcing Bengali on Sylheti speakers any more than we should force Afrikaans on South African Coloureds whose native tongue it may happen by accident of history to be.) But equally, if we believe that the result of a multi-lingual approach will be that all children in the classroom will want to write and explore their own home language, we cannot forbid them from using their 'mother tongue' (once, of course we can stop the terrible oppression which necessitates secrecy of language as a protection from oppression as in the case of many Gypsy groups). We should also never force them - but we cannot forbid them. And we must never allow anyone's language variety to be used as - or to become, despite lip-service to the contrary - a reason for excluding them from equal social/educational opportunities.

Equally, however, we must recognise the disparity between language varieties which are still predominantly oral and those which have an established written tradition. We must value competence in the oral mode which is often the key cognitive base for speakers of languages without a written tradition, from which they approach subsequent cognitive development in written language varieties. And we must not expect every oral variety to undergo some standard transformation to literary status; we must always remember that in the transition from the oral to the written there are losses as well as gains.

REFERENCES

Alladina S. (1991) *Being Bilingual: A Guide for Parents, Teachers and Young People*. Stoke-on-Trent, Trentham Books.

Bakker P. and Cortiade M. (1991) *In the Margin of Romani - Gypsy Languages in Contact. Amsterdam*, Publications of the Institute for General Linguistics, Nr.58, University of Amsterdam

Bakker P and Matras Y. (1997) 'Introduction' in Matras Y., Bakker P., and Kyuchukov H. (1997) *The Typology and Dialectology of Romani*. Amsterdam and Philadelphia, John Benjamins

Hamers J.F. and Blanc M.H.A. (1989) *Bilinguality and Bilingualism*. Cambridge University Press, Cambridge

Kyuchukov H., Matras Y., Bakker P. et al. (forthcoming) *Introduction to Romani*. Interface Collection, Paris and London

Matras Y. (ed.) (1995) *Romani in Contact*. John Benjamins, Amsterdam and Philadelphia

Matras Y. (ed.) (1998) *The Romani Element in Non-Standard Speech*. Harassowitz Verlag, Wiesbaden

Pennycook A. (1994) *The Cultural Politics of English as an International Language*. Longman, Harlow

Sebba M. (1997) *Contact Languages: Pidgins and Creoles*. Macmillan, London

Singh R. (ed.) (1997) *Grammar, Language and Society: Contemporary Indian Contributions*. Sage, London

Singh R (ed.) (1998) *The Native Speaker: Multilingual Perspectives*. Sage, London

Swann, Lord, Chairman (1985) *Education for All: The Report of the Committee of Inquiry into the Education of Children from Ethnic Minority Groups*. Cmd. 9453. HMSO, London

Verma M.K. (1998) *Sociolinguistics, Language and Society*. Sage, London

SECTION ONE

Languages of the Oppressed

Introduction

POLITICS AND LINGUISTICS

This book is about two turning points: a turning point in the discipline of linguistics and a turning point in the practice of education which together challenge racist structures in the most basic element of human culture: the use of language itself. Because we can study the origins of some Creole languages not as textual relics but as living processes, all sorts of questions which traditional prescriptive and descriptive linguistics could disregard become crucial. And because increasing numbers of speakers of these languages will no longer tolerate teachers or anyone discounting them as inferior, these linguistic questions have become political.

Over the past thirty years the development of the study of Creole languages has galvanised linguistics and created a demand by linguists for a new sociology of language, a demand they have largely had to respond to without the help of professional sociologists. The work of a leading traditional scholar of Creole (Le Page and Tabouret 1985) told with great honesty how the abandonment of earlier attempts at a definitive study has been forced by 'new' questions about ethnic identity: can the boundaries of ethnic groups be defined by language variety boundaries? Is linguistic difference the foundation of subjective ethnic identity? What is implied about identity by 'code-switching' (the way in which speakers will switch from, say, Creole or Anglo-Romani to standard English and back even within one sentence)? Social distinctions express themselves as linguistic difference. As Gumperz (1986, p.51) says 'Often the closer two languages or dialects are, the greater the import of the social boundaries which separate them.'

THE NEW LINGUISTICS

There exists a substantial sociology of language written by sociologists which largely passes the linguists by. The sociolinguistics and semiotics of the sociologists concentrates mainly on questions of meanings, interpretation and signification. Though it has absorbed phenomenological perspectives via ethnomethodology and grown away from the linguistic philosophy derived from Wittgenstein, it is still concerned primarily with the elucidation of meaning, with the message, i.e. 'parole' rather than 'langue'. Sociologists, usually staying within one language, often do not even attempt generalisations across languages. Within the confines of a single language conventions are taken for granted, or even endowed with some deep philosophical significance which would not survive translation.

The original problem, which gave rise to the study of foreign languages in the first place, however, was not the philosophy of interpretation, but the mundane task of translation. If one takes upon oneself the task of re-presenting the meaning of an utterance in a different tongue, one has to work on the assumption that the connection between sign and signified is fairly unproblematic.

So long, however, as linguists saw the sets of rules as discrete entities, they could take 'the rules' as given. But when they are studying Creole languages, usually from the vantage-point of a dominant metropolitan language, 'the rules' tend not to be discrete entities. They overlap and join up at the edges as code-switching joins two systems of signification into one. When speakers in conversation map the two sets of rules onto one another they interfere with each other, and the interference is a continuous process, not a stable describable system.

The Creole linguists, then, now have to challenge and deconstruct the 'rules' just as much as sociologists; but the answers given by the sociologists, working largely in a monolingual context, have never been taken up by linguists as relevant. Creolists have to raise questions about the origins and learning of language, (i.e. about the choice and development of 'rules') which the sociologists often think of as disposed of along with Chomsky. Chomsky's transformational grammar, based on an idealised native speaker has been shown by Hymes (1983) to have had negative effects for the study of oppressed languages and linguistic difference. For Bickerton (1981), however, at least, to name one of the more controversial Creolists, it seems that we may have to resurrect the questions Chomsky asked about origins and deep structure of languages, even though at the time Chomsky's idealised and simplified answers may have seemed to discredit the questions themselves. At the point where the academic world of linguistic analysis meets the practical world of language education, 'communicative language theory' tries to go beyond the theory of transformational grammar to emphasise the possibilities of learning through transaction, discovery and awareness of language difference in a student's own social environment (Dalphinis 1986).

SCHOLARS AND 'OBJECTS OF STUDY'

There is a vast gulf between the different sectors of our educational system, and what is taught as true in them. In the lecture-halls and laboratories of higher education critical intelligence enjoys a licence to challenge the conventional wisdom and report the actual results of empirical enquiry. In the school classrooms, which contain the objects of study of the academic linguists, radical criticism is more difficult and more subversive; the verities of previous generations are expected to pass as unchallengeable, and the attitudes that go

Section 1: Introduction

with them produce and reproduce the structures of power and prestige in our society.

The conference from which this book sprang attempted to bridge this gulf. Against the philistinism of those who disregard and disparage the world's oral languages it brought both the anger of community language activists and the scholarly exactitude of academics. The conference was attended by 86 participants from 19 countries. Only 33 of the participants were 'academic' in the sense that they were then employed in higher education; the rest were involved in further or adult education, or schools or community groups. The majority of the participants came from disadvantaged linguistic minorities. The objects of study are now studying themselves.

In his opening speech, on behalf of the Caribbean Communications Project, Eglon Whittingham remarked:

> It is not the existence of a common tongue that has brought us together, but the common experience we share. That experience has seen the effect of politics and power in determining the status of language and, ultimately, people. It is the concomitant social implications that we are here to question. All this is bound up with attitudes and the lust for social control. Society has contrived through various devices to use language for locating people within a social system. Usually, language is used as a determinant of an individual's social status. The individual usually internalises the views and the status assigned, and by doing this, affirms his/her position in society. This has far-reaching implications in societies where literacy and the mastery of the standard variety of the language are given pre-eminence over all other language abilities.
>
> Education is one of the chief vehicles of social control. In this process the emphasis is on the written word, and a particular style of writing at that. Education perpetuates the power of those who have appropriated the right to give legitimacy and approbation to the language, experience and performance of others. Using language as an instrument, the educational systems to which many of us have been exposed polarise the academic and the practical, pure knowledge and applied knowledge...
>
> From the Caribbean perspective, the evolution of Creoles may be viewed in context of the experience of the struggle against racism and oppression. African slaves were seen by their European 'masters' as both physically and mentally inferior in coping with the complex language situations in which they found themselves. Consequently, all the retentions and modifications of their language habits were discredited ... The experience of Afro-Caribbeans in this country attests to this.
>
> This occasion must be seen as a beginning ... an opportunity to clarify issues among ourselves, arrive at a better understanding, establish links, strengthen solidarity in a common cause, and strive to

enlighten and influence those who make decisions about education in this country ... I would like to recall the sentiment of the poet Shelley, in what I consider one of the greatest tributes to languages that do not necessarily employ writing systems: 'He gave man speech, and speech created thought, which is the measure of the universe'.

At the conference everyone became almost lightheaded from the presence of so many others with the same preoccupations, and the pleasure of putting faces to names. Language was also used for its most important purpose, that of celebration. On the second evening of the conference more than a dozen participants contributed to a concert of poetry and song, while on the third and final evening the disco was held up by another half-dozen spontaneous performances. At the same time, however, the conference was also an orgy of work. Note-takers were appointed to report back on all the workshop sessions at a concluding plenary, and all the papers included in this volume were first worked over extensively in the light of the discussion. It is a collective production, that has been revised again and again over 15 years.

In the discussion two concepts were taken up again and again.

First, the identification of 'super-literates' as the movers in a great deal of organised language politics gave participants the opportunity to take a long hard look at their own motivations and interests. The term was introduced at the conference by Morgan Dalphinis and discussed at greater length in a subsequent book (Dalphinis forthcoming). In the modern world the intelligentsia who start to develop literatures in languages without a previously written tradition have almost always become literate in a metropolitan or standard language first before going on to write also in their Creole, Patwa, Romanes or whatever. Their interests and attitudes are distinct both from those of non-literates, and from those who are merely literates, to each of whom literacy in a metropolitan language may appear as the only short-term route to better living standards and social mobility. The 'super-literates' may have a developed critique of the hegemony of imperialist cultures and the illusory nature of the promise they hold out to the non-literate masses in former colonial countries, or to ethnic minorities in metropolitan societies, but they cannot themselves speak for those masses or minorities, much as their talents are needed to pilot any movement through what Churchill (1986) has shown to be the extremely complex variations of language policy in the developed world. Although there is now a more sophisticated academic literature on language policy (Ager 1997; Baynham 1995), the patronising incompetence of the élites revealed by Tollefson (1991), in their efforts to improve the language proficiency of those they term the underclass, continues.

Secondly, as participants from different linguistic and educational situations shared their experiences of trying to create the opportunity for all children to bring their own language with them to school, there was a consensus defining the desired educational language philosophy as 'multi-lingualism'. Alladina's paper opposed this to the dominant racist ideology permeating much of British education, which might be called 'mono-lingualism'. Children can, and should

Section 1: Introduction

develop a broad knowledge of several languages, and the correct situations in which to use them, rather than narrow knowledge of a single standard, combined with a fearful conviction that they could never speak any other tongue. 'Bi-lingualism' as a strategy also reflects monolingual ideology - a grudging permitting of two, instead of one, linguistic standards, rather than a genuine embracing of linguistic diversity.

In the postscript to this volume we consider the prospects for multi-lingualism. It has not exactly triumphed in the period since 1984, although there have been appointments of mother-tongue teachers (though primarily for the Asian language groups) in inner-city areas, despite the Swann Report's rejection of such work in 1985. Gumperz (1986) provided a summing up of the literature criticising notions of cultural or linguistic 'deprivation' while Klein (1986) is perhaps one of the first 'multiculturalists' to treat the implications of multi- lingualism for school libraries seriously.

Monolingual ideology, however, is dominant. The sloppy and complacent liberal defence of British educational practice can bring into question the very possibility of the successful transfer of linguistic competences (cf. Milroy and Milroy 1985). Kalmar (1985) used a comparison of *Inuit Today* newspaper with ethnographic texts of the past to purport to show that 'primitive' languages really can 'evolve' (in a social-Darwinian sense); he completely ignored the effect of power structures of the shape and shaping effect of literacy. Indeed, besides Kalmar, many of the contributors to Olson (1985) seem to display an uneasy awareness that the superiority of European culture can no longer just be taken for granted, and therefore has in some sense to be explained by reference to the special nature of European literacy. In the absence any real data, Winchester (1985) used science-fiction-type speculation to criticise UNESCO's programme on literacy for 'over-optimism' and failing to distinguish the effects of 'high-grade literacy' (ours) and 'elementary literacy' (theirs).

The most worrying, and influential, exhibition of monolingual prejudice, however, occurred in the Swann Report (1985). Our conclusion shows how the Swann report reinforced racist ideas about language by contrasting all other languages to a spuriously universalised 'English' , which is somehow divorced from the ethnic groups of the same name who use it to assure their dominance over other ethnic groups. If the papers in this book serve any purpose at all, it is to present the scholarly and scientific basis upon which the Anglocentric view of language and language teaching will become intellectually untenable.

REFERENCES

Ager D.E. (1997) *Language Policy in Britain and France: The Processes of Policy.* Cassell, London

Bain B. (ed.) (1983) *The Sociogenesis of Language and Human Conduct.* Plenum, NY

Baynham M. (1995) *Literacy Practices: Investigating Literacy in Social Contexts.* Longman, Harlow

Bickerton D. (1981) *The Roots of Language Karoma.* Ann Arbor, Michigan

Churchill S. (1986) *The Education of Linguistic and Cultural Minorities in the OECD Countries.* Multilingual Matters 13, Clevedon, Avon

Dalphinis M. (forthcoming) *Caribbean and African Languages: Social History, Language, Literature and Education.* (Revised Edition). Whiting & Birch, London

Dalphinis M. (1986) 'Language and Communication' in Saakana A.S. and Pearse A. (eds.) *Towards the Decolonisation of the British Educational System.* Frontline/Karnak, London

Gumperz J.J. 1986 'Interactional Linguistics in the Study of Schooling' in Cook-Gumperz J. (ed.) *The Social Construction of Literacy.* C.U.P. Studies in Interactional Linguistics, No. 3, London

Hymes D. (1983) 'Report from an Underdeveloped Country' in Bain B. (ed.) *The Sociogenesis of Language and Human Conduct.* Plenum, NY

Kalmar I. (1985) 'Are There Really No Primitive Languages' in Olson D.R. (ed.) *Literacy, Language and Learning: The Nature and Consequences of Reading and Writing.* Cambridge University Press, London

Le Page R.B. and Tabouret A. (1985) *Acts of Identity: Creole-Based Approaches to Language and Ethnicity.* Cambridge University Press, London

Milroy J. and Milroy L. (eds.) (1985) *Authority in Language.* Routledge and Kegan Paul, London.

Olson D.R. (ed.) (1985) *Literacy, Language and Learning: The Nature and Consequences of Reading and Writing.* Cambridge University Press, London

Swann Lord, Chairman (1985) *Education for All The Report of the Committee of Inquiry into the Education of Children from Ethnic Minority Groups.* Cmd 9453, HMSO, London

Tollefson J.W. (1991) *Planning Language, Planning Inequality: Language Policy in the Community.* Longman, Harlow

Winchester I. (1985) 'Atlantans, Centaurians and the Litron Bomb: Some Personal and Social Implications of Literacy' in Olson D.R. (ed.) *Literacy, Language and Learning: The Nature and Consequences of Reading and Writing.* Cambridge University Press, London

A NOTE ON ORTHOGRAPHY

Unless stated otherwise in specific papers, we will use the orthographies below for the writing of Creole, Patwa and Romani.

For Creoles with English vocabulary, we will use the system of *A Dictionary of Jamaican English* by F.G. Cassidy and R.B. Le Page (1967, 1980, Cambridge University Press, London).

For Creoles with French vocabulary we will use the *St Lucian Creole Alphabet of the National Research and Development Foundation* (1981, Castries, St. Lucia).

For International Romani we use the orthographic conventions adopted by the second World Romani Congress, and used in the journal *Roma*.

Standardisation and Ethnic Defence in Emergent Non-Literate Societies: The Gypsy and Caribbean Cases

Ian Hancock

With non-literate communities so widespread throughout the world, why select Gypsy and Caribbean societies in particular - and why treat them together? There are a number of reasons, historical as well as social. In Britain, where both Gypsies and Caribbean people have settled as non-white immigrants, though separated by some four hundred years, both have come to constitute 'problems' for the host community. I use the term loosely; we may certainly constitute problems for those looking for something to worry about; the sociological literature is full of articles dealing with Caribbeans and Gypsies in terms of being 'problems'. What is less often considered is the other side of the coin: the many problems that the so-called host community presents in turn for Gypsies and West Indians.

We know from experience that in the past, few outsiders have involved themselves with Gypsies or Caribbeans without having some underlying personal motive, whether it has been from a desire to 'improve' our lot for us, or to gather material for a dissertation or a book or, in some cases, to collect information clandestinely to be used by the authorities. Sometimes it has been used to fulfil some romantic fantasies; literature and the media do little to dispel the stereotypes which attract such people.

Gypsies and Caribbeans are immigrants not only in Britain, but also everywhere else except for India and Africa, our ancestral homelands (although it is misleading to think that Gypsy origins are firmly in India, or that all Gypsies today can trace their biological descent to that area, despite its emotional significance for supporters of the nationalist movement; similarly, while pan-Africanism has had widespread support throughout the Caribbean, not all Caribbeans are of African descent by any means; sometimes we find ourselves buying into the stereotypes others have about us, and believing in them as well). Of course, the notion of 'immigrant' is itself a relative one. The British Celts were not particularly pleased at the large-scale influx of Anglo-Saxons into this country sixteen hundred years ago, although the descendants of those Germanic invaders hardly see themselves as immigrants today - indeed, there are Celtic nationals in Britain who would maintain that it is their own people who are made to feel like the interlopers; we are clearly dealing here with an issue of *power*.

Gypsies and West Indians have both been enslaved, and it is because of slavery that huge diasporas of our people have taken place. Emancipation for both came about at more or less the same time, during the middle of the past century. For Gypsies, slavery lasted for five centuries or more, and when anti-slavery movements were becoming vocal in Europe, Gypsy slaves were frequently compared with their African counterparts in the Americas. In 1837, Mihail Kogalniceanu wrote that:

> The Europeans are organising philanthropic societies for the abolition of slavery in America, yet in the bosom of their own continent of Europe there are 400,000 Gypsies who are slaves, and 200,000 more equally victim to barbarousness (1837, p.iv).

Twenty years later in 1857, the historian Vaillant said that those who:

> ... shed tears of compassion for the Negroes of Africa, of whom the American republic makes its slaves, should give a kind thought to ... the Gypsies of India, of whom the European monarchies make their 'Negroes' (1857, p.7).

The Gypsy population in Britain was not subjected to the same kind of slavery as that which existed in south-eastern Europe, but it was nevertheless still harshly treated. At one time, it was a hanging offence merely to be born a Gypsy in England; that policy even exceeded the aims of plain genocide, since it applied in addition to individuals who were not Gypsies, but who were guilty of socialising with them. Simson (1865) and Kinney (1973) have both written about how Gypsies could be made 'slaves for life' in 16th and 17th century Britain and, as in other western European nations, England and Scotland saw one solution to their 'Gypsy problem' in the American colonies. From 1664 onwards, unspecified numbers of Gypsies from those countries were being shipped off to work in the Caribbean and North American plantations. We read in Moreton's account of Jamaica, published in 1793, of Gypsies as young as eleven years old being used for sexual purposes not only by the European overseers, but by the Africans there as well. France, Portugal and Spain were also transporting Gypsies overseas (Hancock 1986a).

Out of these transplanted societies have arisen new cultures, with their roots to some extent intact from the lands of their forefathers, but with branches and leaves which have flourished under different skies. Afro-Caribbean societies have retained much that is obviously African; likewise, Gypsy societies everywhere maintain elements of culture, and especially language, which are traceable to India. Caribbeans of Chinese, East Indian, Irish and other ancestry have had more success in retaining their original character, but in coming into contact with other peoples, under less than ideal circumstances, even these cultures have been modified, and are being modified still.

Over the past century, some scholars have been fascinated by this phenomenon, and have made extensive studies of language and culture in contact. In the West Indies we talk about creolisation, and while the same label has been applied to the Gypsy situation, maybe with some justification, there are significant linguistic differences. For one thing, Gypsies arrived here speaking one language common to the group, Romani, and the intermixing with the local population and with the English language was more or less voluntary, or at least seen as expedient in terms of survival. In some isolated parts of Britain, there are still people who are able to speak the original Romani language, while for everyone else, a new, restructured speech has replaced it. In the West Indies, on the other hand, Africans arrived speaking hundreds of different languages, and were made to integrate with each other rather than with members of the host society. In fact in time, they became themselves the majority society, though until recent times not, politically the dominant one. Again a restructured speech came to replace the earlier languages, and while linguistic particulars may differ, the social consequences in each situation have much in common.

This fact has not escaped some scholars: since John Atkins' observation that the language of the 'creoles' he visited in Jamaica in 1722 was 'a kind of Gypsy gibberish that runs smoothest in swearing', a number of creolists have written more or less extensively on Romani as well, among them Emilio Teza, Adolfo Coelho, Hugo Schuchardt, Charles Godfrey Leland, Peter Bakker, Norbert Boretsky, James Creswell Clough, William Washabaugh, and Dell Hymes. One of the first creolists, Lafcadio Herne, who wrote on Louisiana Creole French, himself came from Gypsy stock. In this book, we continue that tradition.

Another early connection between Gypsies and the emerging Creole societies in the Americas is found in John Stedman's 1790 *Narrative*. Stedman himself was intrigued by Gypsies and asked to be buried next to Bampfylde Moore Carew, his 'kindred spirit', and in his discussion of Sranan, the Creole language of Surinam, he compares some of its vocabulary to Romani (Stedman 1988, p.516). 'Gypsy' languages in the Caribbean have most recently been discussed by Aceto (1997).

Both West Indians and British Gypsies use as their ethnic speech kinds of language which have grown out of contact situations. Both have also arisen from a social mould in which these types of speech have been seen as inferior and inadequate by the respective power structures. This is not uncommon when decisions and pronouncements are made by representatives of those structures; unless they come from members of the communities who themselves aspire to the values of the superordinate society, attitudes such as these are not shared by the speakers of these languages themselves. Unfortunately, the effects of cultural colonisation have been far reaching, and such individuals are rare. There is still a majority of West Indian citizens who will tell you with confidence that their native language, whether it be Guyanese Creolese or Jamaican Patois or Belizean Creole, is broken English, and quite unsuitable for anything other than jokes or Nancy stories. Some people, who, without hesitation, will address an Englishman in that Englishman's native language, would become quite angry should that Englishman attempt to address him in theirs.

In dealing with the status and potential of such languages, we must keep the approaches to these aspects quite distinct; what we may know as linguists to be true, does not always translate in terms of speaker attitude. While language planners can debate over orthography and choice of lexicon, the people in the street may remain unswervingly convinced that their language stigmatises them, and as a result give little or no support to efforts to effect its standardisation. But this is a complex issue, and one squarely based in the individual's social and educational background. In the Caribbean, for example, the working-class masses are often functionally monolingual in Creole and, depending upon the particular country we are talking about, may seldom be in a situation in which the coexistent metropolitan language (usually the language of colonialism) matters much. But middle-class members of the same societies can be very language conscious, and as the teachers and decision-makers in those societies, their attitudes are understandably far-reaching. For those people who, in the current jargon are typed as 'upwardly socially mobile', Creole speech may be too blatant a link with the working-class roots they may have sprung from. In the United States, where Black English issues have much in common with those in the West Indies, the most vigorous opposition to the use of Black English in the schools as a medium of instruction comes not from the white community, but from middle-class black parents, who argue that Black English cannot express everything that International English can, that it is somehow a lazy and ungrammatical deviation from it, and that efforts to use it as a medium of instruction in the schools are just another white plot to keep Black Americans out of the mainstream by denying them access to the language of the power structure. Nor is such reasoning unknown in the Caribbean - especially the kind which stresses the inadequacy of Creole, or which attempts to make a case for its being a reminder of colonialism. Neither of these is valid as I will demonstrate, although there are more persuasive arguments which might be made, of course, for example that the development of local Creoles at the expense of English might fragment the Caribbean nations instead of bringing them close together, or that enormous sums of money would have to be spent to produce educational material in each of the local vernaculars.

Deriving Creole languages from the slave trade and colonialism is one of the false notions about Black history which outsiders have foisted upon the colonised. Stokely Carmichael said that those who are in a position to define others are their masters, and this must be extended to those who define other people's histories too. The slave trade was responsible only for carrying Creole - and I am restricting this discussion only to those Creoles sharing an English - derived lexical base - across the Atlantic, not for creating it. More recent research by creolists and historians, some of them Caribbeans like Walter Rodney, has shown quite clearly that Creole came into existence in a situation of domestic equality before the English became involved in the trans-Atlantic trade. In fact, the English who settled and married into the coastal African societies in the early 1600s and whose children were the first Creoles, were allowed to do so under sufferance from the local African authorities at that time. It was when the English stopped buying slaves from the Dutch in the

Caribbean and began importing their own that this social situation became drastically altered; but by this time, at least two generations of Afro-Europeans-Creoles - had grown up, and their societies become established. It was with these people, and especially with the grumettoes or African porters who worked for them, and not the Europeans that Africans were kept while awaiting shipment. It was from these people that they learnt more or less of the Guinea Coast Creole and brought it with them to the western hemisphere to become one of the inputs into, or components of, the emerging Caribbean linguistic situation (Hancock 1986b, 1987). It cannot, therefore, be argued that Creole is the result of slavery; its widespread use and subsequent establishment in the West Indies was a matter of expediency, just as some African languages also became lingua francas in the same area for a time, even among people who had no historical claim to them, for example Yoruba in Brazil, Efik in Cuba, Congo in Guyana, Mandinka in Grenada or Ashanti in Jamaica.

I have dwelt upon this historical aspect because a knowledge of our true history is a central factor in shaping our revised attitudes towards the languages we speak. We must write our own histories, and not accept unquestioningly the details or our past presented to us in books written by outsiders, whose priorities have almost always been different from our own. As Public Broadcast Service media critic Hodding Carter said in response to a question asking why so little news from Africa was covered in the United States:

> Africa is not viewed as important. It's not the heritage of most of the people watching. It becomes important only when our government says it's of immediate national importance, which usually means an East-West power struggle (Townley 1984, p.4).

Two years later, a similar article in the same magazine reiterated the point: 'Clearly, Africa is not a top priority of television news' (Kalter 1986, p.10). We are minority populations with little representation or influence in the power structure and, by extension the media; our problems, however real to us, seldom touch the day-to-day existence of the mainstream. We only become important, and receive attention, when the government says we are important, which usually means when we are causing that mainstream some kind of discomfort. Otherwise, our function appears to be only to provide a measure by which the majority can recognise the boundaries of its own culture, as Sibley (1981) argues. This requires that minorities, including Gypsies and Caribbeans , be defined by that culture in a manageable way, and part of that involves minimising the legitimacy of our languages and our histories:

> The mental age of an average adult Gypsy is thought to be about that of a child of ten. Gypsies have never accomplished anything of great significance in writing, painting, musical composition, science or social organisation. Quarrelsome, quick to anger or laughter, they are unthinkingly but not deliberately cruel. Loving bright colours, they

are ostentatious and boastful, but lack bravery ... their tribal customs sometimes have the force of law ... they betray little shame, curiosity, surprise or grief and show no solidarity (*Encyclopaedia Britannica* 1956).

The Negro could not be expected to participate in the conquest of the United States. His language consisted mostly, at the time of the Revolutionary War, of grunts, a sign language, and a few words. The jargon of the jungle was in his tongue and the Congo flowed deep in his brain. He was being taught and was learning words sufficient in his new language to make known his wants (Brady 1955, p.12).

Once, however, it has been convincingly demonstrated that all natural languages are the result of human interaction and predictable linguistic development, and that none is in any way inadequate within the culture for which it serves as a vehicle, the first step towards linguistic self-determination will have been taken.

During the Middle Ages, the vernacular of the masses in England was of course English, but the languages of education, politics and the law were Latin and French. English was the target of the same negative attitudes that Creole is often subjected to today; native speakers themselves internalised these attitudes, so that even as late as the middle of the Renaissance, Arthur Golding could refer to English as a 'rude' language, 'voyd of ornate termes'; William Barkar spoke of English as 'our grosse tongue, a rude and barren tongue, when it is compared with so flourishinge and plentifull a tongue [as Latin]'. Roger Ascham called it 'so meanly ... that no man can do worse', while William Adlington thought it was 'barbarous and simply framed' (Williams 1975, pp.87-98). In reaction to these feelings, writers of the time 'gilded' their language with excessive numbers of Latinisms, in an attempt to give it some imagined dignity. It has been estimated that over a quarter of the entire Latin lexicon turned up in the English writing of this period. This is reminiscent to some extent of the highly embellished oratorical register of West Indian English which has been studied by Abrahams and others. While most of this Latin element has not survived, a source-count taken from a modern English dictionary indicates that only 28 per cent of the total lexicon is traceable to the original Anglo-Saxon - a far smaller percentage of items from the core of direct retention, incidentally, than is found in the anglophone Creoles, so-called 'mixed' languages.

While time has lent respectability to English, two factors in particular have had even greater significance: firstly, writings in the native tongue by people such as Gower, or Lydgate, or Chaucer, who were able to demonstrate that the vernacular *could* be used creatively and expressively, and secondly, the spread of English as the vehicle of a powerful colonial, that is political, force.

It must not be imagined that a knowledge of the legitimacy of language history will provide all the answers. Pragmatically we have to accept that linguistic attitudes are a reflection of social ones, and whether it can be shown

Standardisation and Ethnic Defence in Emergent Non-Literate Societies

to the entire academic world that Creoles are models of optimum human grammatical structure, and of immense significance to linguist and geneticist alike, or that Romani is a conservative descendant of noble Sanskrit with conjugations and declensions rivalling those of Latin and Greek, their speakers remain niggers and gyppoes in the eyes of the larger society. As long as we continue to allow ourselves to be defined and evaluated from outside, and as long as we continue to aspire to external norms, the situation is not going to change. I am not proposing separatism here; the world has become far too small for that. Rather, I am proposing that our attitudes towards ourselves be more independent of externally-applied values.

It is sad to me that there are so many parents who have made up their minds not to pass the ethnic language on to their children. I have attended several conferences in the West Indies where there have been individuals who have sat patiently in the back listening to the linguists expounding upon creolisation, only to jump up, finally, in angry desperation to say how *wrong* it is to waste money and energy even to consider such issues, when the same effort could be put into teaching 'good' English more successfully in the schools. I know Gypsy families in the United States in which Romani has been withheld from the children intentionally, with the aim of making them more 'modern'.

Along with these attitudes about language, whether in the Caribbean or the Gypsy situations, there automatically go attitudes about the ancestral cultures and values too; for many West Indians, anything too blatantly 'African' carries with it negative connotation. The very names brought from Africa - *Quashiba, Quaco, Congo, Cuffie* - have become negative in their present-day applications. Yet there is a paradox here, because Creole culture is felt to be the real one; the Afro-Seminole Creoles in Texas for example, find amusement in their own behaviour. They will go to the doctor like anyone else, and even openly ridicule their own folk medicine. But just to be sure, they say, they'll pay a quiet visit to the local Seminole herbalist as well. In the same way, Creole-speaking Louisianans say *Angley sey pu monti, Gombo sey pu paley veritey-la* - 'English is for telling lies, Creole is for telling the truth'. For such groups, language and culture identify them to themselves and to the outside.

Creole societies have a double attitude to the world at large. Outwardly, they belittle the native culture and esteem that of the European, while inwardly they believe the reverse. Similarly, Gypsies maintain that one should be a Gypsy among Gypsies, but act like a *gaujo* (a non-Gypsy) when in that company. The Welsh have a saying, *cenedl heb iaith, cenedl heb galon* - 'a nation without a language is a nation without a heart' - a sentiment echoed by the Surinamese Creole writer J. Koenders, who said *wan pipel di no abi wan tongo, noiti kan de san di fiti na neng fu wan pipel* - 'A people without a language can never be called a people'. One Romani maxim maintains that *amari chib si amari zor* - 'Our language is our strength'. Language and ethnic identity are very clearly bound together for oppressed peoples.

We cannot stop being what we are merely be ceasing to speak our language; speaking English doesn't turn us into Englishmen. By the same token, we cannot fully participate as members of our particular group if we cannot speak the language of that group. Londoners of, say, Jamaican descent who cannot speak Jamaican know how out of place they can feel in a Jamaican-speaking environment. Among Gypsies, fluency in the language is such a powerful ethnic factor that those who are unable to speak Romani are excluded from all kinds of social functions. Such people find themselves in a quandary, since they cannot automatically fit smoothly into any alternate society even if they wanted to - especially if their ethnic or racial differences are readily visible, or if the alternate society is an especially conservative one. Even fully assimilated individuals, for example a sixth-generation American of Chinese descent with no first-hand knowledge of Chinese language or culture, and whose principal diet is coke and hamburgers, will be put into a category on the sole basis of his physical appearance and the stereotypes held about that category, and then be expected to behave accordingly. For others, however, their natural behavioural characteristics may not be easily adjusted; as the Creole proverb says, *yu kyan aid fi-yu grand ina di kabod, bot yu kyaan mek shi duon kaaf (you can hide your grandmother in the cupboard, but you can't stop her coughing).*

I'm not discussing here those individuals who have made the transition, voluntarily or because of family circumstances, and who are comfortable in their acquired identity. There is nothing at all wrong with this. What I'm concerned with instead are the issues surrounding the use of the vernacular language, rather than the imposed, or non-ethnic, language. At the present time, considerable interest exists in creating standardised, written varieties both of various Creole languages and of Romani. In some places, this has been successful; Sranan, Papiamentu and Tok Pisin support growing literatures, for example, but in each case there are clear factors which have made this possible. For the anglophone Caribbean and for Romani, the situation is less straight-forward. I will deal with each situation separately.

THE ANGLOPHONE CARIBBEAN

Throughout the Caribbean there are spoken a great many dialects of what I have called Western Atlantic Anglophone Creole. The whole Atlantic area may tentatively be divided into three: the Eastern or African group, the Suriname group, and the Caribbean group, this last being broadly divided further into the Eastern Caribbean, the Western Caribbean, and the North American. This is a gross over-simplification, but it reflects the diversity which exists, and with which issues of literacy must contend. A more detailed discussion is found in Hancock (1987). The extent of the differences may be illustrated by giving the equivalents of the sentence 'I don't know where your brother found his books' in one Creole from each of these groups:

1. Eastern (African):
    Krio: *a noh no usai una broda bin fen im buk dem*
2. Suriname
    Sranan: *mi no sabi pe a brada fu unu ben feni den buku fu en*

3. Western
> Eastern Caribbean - Antigua: *mi no no we allyu breda min fain i buk dem*
> Western Caribbean - Jamaica: *mi no nuo a wepaat unu breda en fain fi im buk dem*
> North American - Afro-Seminole: *mi na no wiseh hunnuh brada bin fain i buk dem*

Examples like this, however, give a false impression of stability, since with almost no exceptions wherever Creole is spoken, English is spoken too by some section of the same population, and is used in the classrooms and in other official capacities. The result is that for speakers who come into contact with that language, their Creole, whether consciously or unconsciously, is affected to a greater or lesser degree by intrusions from it. This is a characteristic of such bilingual societies, and a great deal of work has been done to try to define its consequences in linguistic terms. Some creolists see the situation as a continuum, with Creole and English at the two ends, gradually shading from one to the other between these extremes. Others maintain that there really exists a set of separate grammars side by side along this spectrum, with the speaker being able to shift along the range from one register to the next. Linguists speak of decreolisation, that is the gradual loss of Creole forms and structures as they are replaced by their equivalents from English, and see this as being inevitable - even desirable. I prefer to call this metropolitanisation, and not to regard it as a necessary process. But however the situation is described, the fact is that not only are there many quite distinct dialects of Caribbean Creole, but there is also a considerable range of varieties of each of these dialects in each location. Do we then treat each as a separate entity, or else attempt to create an artificial 'union' variety?

If the principal argument for fostering the vernacular speech in this way is that it embodies the soul of its speakers and reflects their identity and expresses their way of life more adequately than English can, then a new, artificial variety defeats this purpose quite soundly. Clearly there is little to be gained from creating a pan-Caribbean language; indeed, it can be argued that English already fulfils that purely practical role. Since, with the exceptions of the African and Suriname groups the other Creoles share considerable mutual intelligibility, it seems more logical to develop teaching materials which present an overview of these different dialects so that speakers of any one can be made familiar with those of any of the others. In this way, locally-produced vernacular literature can be retained in the original language and be more widely circulated and appreciated. Without a doubt, the study of Creoles, and especially the Caribbean Creoles, should be made an integral part of the West Indian educational curriculum. I should add too that when Creole is taught as a distinct and separate system from English, and their differences rather than their similarities stressed, students are much more likely to be successful in keeping the two apart. As long as Creole is presented as a 'bad' version of English, confusion must result. Assignments in Creole should be given, and graded as rigorously as those given in English; and just as Creolisms in English are corrected by the teacher, attention should also be brought to the intrusions of anglicisms into Creole.

This leads to a second, and more difficult, issue: if each of the national Creoles is to be developed separately, which variety of each should be chosen? Urban dialects differ from the rural; eastern Jamaican differs considerably from western Jamaican, and northern Antiguan from southern. Berbice Creolese is different from the Demarara dialect; the elderly speak differently from the young, Africans differently from East Indians, and so on. Such diversity is not, of course, restricted to the Caribbean; it is natural to all languages. The same could be said about English, for instance. But English has evolved a more-or-less standardised written variety, which few people actually speak in informal contexts, but which they are taught in the classroom to read and be able to use. Standard English has grown out of the dialects of the educated: the writers and politicians who gravitated to the London area in the sixteenth and seventeenth centuries, and who did most of the writing and talking. And so it seems to be with the emergence of written Creole; it seems very much to be in the hands of the novelists and poets, and perhaps this is inevitable, for although it may be argued that such people constitute an educated elite, and are thus to some extent remote from the folk, they are also more likely to be aware of the formal differences between the vernacular and international written English.

The more basilectal, or conservative, any Creole is, the more it will have in common with other, related Creoles and the less it will be like English. The selection of such a variety would have the advantage of keeping the two systems, Creole and English, more distinct from each other and consequently not so susceptible to cross-interference. The phonology of the basilectal varieties is also more easily represented orthographically since its inventory of vowels is usually smaller, and it is worth considering that a non-English-based spelling system for the Creole would also serve to emphasise its distinctiveness from English.

It may be objected to that conservative or "deep", Creole is not representative of the majority of speakers, and is associated with a lack of formal education and sophistication. These are valid points, since they are very real feelings for very many people; but written English is not the speech of the majority either, and the fact that the use of Deep Creole may raise a smile is a reflection of social attitudes resulting from the notion that the more like English one's speech is, the better it must be. This kind of colonial brainwashing is counter-productive, and must be dealt with as a part of the overall Creole language programme. Language planners for Hindi, or Indonesian, or Hebrew, among others, have not hesitated to draw upon older, even obsolete forms to tailor them to the requirements of modern technology, and have seen this preferable to the wholesale adoption of foreign (and usually English) vocabulary.

Whatever standard variety is decided upon, it will not be the natural speech of the entire population. No speech community in the world could make such a claim. The only alternatives are to have several different standards, which is hardly practical, or to have no written standard at all. The latter possibility has its adherents, who see no reason to cultivate the vernacular when written English is already available; but if nothing else, this would ensure that the capacity for written expression would remain the domain of just a few, who would nevertheless continue to represent Creole speech anyway in their writings, usually only direct speech, in an impressionistic, English-based orthography.

ROMANI

Those who feel that reducing Creole to a standard written form takes something away from the language, would find considerable support among the Romani-speaking population. Not only is there widespread opposition to literacy itself, but it is popularly believed by many Gypsies that it is impossible to write Romani at all, and that learning to do so can lead to sickness.

I have in my files an article which appeared some years ago entitled 'Cure for a Gypsy curse'. Although the title panders to popular stereotyping, the 'curse' referred to is illiteracy. The opening line beings 'It is essential that Gypsy children ... should go to school' (Gibbard 1973, p.30). Practically without exception, all of the literature dealing with literacy assumes automatically that it must be the desired goal. Among many Gypsy groups, however, too much formal learning is seen not only to be debilitating, but as a threat to the Romani way of life. There are a number of reasons for this: 'formal' education is usually in terms of the majority culture, making no concession to the often quite divergent values of the Romani-speaking students in the classroom. Also, because most schools are not now segregated according to sex, parents are extremely reluctant to permit their children to share a classroom with non-Gypsies because of the risk of romantic involvement.

While in the USA at least, a basic knowledge of reading and writing is increasingly becoming considered a practical asset - for example when consulting road maps or street and business signs, or for writing one's own receipts - it is commonly felt that women should not be privy to these skills. At the present time, the majority of Gypsies in the United States have only basic literary skills, although the situation is changing. What this change will mean to the maintenance of traditional Romani values, however, remains to be seen. From the sociologist's point of view, the differences between a literate and a non-literate society are crucial:

> In non-literate society, every social situation cannot but bring the individual into contact with the group's patterns of thought, feeling and action: the choice is between the cultural tradition - or solitude. In a literate society, however, and quite apart from the difficulties arising from the scale and complexity of the 'high' literate tradition, the mere fact that reading and writing are normally solitary activities means that insofar as the dominant cultural tradition is a literate one, it is very easy to avoid (Goody and Watt 1968, pp.59-60).

For many Gypsy groups, the maintenance of a non-literate tradition has become institutionalised, serving as a means of sustaining non-acculturation. This operates in four specific ways (adapted from Hancock 1975, pp.43-48):

1. The minimisation of time spent in school reduces proportionately the influence of the teacher's set of values on the Gypsy child, and effectively eliminates peer-group pressure from the other children - two of the most pervasive forces in the socialisation process;
2. Illiteracy hinders any socialisation in the direction of the majority culture through the written word, and forestalls identification with historical and cultural heroes through books and novels;
3. Illiteracy strengthens the likelihood that Romani will remain the first language of the individual, with the resulting reinforcement of group values which occurs when he speaks mainly to and in the company of other Romani speakers, and lastly;
4. Illiteracy curtails defection to the majority culture via the occupational route, as (within the non-Gypsy milieu) only the most menial, physically strenuous and low-paying jobs are available to illiterates.

There persists among non-Gypsy scholars of Romani culture the type of individual who feels that such resistance to acculturation is right and proper, and that Gypsies who do not conform to the 'urzigeunerisch' stereotype have lost something of their Gypsiness; the literature, both scholarly and journalistic, is full of essays expressing disappointment on the part of the observer that the Gypsies they are reporting on wear suits, or live in houses, or are able to read and write. And yet it must be remembered that Gypsies have survived by constantly adapting to the changing environment - indeed by staying a couple of steps ahead of the society around them, while maintaining the linguistic and cultural core to which the ethnic identity is anchored. If staying ahead means acquiring literacy, this will be accommodated as needed.

Since the end of the Second World War, in which upwards of a million Sinti and Roma were murdered, the nationalist movement has gathered considerable force, one of the most significant achievements being admittance of the International Romani Union to the United Nations Organisation in 1979. While this has lent volume to the Gypsy voice, and has brought about the beginnings of positive change where our protests formerly fell on deaf ears, it has also thrown Gypsy politics into the international arena, with the result that communication on a world-wide scale has become essential. This in turn has meant that the only common means of achieving this, i.e. through the ethnic language, has become a crucial issue, although in his extensive study entitled *Linguistic Minorities in Western Europe*, Meic Stephens (1976, p.xiii) decided not to include Romani:

> ... the Rom have also been omitted, because in Western Europe their situations are *sui generis* and their problems neither linguistic nor territorial.

Standardisation and Ethnic Defence in Emergent Non-Literate Societies

Some years ago, I prepared a study dealing with the problems of creating a standardised dialect of Romani (Hancock 1975, 1977). The historical and social discussion may be summarised then as follows:

1. Although it seems probable that there were at least three separate and independent migrations of peoples from India out of the sub-continent, speakers of Romani entered Europe seven centuries ago as one people sharing one language and one identity.
2. Because of both historical and contemporary factors, not least anti-social pressures from the surrounding societies which continue to divide the Romani-speaking populations, there are today a great many widely differing dialects of that language, and as many groups socially isolated from, and even hostile to, each other.
3. Perhaps the greatest obstacle to achieving political and cultural unity is the lack of communication among the various Romani groups in Europe, Australia and the Americas.
4. It may be assumed that progress towards reunification would be more easily made if a common dialect were available to all groups. The achievement of linguistic reunification would be the first step toward reunification as a people.

The problems associated with these suppositions were summarised in (Hancock 1977) follows:

5. No single dialect spoken anywhere is so close to the common protoform that it may be adopted without modification; in other words, whatever dialect is chosen will have to be adapted to a more acceptable international form, especially lexically, phonologically and orthographically. It may be necessary to cultivate two standardised dialects: one for northern and one for southern Europe.
6. Using existing means of education, the propagation of such a standard or standards will be very unevenly achieved. Settled, already literate Rom, such as predominate in eastern European countries, will have a far better opportunity to acquire the dialect(s). For illiterate Rom, the task would be much harder.
7. Not all Rom everywhere will ever learn, or be disposed to learn such a dialect. This will create a 'linguistic elite' consisting only of those who have learnt the new international standard. The rights of those whose way of life or whose attitude toward literacy keeps them separate from the literate community must not be jeopardised as a result of their circumstances.

So far, achievement in this direction has been slow; while the number of literate Rom continues to grow, the dialects and orthographies they use reflect a great many different backgrounds. If a Rom has learnt to read at all, it has been in the national language of his country, which is why it is so widely held that Romani can't be written: a person familiar only with English spelling conventions, for example, would not be able to represent Romani phonology very accurately in writing using them. An elite, however, has begun to emerge: leaders in the Romani Union have such non-traditional occupations as journalists, lawyers, engineers and even medical doctors, professions which certainly alienate them from some sections of the Gypsy population. It is to be regretted that elitism is seen in terms of the values traditionally associated with western materialism, and that being 'educated' is automatically interpreted as being schooled; individuals extensively knowledgeable in Romani medicine, or oral literature, or history, may be seen as wise, or venerable, but unless they had been to school, never educated.

At present, while Romani is the common medium of written communication, each writer in each country tends to use his own dialect and his own spelling conventions even when communicating internationally. Clearly this is far from satisfactory, although it is becoming apparent that as such communication increases, those using the language are beginning to make concessions to the other writers and their dialects.

Lexical items with too local an application are avoided; spelling seems to be gravitating towards a modified Serbian system, probably because the greatest number of Romani-language publications used to be produced in that country and in Sweden, which has already published several books in Romani using a Slavic-type orthography as well. The success or failure of the new official orthography approved by the voting body at the Fourth World Romani Congress in Poland in 1990 remains to be seen.

For both Creole and Romani, the emergence of written standards and uniform orthographies seems to be in the hands of the writers rather than of the academicians; the latter have had less success in the long run than the former, and perhaps this is as it should be. Language, we should remember, is a spontaneous, human, creative art; to shape it on paper into something too remote from natural speech is to stifle its capabilities. Human language does not exist in the abstract, nor does it independently live, until it is given life in the mouths of its speakers.

REFERENCES

Aceto M. (1997) 'Synactic Innovation in a Caribbean Creole', *English World-Wide*, XX
Atkins J. (1735) *A Voyage to Guinea, Brasil and the West Indies*. London
Brady T.P. (1955) *Black Monday*, Citizens' Council of America Publications. Jackson
Gibbard G. (1973) 'Cure for a Gypsy Curse', *Observer Magazine*, 17 July, pp.30-32
Gilbert G. (ed.) (1987) *Essays in Memory of John E. Reinecke*. University of Hawaii Press, Honolulu

Goody J. (1968) 'The Consequences of Literacy' in Goody J. and Watt I. (eds.) *Literacy in Traditional Societies*. The University Press, Cambridge, pp.27-68

Goody J. and Watt I. (eds.) (1968) *Literacy in Traditional Societies*. The University Press, Cambridge

Hancock I. (1975) *Problems in the Creation of a Standard Dialect of Romani, Part 1: Orthography*. ERIC, Washington

Hancock I. (1977) *Problems in the Creation of a Standard Dialect of Romani, Part 2: Grammar and Lexicon*. Report presented before the Sixth Annual American Council Conference on the Teaching of Foreign Languages, San Francisco, 24-26 November

Hancock I. (1986a) *The Pariah Syndrome: An Account of Gypsy Slavery and Persecution*. Karoma, Ann Arbor

Hancock I. (1986b) 'The Domestic Hypothesis, Diffusion and Componentiality: An Account of Atlantic Anglophone Creole Origins' in Muysken P. and Smith N. (eds.) *Substrata Versus Universals in Creole Genesis*. Benjamins, Amsterdam, pp.71-102

Hancock I. (1987) 'A Provisional Comparison of the Anglophone Atlantic Creoles' in Gilbert G. (ed.) *Essays in Memory of John E. Reinecke*. University of Hawaii Press, Honolulu, pp.43-113

Kalter J.M. (1986) 'The Untold Stories of Africa: Why TV Is Missing Some Big Ones', *TV Guide*, 24 May, 34(21), pp.2-12

Kinney A.F. (1973) *Rogues, Vagabonds and Sturdy Beggars*. The Imprint Society, Barre

Koenders J.G.A. (1975) 'Selections of His Writing' in Voorhoeve J. and Lichtveld U.M. (eds.) *Creole Drum: An Anthology of Creole Literature in Surinam*. Yale University Press, New Haven, pp.135-163

Kogalniceanu M. (1837) *Esquisse sur l'Histoire, les Moeurs et la Langue des Cigains*. Behr Verlag, Berlin

Moreton J.B. (1793) *West India Customs and Manners*. London

Muysken P. and Smith N. (eds.) (1986) *Substrata Versus Universals in Creole Genesis*. Benjamins, Amsterdam

Sibley D. (1981) *Outsiders in Urban Societies*. Basil Blackwell, Oxford

Simson W. (1865) *A History of the Gipsies*. Sampson, Low, Son & Marston, London

Stedman J.G. (1790, 1988) *Narrative of a Five Years Expedition Against the Revolted Negroes of Surinam*. The John Hopkins University Press, Baltimore

Stephens M. (1976) *Linguistic Minorities in Western Europe*. The Gomer Press, Llandysul

Townley R. (1984) 'The Wars TV Doesn't Show You', *TV Guide*, 18 August, 32(33), pp.2-5

Vaillant J.A. (1857) *Les Rômes: Histoire Vraie des Vrais Bohémiens*. Dentu & Cie, Paris

Voorhoeve J. and Lichtveld U.M. (eds.) (1975) *Creole Drum: An Anthology of Creole Literature in Surinam*. Yale University Press, New Haven

Williams J.M. (1975) *Origins of the English Language: A Social and Linguistic History*. Macmillan, New York

Towards a Typology of Unwritten Languages

Donald Kenrick

INTRODUCTION

Of the 5,000 or so languages in the world only about 500 have a written tradition (Gunnemark and Kenrick 1986). This paper will set up a system of classification of the other 4,500 or so. There are a number of ways in which this could be done, but I think the most useful is to ask the question: 'Why do the speakers of language X not write their language?' Before we do this, however, we need to define the terms 'a language' and 'a written tradition'.

A language

It has been said that a language is a dialect with a gunboat. Although this definition causes problems with landlocked tongues such as Romantsch, it does give a succinct indication of the difference. In other words, a dialect becomes a language in its own right when it has an independent social or political status. Voegelin and Voegelin (1977) use such a definition to arrive at the figure of 5,000.

A written tradition

For a language to have a written tradition there must be writings in it addressed to the speakers of that language.

A language may have a tradition of oral literature, which may lead to traditions of drama and radio broadcasts, without having a written tradition. In fact, it is not unknown for radio broadcasts, say in Krio, to be made via simultaneous translation from another language such as standard English. So, although we should not forget the value of radio in developing a language, in the way, for example, that Radio Hargeisa has done for Somali, we will not include as having a written tradition languages which are written down only informally by actors or radio announcers.

A language does not have a written tradition merely because folktales have been published in a phonetic script in the Journal of Anthropological Linguistics. In the case of Welsh Romani, for example, the corpus of writing largely consists of folktales published in the Journal of the Gypsy Lore Society and translations of parts of the Rubaiyat of Omar Khayyam (1899, 1902, 1907) all written by non-native speakers. As few of the speakers of Welsh Romani could read English or Welsh, and almost none could read Romani, we will not class Welsh Romani as a language with a written tradition. Kloss and McConnell (1978), reached a figure of 1,500 written languages only by including many where the few writings that exist are translations (of parts of the bible or of Lenin) and the work of non-natives.

It is vital to distinguish between those languages which have a native written tradition, and those where most of the material at present available in written form is alien to the cultural values of the community. If the only materials are translations and prayers used by missionaries from an outside religion and proclamations from a distant government forbidding, say, the wearing of native dress, could we then say that this language has a written tradition ? The purpose of starting to write may be not so much to permit the development of one civilisation as to impose another.

In the UNESCO (1953) report on the use of vernacular languages in education 'a vernacular' was defined as 'a language which is the mother tongue of a group which is socially or politically dominated by another group speaking a different language'. With regard to these groups the report declared:

1. Every child of school age should attend school.
2. Every illiterate should be made literate.
3. The best medium of teaching is the mother tongue of the pupil.

This still, however, leaves the way clear to use the mother tongue as the language of instruction, but to teach children (and adults) to write in a second language. For example, in primary schools in Paraguay, Guarani is used for speaking alongside Spanish, but Spanish is the only language used for reading and writing. It is not until the secondary stage (by which time many of the native speakers have ceased attendance) that Guarani is used as a written medium (Engelbrecht and Ortiz 1983).

A TYPOLOGY OF REASONS FOR THE LACK OF A WRITTEN TRADITION

The speakers are illiterate

1. The speakers of language X at this stage in their economic and social development do not want or need to write their or any language. There are communities of subsistence farmers and hunters and gatherers, most of whose day is spent in survival, in obtaining food, clothing and shelter. They have no electricity and reading would be impossible after dark. They may have strong oral traditions, songs, folktales and ceremonies with dances, but if they have a need for a written language they do not feel it.

2. Ethnic groups at a more complex economic level, who, sometimes at least, feel a need to write and read, but are nonetheless illiterate because no-one from inside or outside the group has put the language into writing or set up a system for teaching it. It might be possible for an outside agency to work with native speakers to develop or adapt a system of writing for the language. But this has not happened. Perhaps outside agencies are too busy expelling the group from its ancestral lands or building up their own culture. Amongst women of the Fur in Sudan there is 0% literacy. As the men have some degree of literacy in Arabic, there would seem to be a need or use for the women also to be able to read and write, but the lack of resources and the subordinate role of the women means they cannot.

It has happened many times in history that a resourceful person in an ethnic group has developed a writing system internally. This may be an adaptation of an existing outside one or a new system inspired by noticing that other - more powerful - groups do have a writing system. It has been suggested that the Semitic/Latin alphabet was the work of such an innovative individual inspired by observing the way the Egyptians committed their language to writing. A more recent example is that of the Cherokee. In 1821 after twelve years of work an American Indian, Sequoyah, produced a syllabic alphabet for the language of his people. He was convinced that the power of the white man lay in letters. Within three years enough people had learnt to read to justify the production of a newspaper and the script was still in use fifteen years ago by some 12,000 persons in Oklahoma and Carolina (Ferguson et al. 1981).

There are speakers who are literate, but in another language

At a certain point it is likely that a movement for literacy will begin either from within or from outside the group. In both cases, however, it is possible that the literacy campaign will be conducted not in the speakers' own language, but in that of a more dominant group. This may happen for a variety of reasons. Let us consider possible answers to the question: 'Why might the speakers of language X write language Y rather than language X?'

Prestige considerations.

An example might be Berber, in the predominantly Muslim countries of North Africa. Arabic has prestige because of its role in Islamic teaching. It is only in countries such as Mali where Islam shares prestige with Christianity, and Arabic shares historical significance with the ex-colonial languages, that Berber (in the Tamashek dialect) is widely used on the radio and is developing a literary use.

In Guatemala, Jacaltec, spoken by some 12-20,000 persons, used to be in the shadow of Maya and Quiche. Then, after the Spanish conquest, Spanish became the dominant tongue. A writing system has been developed by missionaries, but the people are reluctant to use it. One speaker told a visiting linguist, 'Our language has no grammar and there are no schools. How can we write it?' She was unwilling even to transcribe a tape as there was no standard form and she did not know how to deal with different individual idiolects.

Hua (Papua New Guinea) faces several problems, of which lack of prestige is one. There are 3,000 first language speakers of whom only two are monolingual. Marriage alliances are normally contracted with speakers of other languages and the women join their husband's family. So, traditionally, women Hua speakers marry speakers of Gimi and go and live with Gimi speakers. The children are brought up bilingual in Hua and Gimi and may learn a third language (e.g. Siane) when they marry. There are two languages with prestige menacing Hua: standard English and Tok Pisin (Pidgin English). The under-20s all know Tok Pisin from work situations and it is now becoming the language of married couples from different language groups. It is entering the oral language usage of first language speakers of Hua in certain defined situations, such as playing cards, or while drinking. In these circumstances Hua is not developing as a written language. This function is served by English or Tok Pisin.

The prestige language may be an older form of the currently spoken language. Examples are Arabic, Greek (see Roussou's paper in this book) and Assyrian. In these cases power does not rest with an outside dominant other language, but with the intelligentsia who through their education have mastered the old written language. In Sweden the authorities found that the Assyrian written language was so far removed from the spoken language of the children that teaching it hampered the acquisition by young children of both Assyrian and Swedish. They therefore developed readers in the Latin alphabet for modern spoken Assyrian, and these were used in Swedish schools.

Maltese, originally a dialect of Arabic, only became a written language in its own right because Malta is a Catholic, not a Muslim country, and therefore no prestige is attached to the older Koranic form of Arabic.

The existence of a related language with a long written tradition can also militate against the development of writing in the minority language. Speakers of Bhojpuri write in Hindi, and speakers of Kachchi write in Gujerati and use it in formal situations (see Alladina's paper in this book). As in the Swedish Assyrian experience noted above, there are experiments in devising Latin alphabets for mother tongue teaching for emigrant communities of such groups, for example with Berber in Norway, and in East London with Sylheti, the spoken language of most London Bengalis. Luxemburgisch has managed to develop as a literary language because of the desire of its speakers to remain independent politically from both France and Germany.

The prestige of a dominant language can mean that parents see their home language as a hindrance to their children's social mobility. Many parents in Peru were against the introduction of Quechua into local schools. They wanted their children to spend as much time as possible learning Spanish to help them in obtaining work. The same argument has been raised by some Caribbean parents in Britain who have opposed the introduction of Creole songs and poetry even in Caribbean Saturday supplementary schools.

A language may also be seen as a survival of colonial oppression and therefore something to be abandoned rather than cherished. This argument was used about Tok Pisin in Papua New Guinea. That language has now reached the position of being used in Parliamentary debates and reports, but many other Creoles are still seen as shameful by their speakers. Some speakers of St. Lucian Patwa will apologise for using 'broken French' in front of an outsider and talk to their children only in English.

Economic considerations

Economic considerations, real or imagined, often militate against the development of a written language. It is often stated, for example, that Mexico cannot afford to set up education projects in its indigenous languages. Indeed, in some countries, even some written languages are not used in Higher Education because of the cost of developing textbooks. Medicine in Egypt and sociology in Iceland both have to be studied through the medium of a foreign language.

In the years since it became culturally independent of Denmark, Greenland, with a population of 55,000, has developed a national written language based only on the western dialect. They felt unable to afford the luxury of a separate written language for the several thousand speakers of the eastern dialect. Also, it is likely that any attempt to develop two languages on the island would mean that Danish might regain its earlier position of prestige.

Considerations of national unity

a. Use of language X is discouraged
This argument places the perceived linguistic needs of nation-building above the educational needs of individuals. For example, in the Philippines, although there are moves to introduce literacy programmes in some minority vernaculars, such as Zamboangueno, on Mindanao, the dominant sentiment of politicians and linguists was to develop one existing language, Tagalog, under the name of Pilipino, to fill the role of a national language. There is now a committee engaged on producing a new national language, to be called Filipino, as a union dialect of many language varieties of the islands.

The desire for national unity may spring from left or right wing political theories. The French Revolution may have dealt a severe blow to the aristocracy, but it also menaced the survival of Breton, Basque and other vernaculars which were actively repressed in France. In Romania Tartar-speaking parents are told by their children's teachers not to use the language to the children as this will hinder their progress in Romanian.

b. Use of language X is forbidden
This is the most extreme case. The prime example is Kurdish. It has a written tradition in the USSR but is banned in Turkey and from time to time in Iran, Syria and Iraq.

Another example is Carpatho-Ruthenian or Rusinian. It has a limited literary use in the USA among older immigrants, but not in its homeland. When the greater part of Rusinian-speaking territory was annexed to the USSR after 1945, Rusinian was replaced by standard Ukrainian in the schools. The same happened later in Czechoslovakia and Hungary. In Poland there were efforts to convince its speakers that Rusinian was a dialect of Polish and that they should have their education through Polish (although Ukrainian is currently an alternative). The situation has been made worse for the preservation of the language in Poland by the removal of its speakers from their home villages to other areas. In Yugoslavia, however, Rusinian was a recognised literary language. So Marx was available in it only in Yugoslavia (Kloss and McConnell 1978, p.561)

In Peru, Aymara and Quechua were introduced into schools in 1978. After a change of government in 1980 they were again banned. In a similar way the Bulgarians prohibited the use of Macedonian and declared it to be a dialect of Bulgarian after the political split with Tito in Yugoslavia. There is pressure on Turkish schools in Bulgaria to change the language of instruction to Bulgarian, and the use of Romani even in songs is discouraged, except in folkloric restaurants for tourists.

The suppression of a written language or the refusal to let it develop is often accompanied by attempts to stop children even speaking it. The 'Welsh knot' was a piece of wood tied around the neck of a child heard speaking in Welsh at school. If another child then spoke the language the knot was passed over. This of course encouraged children to report each other for speaking their own language, as at the end of the week the child with the knot on its neck received a beating. The same system was used to try to kill off Irish and Scottish Gaelic. One of the few living speakers of Manx (who learnt it from his grandmother) tells of how he was punished at school around 1945 for teaching the Manx numerals to his classmates during the break period. Such methods have also been used against the Lapps and Australian Aborigines in this century.

Considerations of numbers

It is sometimes alleged that there are too few speakers to create a literary language. For example in the USSR the 1,065 speakers of Saami (according to the 1971 Census) have not been able to sustain a written language and now use Russian. The Soviet Union, however, contained also examples of very small language communities where a literary tradition has been created and sustained over the past fifty years: Selkup with 2,186 speakers, Mansi with 4,037 speakers and Nivkh (or Gilyak) with 4,420. Outside the USSR, in the Faroes, a population of 40,000 maintains a flourishing literary language.

The bible societies are prepared to work with very small language groups, perhaps more so since the invention of the xerox machine. Translators have prepared portions of the scriptures for the 1,000 speakers of Alta in the Philippines and the 2,500 Yuracare in Bolivia (Grimes 1984).

Restriction to use by élites

There are cases where, as Goody (1968) says: '... literacy is culturally limited to sacred uses and literary skills deliberately or practically restricted to an elite group'.

In some parts of West Africa, Mandinka bards are opposed to writing down songs as they would lose their role (and income) as people who can recite them by heart. Elsewhere in west Africa, in Liberia, the traditional Vai script is taught only to boys as a rite de passage at puberty. It is never used after being learnt, in order to keep it secret from younger boys and females.

In Seal Bay, Alaska, only a limited number of adults could read the church service in Aluutiq, which was used alongside Church Slavonic, also known only by a few men. The policy of the education board from 1931 to 1960 of suppressing native Eskimo and Indian languages so that few children even learnt to speak, let alone write the language gave these local lay readers a prestigious role, which was lost, however, after the coming of a full-time priest who spoke only English and dropped both Aluutiq and Church Slavonic from the services (Reder and Green 1983).

Considerations of secrecy

Some languages serve to enable their speakers to communicate in the confidence they will not be understood by non-members of their community. In the 1970s some Gypsy activists in England opposed Romani (even in a foreign variety) being taught at evening classes in London. After threats to the Principal of the evening institute concerned, the course had to be moved to a different location. In the same way readers of *Romano Drom* newspaper expressed doubts at the wisdom of advertising a correspondence course in Romani. The fear was that police and local authority officials would learn the language and then the Gypsies would not be able to discuss secretly such matters as where they could move to when their caravans had been forcibly evicted.

As Papenbrok points out in this volume, for the German Sinti Gypsies such fears became reality in the Nazi period, when non-Gypsies who had learnt the language took part in the police interrogations to establish family trees and hunt out Gypsies hidden in the house-dwelling community. As a result of this experience there has been strong opposition even to recording of songs in the language.

CONCLUSION

Several of these reasons may be present at the same time in the case of any particular language without a written tradition, or one reason may succeed another. Romani, for example, may be becoming less secret; but even when its speakers decide they do want to read and write it, they still lack power and their language still lacks prestige. The purpose of this book is to explore both the similarities and the differences in the social and sociolinguistic situations of these oral tongues, and where the reasons for their not being written are outside pressures rather than the will of the speakers, to show the way forwards towards the status of a written language.

REFERENCES

Englebrecht G. and Ortiz L. (1983) 'Guarani Literacy in Paraguay', *International Journal of the Sociology of Language*, 42

Ferguson C.A. et al. (eds.) (1981) *Language in the U.S.A.*. Cambridge University Press, Cambridge

Goody J. (1968) 'The Consequences of Literacy' in Goody J. and Watt I. (eds.) *Literacy in Traditional Societies*. Cambridge University Press, Cambridge

Grimes B.F. (ed.) (1984) *Ethnologue: Languages of the World*, 10th Edition. Summer Institute of Linguistics, Dallas

Gunnemark E. and Kenrick D. (1986) *A Geolinguistic Handbook*. Gunnemark, Gothenburg and London

Kloss H. and McConnell G. (1978) *Written Languages of the World*, Volume 1. Laval University, Quebec

Omar Khayyam (1899) tr. Axon W.E.A. and Crofton H.T. 'Homer Tankeromengro 'dre' Ro'manes', *Manchester Quarterly*, 18, p.209

Omar Khayyam (1902) tr. Sampson J., ill. John A. *Omar Khayyam bish ta dui gilia chide are volshitka Romani chib*. D. Nutt, London

Omar Khayyam (1907) tr. MacAlister Sir D. 'Tanangreske Shtarenge Gilia' in MacAlister Sir D. *Echoes*. Macmillan and Bowes, Cambridge

Reder S. and Green K. (1983) 'Contrasting Patterns of Literacy in an Alaskan Fishing Village', *International Journal of the Sociology of Language*, 42

Voegelin C. and Voegelin F. (1977) *Classification of the World's Languages*. Elsevier, Holland

UNESCO (1953) *The Use of Vernacular Languages in Education*. Paris

SECTION TWO

The Emergence of Literary Languages

Introduction

Many of those involved with Creole, Patwa, and Romanes outside of Eastern Europe tend to believe that the problems of their language struggle are different in kind to those that established literary languages have had, if not unique. Friedman's paper on the Balkans presents an invaluable corrective to such ethnocentrism. In the past 750 years in Eastern Europe the emergence of new literary languages from languages without written traditions has been a continuous process. Macedonian, the last completed example given by Friedman, only became an official language when people now in old age were young adults. Romanes language campaigners, therefore, have a live exemplar. There exist in that part of the world general societal expectations, almost a set of ground rules, a set of legitimating preconditions for the attainment of official linguistic status.

Friedman is very clear, however, that although linguists can contribute to and describe the linguistic changes involved in the emergence of a literary language, the determining factors have to do with power and politics. The categories of Lenin's and Stalin's writings on nationality and language, in terms of which the 'rules' of many of the Balkan states were then officially couched, themselves respond to the material reality of ethnic division under the Tsars, and the millet system of the Ottoman empire. In linguistic studies in this field, therefore, there is a very close relation between analysis and advocacy. Advocacy in language campaigns always requires linguistic analysis for support and legitimation; and analysis finds it almost impossible to operate without some value presuppositions; as J.S. Pathania pointed out in a memorable communication to the conference, even the very fact that the linguistic analysis is written in one language rather than another has political implications.

It is to these implications that Devonish addresses himself, laying in his paper some of the groundwork for a self-generated Creole normative grammar written in Creole. It is, in fact, an example of the political linguistics that Friedman has discussed, as is the paper by Acton, Marselos and Szego on Romani. Roussou, however, is in a sense commenting on the reasons for the failure of Cypriot Greek to fulfil a literary promise which began much earlier, leaving Cypriot children with many of the same problems faced in school by other speakers of languages without a written tradition.

An important element in the establishment of many literary languages (English not least among them) has been the production of sacred religious texts, especially the Bible. This continues to be important in the Third World (see Levinsohn in Section 5) and for Romani, as Ellingworth shows.

A number of common themes emerge in these papers, such as the pivotal role of intellectuals whose situation may be far removed by barriers of education, multilingual literacy, social class and politics from the majority of an oral language community. Ellingworth's warnings about Einzelgänger are as firm as those of Dalphinis about super-literates. Finally, one can also draw conclusions from these papers about the need for some kind of linguistic theory to be present in the school curriculum itself. The old school grammars of English or Katharevousa have been discredited both as unscientific and as elements in the maintenance of oppressive social orders, but their disappearance has left a gap as yet unfilled. Unless children learn some way of understanding how utterances are structured, of how in different circumstances we can, without even thinking about it (until we are made to think about it at school) distinguish native speech from that of, say, a foreigner failing to reproduce native speech, then exercises like translation between languages, or even a conscious control of one's own tongue become impossible. Devonish in particular makes it clear that a new linguistics has to root itself in different vernaculars, and in education, for a multilingual society to flourish.

Historical, Nationalistic, and Linguistic Considerations in the Formation of Literary Languages: Past and Current Problems in the Balkan States

Victor A. Friedman

The processes which led to and continue to affect the formations of the modern literary languages of the Balkan peninsula have their parallels elsewhere in the world; yet the Balkans constitute a unique 'living laboratory', due both to the great diversity of languages, and to the fact that these processes are well-documented, relatively recent, and on-going. The relationship of linguistics to the developments in these languages has undergone a number of vicissitudes. Map One shows the provinces, regions and states of particular relevance to this article.

ORIGINS OF MODERN LITERARY LANGUAGES

We consider here six language groups: Greek, Turkic, Romance, Albanian, Slavic and Indic. Each of these groups is represented by one or more literary languages ranging from well-established to nascent. Some of these languages have claims to older written traditions such as Ancient Greek and Old Church Slavonic. These traditions were interrupted because, as the International Commission of Enquiry into the causes of the Balkan Wars wrote:

> ... the Turkish conquest came, levelling all the nationalities and preserving them all alike in a condition of torpor, in a manner comparable to the action of a vast refrigerator (d'Estournelles de Constant et al., 1914, p.29).

This break is crucial in understanding the relationship of Balkan literary languages to contemporary languages without written traditions. After the 'refrigeration', the thaw entailed by the disintegration of the Ottoman empire faced the peoples of the Balkans with the task of creating literary languages on the basis of vernaculars which had completely lost touch with their literary variants, if such there had been in the first place, to such an extent that they were operating, in essence without a continuous written tradition. As a result the problems were and are precisely those faced by any language attempting to establish itself as a medium of written communication, with all the socio-cultural and political significance thus entailed.

In addition, the extra-linguistic factor of ethnicity must be taken into account. Much modern thinking makes mother-tongue the most important determinant of ethnicity. In the Ottoman empire, however, religion was of primary importance as the definer of millet (nationality). Under this system all adherents of the Orthodox Christian Church headed by the patriarch of Constantinople were 'Greeks' while all adherents of the state religion of the Turkish Empire, that is Islam, were 'Turks'. The Greek Orthodox church gradually took advantage of its privileged position in Constantinople to eliminate the autocephalous Bulgarian and Serbian Churches (in 1765 and 1767 respectively).

Thus Bulgarians, Serbs, and all other Greek Orthodox peoples in European Turkey were treated as ethnic 'Greeks' who happened to speak some other language. Likewise the Moslem Albanians, Bosnians, Pomaks, and Torbesh were all 'Turks'. This identification of religion and ethnicity bears not only upon the developments of previous centuries, but also upon current trends.

The definition of the terms 'literary' and language' are problematic. Although both are linguistic, their definitions are largely extra-linguistic, that is, mainly political. It has been said that a language is a dialect with an army of its own. Thus, for example, the Germanic speaking peoples of Scandinavia have no less than three mutually comprehensible languages, while people in Italy, China and the Arab world speak mutually incomprehensible dialects of the same language. In the Balkans, as elsewhere, the situation is complicated in that linguistic and associated ethnic claims are intimately connected with territorial and other political claims. For this paper, however, I will accept the definition of a 'literary language' as one which is codified and used in all spheres of a given political or ethnic unit's national life (Close 1974, p.31). I will also use the term 'literary' to cover the terms 'standard' and 'national' applied to languages; these are important distinctions, but do not affect the considerations of this paper. I will define the following Balkan languages as literary: Greek, Turkish, Romanian, Albanian, Macedonian, Bulgarian and Serbo-Croatian. In addition I will discuss Romani, Aromanian, Moldavian, Croatian and Bosnian in so far as these shed valuable light on processes of development.

POLITICAL CONFLICTS AND LANGUAGE DEVELOPMENT

Greek

The standardisation of Modern Greek has suffered considerably at the hands of linguists due to the diglossia which their disagreements encouraged. Greek diglossia goes back to before the beginning of the Christian era when teachers

The Balkan States: The Formation of Literary Languages

THE BALKANS
VICTOR A. FRIEDMAN

NOTES
1. Disputed parts of former Yugoslavia (Eastern Slavonia, Republika Srpska, Herceg-Bosna) are not specified.
2. Slovenia and Croatia do not consider themselves to be part of the Balkans.

and writers began to attempt to imitate Classical Attic, and actively discouraged the speaking and writing of the common Greek language of their time (Browning 1983, pp.44-45). This artificial atticising Greek was the ancestor of Byzantine Greek, the official language of the Byzantine empire, and began the tendency which culminated in the current diglossia. By the beginning of the nineteenth century, as Greek independence became a real possibility, several opposing linguistic camps emerged: one wished to continue the tradition of Byzantine Greek, another wished to return to classical Greek, a third wished to 'purify' the spoken language of its post-classical elements, and a fourth wished to use the actual spoken language as the basis of the literary language. In the years immediately after independence (1821), the Peloponnesian dialects came to form the basis of a demotic koine (dhimotiki). When Athens became the official capital in 1833, the Athenian dialect was overwhelmed by the flood of newcomers; the contemporary demotic standard is based on the speech of the capital, which in turn has its origin in the speech of the Peloponnese. During the years which followed the establishment of independence, however, a period of political reaction set in as and with it came linguistic reaction: the rise of puristic Greek, katharevousa. Katharevousa is not the descendant of Byzantine Greek, but is rather atticised demotic, a mish-mash of archaic, pseudo-archaic and contemporary forms. During the twentieth century, the opposition between katharevousa and demotic has come to embody the political opposition between the right and the left. Under liberal governments, demotic was used in elementary school instruction and there was hesitation in the use of katharevousa elsewhere. Under right-wing governments such as the military junta of 1967-1974, demotic was banned from all spheres of public life. Since the overthrow of the junta in 1974, demotic has replaced katharevousa everywhere in both public and private life, although katharevousa must still be studied due to the literature written in it. The orthography of demotic, however, has remained relatively conservative and is generally perceived as a valuable link with the past. There are those who would reform the spelling to conform with pronunciation, but they can be compared to those who would radically reform English spelling.

Turkish

The development of literary Turkish provides an interesting contrast with that of Modern Greek. In the course of its use as the official language of the Ottoman empire and the political centre of the Islamic world, Osmanli, that is, Ottoman Turkish, incorporated so much Arabic and Persian vocabulary, syntax and even morphology and phonology that by the nineteenth century this language was incomprehensible to the ordinary speaker of what was called 'kaba türkçe', 'vulgar Turkish'. Lewis (1967, p.xx) says it was as if we said 'What is the conditio of your progenitor reverendus?' instead of 'How's your father?' The Tanzimat of 1839, which stemmed the tide of Arabic and Persian borrowing, brought in a period of reform. No real progress was made, however, until after 1923, when Turkey became a republic headed by Atatürk. In 1928 he switched the whole country, virtually overnight, to a Latin alphabet orthography which he had devised in consultation with linguists. The change of alphabet greatly facilitated the process of eliminating or naturalising Arabic and Persian vocabulary, not only by cutting off the link with those languages, but also by rendering phonological irregularities predictable from the Arabic orthography opaque (Perry 1982, p.16). In 1932 Atatürk founded the Turkish Language Society and held the first Turkish Language Conference. His intention was to create a literary Turkish based on the common spoken language and purged of that part of its Arabic and Persian component which had not entered common usage. The Turkish Language Society was charged with creating new vocabulary based on dialect words, borrowing from other Turkic languages, and, most important, new derivations based on roots already present in the language.

The extremist purism of the Turkish Language Society during the 1930s, however, gave rise to one of the most bizarre linguistic theories ever to emerge from a standardisation movement, the so-called Sun Language Theory (Günes Dil Teorisi). According to this theory all human language originated from man's utterance of the primal syllable A(g), and all words of all languages can be derived by a series of formulae from this primal syllable. In addition it was claimed that Turkish was the mother of all languages (Tankut 1936). While this theory rendered most Turkish theoretical linguistic work of the period invalid, it did have the positive effect of tempering radical purism; for if Turkish was the mother language, then Arabic and Persian words in it were ultimately of Turkish origin, and could thus be claimed as native Turkish. It is even suspected that Atatürk himself launched this theory for the purpose of controlling the radical purists (Heyd 1954, p.34). It is in the role of purism that Greek and Turkish present an instructive contrast. The purism of Greek is archaising and politically conservative, that of Turkish is innovating and politically liberal or radical. During the most recent period of military rule in Turkey, when public discussion of politics was forbidden, right and left wing newspapers began to editorialise on linguistic usage. The former, led by Tercüman, attacked the Turkish Language Society as too radical; the latter, led by Cumhuriyet defended it. Both sides did so in the name of Atatürk, the former claiming that the Turkish Language Society had gone too far, the latter claiming that it was carrying on his mission.

Romanian

The case of Romanian differs from both Greek and Turkish. The earliest document in Romanian is a letter from 1521. With the Turkish conquest, Greek gradually became the dominant language in Wallachia and Moldavia due to the millet system, because the majority of the population was Orthodox Christian. The situation in Transylvania was considerably more complicated. After the reformation Transylvania had four official religions: Catholicism, Unitarianism, Calvinism and Lutheranism. The ruling classes had two languages: Hungarian and German. The majority of the population consisted of disenfranchised Romanian-speaking Eastern Orthodox serfs. As education was tied to class and religion, there were no Romanian schools. During the eighteenth century, the Habsburgs introduced the Uniate Church into Transylvania, in an attempt to Catholicise the Romanian speaking majority and thus promote centralisation and the integration of Transylvania into their empire. The result was that Romanians were exposed to education, learned that their language was descended from the Latin of the 'noble Romans' who had ruled a vast empire, and thus acquired a new sense of dignity before their German and Magyar masters. The resultant movement, called Latinism, served as the basis of Romanian nationalism and the development of the Romanian literary language (Verdery 1983, pp.84, 108-121). The movement spread also to Wallachia and Moldavia. The subsequent rise of literary activity was particularly concerned with lexicographic considerations and the relationship of Romanian to Latin and the living Romance languages that already had literary traditions, especially French and Italian. This was particularly true in the coining of neologisms and the devising of an orthography: French was more important for the former and Italian for the latter. The dialectal base of the literary language which emerged was that of Wallachia, particularly Bucharest. There were early attempts to create a literary Romanian which combined Aromanian and Daco-Romanian dialects, but these were abandoned as impractical (Close 1974, p.67). In 1859 Moldavia and Wallachia were for all practical purposes united into an independent country, and the Cyrillic alphabet which had been used for Romanian since the sixteenth century was officially replaced by a Latin orthography. Transylvania became part of Romania between 1918 and 1920.

Unlike Greek and Turkish, in which the divisions have been language-internal, the divisions affecting Romanian have been external, Moldavian on the one hand, and Aromanian (Macedo-Romanian) on the other. As a result of the annexation of Bessarabia by the Russian empire in 1812, the principality of Moldavia was divided in half. The half that remained dependent on Turkey formed part of independent Romania in 1859. Bessarabia became part of Romania in 1919 and was re-annexed by Russia in 1940. During the inter-war period Russian claims to Bessarabia were historico-political: the 'people' of Bessarabia wanted to live in a communist state. After World War II, however, the Russians could no longer use this argument, since Romania was also a socialist country, and so the concept of a separate Moldavian nationality with its own Moldavian literary language was pursued in earnest (King 1973, pp.100-105). As Dyer (1985) has shown, however, literary Moldavian is based on the same Wallachian dialects that serve as the basis of literary Romanian. The only significant differences between the two literary languages is that the former uses a Cyrillic orthography and has a larger component of East Slavic loanwords.

Aromanian, the Romance language of the scattered groups living in Albania, Greece, and Macedonia, had separated from Daco-Romanian by the tenth century. While it could not be integrated with literary Daco-Romanian for a variety of reasons (Close 1974, p.67), the fact that it does not constitute a separate literary Balkan language is worthy of comment in the context of the pluralist policies of Yugoslavia, particularly Macedonia. It would appear that religion is still an important defining ethnic factor, in so far as all the Muslim non-Slavic minorities of Macedonia have or are obtaining a large measure of cultural autonomy, whereas the Aromanians, who constitute the largest Christian non-Slavic minority (0.5% of the population) do not have such rights.

Albanian

Like Romanian, Albanian did not have an ancient literary tradition. The earliest document is a baptismal formula embedded in a Latin text from 1462. While Albania was under Ottoman rule, an Albanian literature did develop among the Albanians who had fled to Italy, the Arbëresh, but this did not have much effect on events in Albania. The Albanians were divided among three religions, Catholics (10%), Orthodox (20%) and Muslims (70%), (Byron 1979a, p.17) and the millet system worked especially to their disadvantage. The Orthodox were subject to Hellenisation, the Muslims were considered 'Turks' and therefore denied linguistic rights even after various Christian peoples had begun to gain theirs, while the Catholics were few, and largely isolated in the mountains of the North, although there was a significant community in Scutari (Skendi 1980, pp.187-204). The millet system also put the Albanians in danger of being completely partitioned by their Greek and Slavic Christian neighbours as the Ottoman empire was disintegrating, and so in 1878 in the wake of the Congress of Berlin, a group of Albanians formed the League of Prizren to promote Albanian nationalism, defend Albanian territorial integrity, and promote the Albanian language (the one national characteristic that cut across religious boundaries). A key issue was the choice of an alphabet. Each of the possibilities had religious implications: Arabic implied Islam, Greek implied Orthodoxy, and Latin implied Catholicism. Cyrillic was also used, especially in Macedonia, but was never a serious national contender. In the case of the Latin alphabet the choice of symbols and digraphs was of interest to the European powers, because they were sponsoring schools and seeking to extend their influence in the area. Thus, for example, Austria-Hungary and Italy, which were both publishing textbooks and sponsoring schools, purposefully supported differing orthographies (Skendi 1980, pp.218-220). In 1908 the Young Turks came to power and the Albanians were briefly permitted linguistic freedom. That same year the Albanian Alphabet Congress of Bitola (Monastir) was a key step leading ultimately to the current Latin orthography. Fearing that an Albanian literary language might lead to an independent Albanian state, the Young Turks attempted to suppress the Latin Alphabet, but in vain. Independence was declared in 1912, and from then till 1945 the main focus of linguistic effort was the dialect question. Albanian has two very different dialect groups: Geg (North) and Tosk (South). In the early years of independence people wrote more or less in their own dialects and attempts at dialect integration were threatened by a high degree of artificiality, as for example in Faik Konitza's suggestion that the Geg indefinite article nji and the Tosk indefinite article një both be used in literary Albanian, the former for feminine nouns and the latter for masculine, although in fact no Albanian dialect ever makes a gender distinction in the indefinite article (Byron 1976, p.50). Under King Zog (1925-1939), efforts were made to base a literary standard on the Southern Geg dialect of Elbasan, but serious standardisation did not progress until after the second world war.

At this point it should be noted that the region of Kosovo, which is predominantly Albanian, was awarded to the Kingdom of Serbia in 1913, and subsequently became part of Yugoslavia. In Albania the number of Gegs only slightly exceeds that of Tosks, but Gegs are the only Albanian group in Kosovo, and the overwhelming majority of Macedonia's 23% Albanian minority. After 1945 the Tosk dialect of Korçë gradually emerged as the basis of the standard in Albania, while Albanians in Yugoslavia continued to pursue standard Geg. The Yugoslav government tried to encourage the idea that there were two separate nationalities and languages (Albanski in Albania versus Shiptarski in Yugoslavia) but this failed. In 1968 the Albanians of Kosovo officially accepted the Tosk-based literary standard of Albania, thus producing gjuha unifikuar, the 'unified language' (Byron 1979b).

Kosovo intellectuals, however, keep length and nasality in their speech, and efforts have been made to introduce certain Geg features into the standard, e.g. the reflexive pronoun i vetë which expresses a distinction lacking in most Tosk dialects, but the literary standard is still Tosk in the vast majority of its features.

South Slavic

The South Slavs have been considerably more fragmented than the other language groups considered so far. The territory of modern-day Yugoslavia was divided between Austria-Hungary and Turkey at the beginning of the nineteenth century. Autonomy, independence, and unification were achieved in bits and pieces during the next hundred years. During the nineteenth century the literary languages of the West South Slavs (Serbs, Croats Bosnians, and others) were characterised by increasing unity while those of the East South Slavs (Bulgarians and Macedonians) tended towards division.

The differences among the West South Slavs were considerable. Serbs are Orthodox and use Cyrillic; Croats are Catholic and use the Latin alphabet. Croatian dialects diverge from one another much more than Serbian dialects. Croatian tends to borrow from Latin and German and tends to create neologisms whereas Serbian is more likely to borrow from Greek and Turkish and accept loanwords from other Slavic languages, e.g. Croatian kolodvor, Serbian stanica, 'station'.

A major dialectal division cutting across these lines is the reflex of Common Slavic *e (the choice for example between snig, sneg, and snijeg for snow). In 1850 Serbian and Croatian linguists and intellectuals signed the knjizhevni dogovor ('literary agreement') in Vienna, agreeing to adopt a Herzegovina-based 'ijekavian-shtokavian' standard developed by the Serb Vuk Karadzhic as a common literary language. This was a compromise for both sides brought about by the political necessity of having a common language. Vuk's language, however, met with stiff resistance in Serbia, where it was not officially adopted till 1868. The Serbs had been using a form of Church Slavonic called Slavenoserbian, which had an established literary tradition and orthography, albeit no direct connection with the spoken language. Vuk not only rejected the vocabulary and grammar of this language, advocating instead the use of the vernacular, but he also reformed its Cyrillic orthography, eliminating obsolete letters, and, following the principle of one letter per sound, introducing the grapheme <j> from the Latin alphabet. This last move outraged many Serbs because of its Roman Catholic implications. The majority of Serbs, however, never accepted the ijekavian pronunciation, and ironically enough, Vuk's ijekavian standard came to be identified as Croatian. In 1954 a new agreement was signed in Novi Sad in which the various Serbo-Croatian speaking peoples of Yugoslavia reaffirmed their commitment to a unified literary language. In March 1967, however, a group of Croatian intellectuals issued a manifesto proclaiming Croatian as a separate language, and problems continue to this day. In recent years the Serbo-Croatian speaking Muslims who constitute the plurality in Bosnia-Herzegovina, and who are recognised as a separate ethnic group, Muslimani (now Bosniacs), have also been agitating for a separate codified standard distinct from both Serbian and Croatian. Further conflict is created by the prestige dialects of the Serbian and Croatian capitals (Belgrade and Zagreb), which both differ from Vuk's standard (Magner 1981). Thus the centripetal forces of the nineteenth century have been replaced by centrifugal ones in the twentieth (Naylor 1980).

The situation of the East South Slavs, the Bulgarians and the Macedonians, has been quite different. As a group they were threatened by hellenisation during the first half of the nineteenth century due to the millet system, but with the establishment of an independent Bulgarian church (the Exarchate), different tensions began to manifest themselves. Two centres of Slavic literacy had arisen during this period: one in south- western Macedonia and one in northeastern Bulgaria. The people of the southwest had a distinct regional identification as Macedonians, and with the uncompromising attitude of the users of the northeast Bulgarian standard, especially after the establishment of the Exarchate, came the development of a separate ethnic and linguistic consciousness among many Macedonians. In dialectal terms, there is a relatively thick bundle of isoglosses, coinciding roughly with the Serbian-Bulgarian political border, which fans out when it reaches Macedonia, so that the dialects of Macedonia are transitional between Serbian and Bulgarian. Serbia and Bulgaria also had conflicting territorial claims to Macedonia (as did Greece), and they tried to support these claims by linguistic arguments, as well as by force of arms as in the second Balkan war of 1912 (Belic 1919, p.250, Vaillant 1938, p.119). The official Bulgarian attitude to this day is that Macedonian is a 'regional variant' of Bulgarian (B.A.N. 1978).

A comparison is sometimes made between Macedonian and Moldavian (King 1973, pp.100-102). The claim is that just as the Russians have fostered a Moldavian language in order to justify the annexation of Bessarabia from Romania, so the Yugoslavs have created a Macedonian language to justify their territorial claims against Bulgaria. There are, however, considerable differences between the two situations. Macedonian linguistic separatism is attested in print since 1878, and the first definitive outline of the bases for a Macedonian literary language dates from 1903, while Macedonia was still a part of Turkey (Friedman 1975). Thus, while the official recognition of a separate Macedonian language and nationality may well be in Yugoslav interests, the fact remains that this language and ethnic identification arose among Macedonians themselves quite independently of Yugoslav interests, before such interests even existed. The same cannot be said of Moldavian, since Bessarabia had already been annexed to Russia in 1812.

After the second Balkan war, Macedonia was divided among Serbia (later Yugoslavia), Greece and Bulgaria. In Greece, Macedonians have been subjected to gradual but unrelenting hellenisation. In Bulgaria, only the Bulgarian language has been permitted in Macedonia, except during the period 1946-1948 (from the end of World War Two to the Tito-Stalin break), when Macedonian was recognised in Bulgaria as a minority language. In Yugoslavia Macedonian was treated as a Serbian dialect between the two world wars, but literature was published and plays were performed in it as 'folklore and dialect literature'. On August 2nd, 1944, in keeping with Tito's pluralist nationalist policy, Macedonian was officially recognised as a separate literary language in Yugoslavia. The basis was the speech of the West Central dialect region, and a generation of young linguists set about establishing norms. There was a brief period when some people proposed waiting until a team of Russian experts could be brought in, but this proposal was not accepted (Friedman 1985). The orthography follows the principles of Serbian rather than Bulgarian.

Macedonian presents one of the few examples where linguists participated in a more rational arrangement of dictionary entries. Following the classical tradition, the codifiers of the literary language at first listed verbs by the first singular (present). In literary Macedonian, however, a verb can have one of three stem-vowels (/a/, /e/, /i/) in all persons of the present except the first singular (and third plural), where this opposition is neutralised (only /a/ occurs). An American linguist, Horace Lunt, convinced the codifiers to use the third singular, which clearly shows the present stem, rather than the first singular as the standard citation form (Lunt 1951). This not only gave the dictionary entry more predictive power, but also helped spread the standard use of stem-vowels, an area of considerable dialectal variation. A major problem for literary Macedonian is the fact that Skopje, the capital and principal cultural centre, is outside the West Central area and is subject to considerable Serbo-Croatian influence. Nonetheless, an entire generation of speakers educated in the literary language has grown up, and they can and do use it consistently.

Literary Bulgarian, like Serbo-Croatian and Greek, had to face threats from archaisers who wanted Church Slavonic to become the official language of the emerging Bulgarian state. Having overcome these (although Bulgarian orthography was not completely modernised until 1944) as well as the hellenisers mentioned earlier, the creators of the literary Bulgarian were faced with the task of integrating a number of divergent dialects. On the whole, however, having experienced increasing centrifugal tendencies in the nineteenth century and a definitive split in the twentieth, the two East South Slav literary languages are currently characterised by tendencies to unify around their respective standards, as opposed to the increasing fragmentation of West South Slavic.

Romani

Although literary activity in Romani dates only from the early years of this century, a number of attempts have been made to use it in at least some of the functions of a literary language in literature and education, in the USSR, Scandinavia and elsewhere. The past decade or so has seen a significant upsurge in Romani nationalism, and concomitant with these activities there have been renewed attempts to create a Romani literary language (that is, a unified, standard language). Activities within the scope of this paper had one of their most important starting-points in southern parts of the former Yugoslavia, which has the largest settled Romani population. Of particular significance was the publication of a bilingual edition (Romani and Macedonian) of a Romani grammar in Skopje in 1980 (Jusuf and Kepeski 1980). This grammar is a significant signal of the efforts to create a Romani literary language for use in schools, and can be compared with certain Macedonian works by Gorgi Pulevski from the end of the nineteenth century (Friedman 1975). Both reflect the rising national consciousness of their respective peoples, both are polyglot as a reflection of the linguistic situations of their respective users, and both reflect a lack of consistency and standardisation characteristic of the pre-codified stage of a nascent literary language. In the case of Macedonian, Pulevski's work, like other manifestations of Macedonian nationalism at that time, was lost or suppressed for many years, although the results achieved in 1944 were consistent with the beginnings signalled by it. In the case of Romani, Jusuf and Kepeski's grammar may be able to serve as the starting point for a Romani literary standard, at least in Macedonia and adjacent parts of Serbia and Kosovo.

The chief problems facing all attempts at a Romani literary standard are the integration and selection among divergent dialects and the expansion of vocabulary. Jusuf and Kepeski draw on the three main dialects of Skopje: Arlija, Dzhambaz and Burgudzhi. The Arlija dialect is the oldest in Skopje and serves as the principle one for the grammar, but the authors' main approach to dialect selection is to avoid it: they randomly use different dialect forms throughout the text, including some of the paradigms. For the expansion of vocabulary, Jusuf and Kepeski have followed the practice endorsed by the World Romani Congress, of borrowing words from Hindi. Unfortunately, they have not adapted these borrowings to Romani phonology; for example, they spell words with voiced aspirates, which are quite foreign to the Romani sound system, for example, bhavi, 'consciousness'. Another important issue is that of the choice of orthography. Jusuf and Kepeski chose the Latin alphabet with a Yugoslav-based spelling, although they also supply a conversion table for a Macedonian-based Cyrillic alphabet which they use when citing Romani forms in their Macedonian text. The bialphabetical linguistic practice which is already well-established in Yugoslavia made this obviously internationally aimed option easier.[2] We should also mention here the suggestion of Cortiade (1984) to overcome certain dialect differences by means of the use of morphophonemic symbols in the spelling system, e.g. orthographic <Romeça> for phonetic (romesa)/(romeha)/(romeja)/(romea), 'Rom', instrumental case, where the various realisations of what was originally intervocalic /s/ are readily predictable. In other environments, however, there is a considerable variation in the treatment of /s/, and so ultimately a choice will have to be made. Cortiade has argued that one of the more conservative Balkan dialects should serve as the basis of literary Romani, since various innovations are predictable in terms of the original base, but not vice versa.

When we look at the factors which have led to the selection of dialect bases for the various Balkan literary languages, we see a combination of political, cultural and numerical considerations. Thus, for example, in the case of literary Macedonian, the choice of the West Central dialect was motivated by three major factors: it was the most distinct from both Serbian and Bulgarian, it was the single largest relatively homogeneous dialect region, and it was the most readily comprehensible by the largest number of speakers from other regions. In the case of Serbian, Vuk Karadzhic chose his native dialect. The victory of literary Tosk over literary Geg as the basis of Standard Albanian is due at least in part to the fact that the majority of the leaders of post-war Albania were Tosks (Byron 1979a). In Bulgaria and Greece, the dialect in the first area to become independent of Turkish domination ended up as the basis for the literary language, although other factors (shift of capital in Bulgaria, diglossia in Greece) have significantly complicated the picture. Similarly, in Turkey and Romania, it is the dialects of the capitals which have had the prestige to serve as the bases of the literary languages, although in the case of Romania, the original impetus came from outside the literary region. In this context, it can be said that the considerable Romani literary activity outside of the Balkans will also have to be taken into account, but the precise outcome of interaction and integration remains to be seen.

We see therefore that the use of linguistics in the formation of literary languages and the affirmation of nationalism has had a wide variety of effects. Historical linguistics has been used by archaisers and purifiers, especially in the cases of Greek and Turkish. On the other hand dialectology has been the key to efforts of separatism and unity among the Slavic, Romance and Albanian languages. To these latter can now be added Romani. In the fixing of orthographies, phonology has played a role in all but Greek, which has retained its historical spelling. All of the other languages claim 'phonetic' spelling, although in fact phonemic would generally be a better term. Of the

Slavic languages, Bulgarian is distinguished from Serbo-Croatian and Macedonian by a greater tendency towards morphophonemic spelling and as a result of the 1944 spelling reform, Bulgarian also has a few morphologically conditioned pronunciations of a type not found in Serbo-Croatian and Macedonian. Another example of a phonological phenomenon affected by standardisation is the automatic devoicing of underlying voiced consonants in final position. This is absent in Greek, Romanian and Serbo-Croatian, but uniformly present in Macedonian, Bulgarian and some dialects of Albanian and Romani. The approach in the Slavic languages is to portray the underlying phoneme orthographically, e.g. narod/narodi, /narot/-/narodi/, 'people/peoples'. In Turkish, after considerable vacillation, the current orthographic practice favours phonetic representation, e.g. cep/cebim 'pocket/my pocket'. In the case of Albanian, the central dialects are characterised by final devoicing, a feature absent both further north and further south. In this instance language planners eventually opted for spelling final voiced consonants, e.g. zog/zogu, 'bird/the bird', despite the fact that this does not represent the pronunciation of the Tosk region whose dialects form the basis of the standard language. The spelling of final voiced consonants is helping to spread the pronunciation to areas where it is not native. On this point as on others Jusuf and Kepeski's Romani grammar uses alternatives without selecting between them e.g. in the spellings dad and dat, 'father'. The general tendency in most works written in Romani so far, however, has been to spell with voiced final consonants.

In the realm of morphology we have seen how the alternatives offered by different dialect forms can be used to enrich the literary language, or to create artificial distinctions. In the case of syntax and lexicon, the dialects (and earlier stages of the language) can be used to enrich the literary language; a key issue for these, however, (which does not affect phonology and morphology in the same way) is the extent of foreign lexical borrowing and syntactic imitation of foreign models. This has been an especially important issue for Macedonian, where the tremendous influence of Serbo-Croatian after 1945 threatened to alter its syntactic patterns significantly. Concerted efforts on the part of both codifiers and users of the literary language have succeeded in reversing this trend, however.

CONTEMPORARY SOURCES OF AUTHORITY IN LANGUAGE CODIFICATION

Each of the socialist countries, Albania, Bulgaria, Romania and each republic and autonomous region of the former Yugoslavia has an academy of sciences and an institute of language. The institutes are responsible not only for linguistic research but also for developing and defining literary norms and publishing grammars, dictionaries and other authoritative works. Each institute has its journal in which both theoretical and practical linguistic questions are addressed. The Institutes are not the only sources of normativisation, however. There are also Teachers' Unions and other language organisations which publish linguistic or language journals on a more popular level and which are devoted to practical considerations of usage and codification. Similar linguistic topics are also discussed in the daily press, and there are many popular books on 'language culture', that is, normative usage. As a result, the codification of literary languages has developed in part through dialogue between codifiers and users.

In Greece and Turkey, language codification has been more closely tied to political parties, and linguistic tendencies are associated with political tendencies. (This is not to say that language was divorced from politics in the socialist Balkans, but only that codification has not been subject to the same types of vicissitudes in a one party system as in a multi-party system.) Although the Turkish Language Society functions in a manner similar to that of the institutes described above, neither Greece nor Turkey has quite the same type of institution due to differences in sociopolitical structure, and the Ministry of Education frequently plays a more active role in decision-making.

In future language planning and standardisation in the Balkans, linguistics can be used to advance compromise solutions to specific problems, choices or interpretations, or it can be used to justify divisive tendencies which are always potentially present. In Greek and Turkish, special problems are created by the strength of archaising and puristic tendencies, while the Slavic and Albanian literary languages face special difficulties due to the fact that their cultural and political capitals are located outside the region where the literary dialectal base is native. In Romani the chief problems which must be faced are dialectal compromise and vocabulary enrichment, and as these processes are still in their early stages, there is much that linguistics and the previous experiences of other languages can contribute.

NOTES

1. In this paper, I take the most widely accepted definition of the term 'Balkan', that is, the peninsula comprising the modern nations of Albania, Bulgaria, Greece, Romania, the former Yugoslavia and European Turkey (Turkish Thrace). A more detailed treatment of some of the themes of this paper appear in my article 'Linguistics, Nationalism, and Literary Languages: A Balkan Perspective' in Raskin V. and Bjorkman P (eds. 1986) *The Real World Linguist: Linguistic Applications in the 1980s*, Ablex, New Jersey, pp.287-305. A number of changes have occurred since this paper was originally written, especially in former Yugoslavia. Nonetheless the basic facts are accurate.
2. The former Soviet Union provides an instructive contrast. There, Romani, like all other national or literary languages except Estonian, Latvian, Lithuanian, Armenian, Georgian, and Yiddish, had to use a Russian-based Cyrillic alphabet.

REFERENCES

B.A.N. (1978) 'Edinstvo na bulgarskija ezik v minaloto i dnes', *Bulgarski ezik*, 28(1), pp.3-43
Belic A. (1919) *La Macédoine*. Bloud & Gay, Paris
Browning R. (1983) *Medieval and Modern Greek*. C.U.P., Cambridge
Byron J. (1976) 'Faik Konitza dhe gjuha letrare shqipe' in Licho E. (ed.) *Faik Konitza 1876-1976*. Vatra, New York, pp.49-51
Byron J. (1979a) *Selection Among Alternates in Language Standardization: The Case of Albanian*. Mouton, The Hague
Byron J. (1979b) 'Language Planning in Albania and in Albanian-speaking Yugoslavia', *Word*, 30(1-2), pp.15-44
Close E. (1974) *The Development of Modern Rumanian*. O.U.P., London
Cortiade M. (1984) *Romani fonetika thaj lekhipa*. Filan Than
Dyer D.L. (1985) 'Moldavian Linguistic Realities'. Paper presented at 4th International Conference on Non-Slavic Languages of the Soviet Union, University of Chicago, May 1985
Du Nay A. (1977) *The Early History of the Rumanian Language*. Jupiter, Lake Bluff, Il.
d'Estournelles de Constant Baron et al. (1914) *Report of the International Commission of Inquiry into the Causes and Conduct of the Balkan Wars*. Carnegie Endowment for International Peace, Washington D.C.
Friedman V.A. (1975) 'Macedonian Language and Nationalism in the Nineteenth and Early Twentieth Centuries', *Balkanistica*, 2, pp.83-98
Friedman V.A. (1982) 'Reportedness in Bulgarian: Category or Stylistic Variant?', *International Journal of Slavic Linguistics and Poetics*, 25 and 26, pp.149-163
Friedman V.A. (1985) "Sociolinguistics of Literary Macedonian', *International Journal of the Sociology of Language*, 52, pp.31-57.
Heyd U. (1954) *Language Reform in Modern Turkey*, Oriental Society, Jerusalem
Jusuf, S. and Kepeski, K. (1980) *Romani Gramatika - Romska Gramatike*. Nasa Kniga: Skopje.
King R.R. (1973) *Minorities Under Communism; Nationalities as a Source of Tension Among Balkan Communist States*. Harvard, Cambridge, Mass.
Lewis G.L. (1967) *Turkish Grammar*. O.U.P., London
Lunt H. (1951) 'Morfologijata na makedonskiot glagol', *Makedonski jazik*, 2(6), pp.123-131
Magner T.F. (1981) 'The Emperor's New Clothes, or a Modest Peek at the Serbo Croatian Accentual System', *General Linguistics*, 21(4), pp.248-258
Naylor K.E. (1980) 'Serbo-Croatian' in Schenker A.M. and Stankiewicz E. (eds.) *The Slavic Literary Languages*. Yale Concilium on International and Area Studies, New Haven
Perry J.R. (1982) 'Language Reform in Turkey and Iran'. Paper presented at the Atatürk Centennial Symposium, University of Chicago, 5 June
Skendi S. (1980) *Balkan Cultural Studies*. East European Monographs, Boulder CO.
Tankut H.R. (1936) *Güne-dil teorisine göre dil tetkikleri*, State Publishing House, Istanbul
Vaillant A. (1938) 'Le problèm du slave macédonian', *Bulletin de la Société de Paris*, 39(2, 116), pp.194-210
Ventcel T.V. and Cherenkov L.N. (1976) 'Dialekty cyganskogo jazyka', *Jazyki Azii i Afriki*, 1, pp.283-339
Verdery K. (1983) *Transylvanian Villagers: Three Centuries of Political, Economic and Ethnic Change*. University of California, Berkeley

On the Writing of Normative Grammars for Caribbean Creole Languages: The Case of Guyanese Creole

Hubert Devonish

INTRODUCTION

One result of Caribbean Creole languages' expansion of functions in the area of writing is concern about the question of 'correctness'. In the area of spelling, the development and popularisation of suitable orthographic conventions are sought. For 'correctness' in word use, dictionaries and technical word lists would provide a solution. The focus of this paper is the problem of 'correctness' in the area of Creole morpho-syntax, that is, what is commonly referred to as the 'grammar' of the language.

The writing of normative grammars for Caribbean Creole languages would provide a way of establishing 'correctness' in the area of their morpho-syntactic systems, but we have to be clear about the kind of sociolinguistic circumstances into which these grammars would be introduced, and the kinds of language attitudes and behaviour which such grammars would be expected to promote, and the precise nature of the 'correctness' which such grammars would be expected to develop within the speech community.

This paper presumes there will be no policy to impose on the population any single variety of the language as the sole standard form, but rather, to the degree that standardisation is desirable, it should be allowed to emerge naturally and by popular consensus over a period of time. The normative grammar should therefore possess a flexibility which would promote rather than hinder the development of this consensus, and allow for continued variation where consensus is either not possible or not desired by members of the speech community.

What, then, would be the morpho-syntactic norms promoted as 'correct' by such a normative grammar? It would have to identify as recommended those forms which are shared by the widest range of Creole language varieties in the speech community. Such a grammar would also have to list the other variant forms used, ranked according to distribution rather than simply labelled 'correct' or 'incorrect'.

On Writing of Normative Grammars for Caribbean Creole Languages

We have to be clear about the purpose of these recommendations. An 'official' language, or one granted 'official status' is for use within state institutions. Officially controlled or influenced educational, mass media and other institutions direct communications at the mass of the population. The very centralised nature of these sources of communication tends to require some degree of normalisation within language varieties used in official domains. Without in any way condoning the degree of centralised government control which exists in most Caribbean Creole-speaking communities, some degree of centralisation is presumably always going to be necessary. The recommendations in a normative grammar of Guyanese Creole would therefore be primarily directed at its official use, and would aim at a variety of the language which first provides the maximum degree of intelligibility for the widest cross-section of the Guyanese population, and secondly does not appear to favour any one section of the speech community at the expense of other sections.

What, however, about those Creole forms not recommended by the normative grammar? They would, of course, continue to be used by those speakers who currently employ them. The fact that they are not recommended in the normative grammar ought not to represent any attempt to suppress them. The non-recommendation of these forms in the normative grammar would be directed at the language use of a small number of persons operating in a limited range of public communication. The inclusion of non-recommended forms within the grammar would both give those forms legitimacy and allow the grammar to serve as a valid reference for all the varieties of the language. This general legitimising function is far more important than that of recommendation versus non-recommendation of particular variant forms.

A normative grammar which has as one of its goals the provision of a reference point for all the varieties of Creole in a country like Guyana, is a basic ingredient in the development of a democratic and decentralised official language policy. Such a policy would encourage the use of all varieties of Creole, in speech and writing, for official as well as non-official functions. The only exception would be those communications originating from institutional centres. Here, the forms recommended in the normative grammar would be employed. The presentation in the normative grammar of the range of possible variant forms, recommended or otherwise, allows those who use the grammar to familiarise themselves with Creole forms which they do not actively use. In circumstances where the bulk of the population has a passive or receptive competence in varieties other than those which they speak natively, it would be possible for any speaker to use any variety of Creole in a public communication situation, without worrying about whether the variety chosen is unfamiliar to any section of the audience. It is easier to encourage receptive competence in varieties which are unfamiliar, than to force a large section of the population to produce actively some set of standard Creole forms which they may not normally use actively.

LINGUISTIC DESCRIPTION IN THE NORMATIVE GRAMMAR

In the case of Guyanese Creole, there is a growing body of material concerned with the linguistic description and analysis of particular aspects of the language (Bickerton 1975; Rickford 1979; Gibson 1982). These works, however, are highly specialist studies, accessible only to a handful of people with training in linguistics. Also, each of these works tends, for reasons of practicality, to focus on a particular sub-system within the overall linguistic system of the language. This creates the danger that sight may be lost of the role which the sub-system plays within the overall linguistic system. These works also tend to be carried out within quite specific theoretical frameworks. Apart from the issue of the extent to which the theoretical approaches adopted are appropriate for describing the Guyanese Creole language data, there is the problem presented by the lack of compatibility between the various approaches.

Nonetheless, these works constitute a vital input into the writing of a normative grammar, but for many of them to be of any use, steps have to be taken:

1. to extract the various insights provided from within the narrow theoretical and analytical strictures within which they may have been originally presented;
2. to integrate these insights into a general analysis of the linguistic system;
3. to present them in a manner which would attempt to reflect the way that a native speaker, uninfluenced by grammatical notions derived from formal instruction in English, would perceive that his language operates.

The problem which faces any attempt to take steps (i) and (ii), lies in the tendency, even in modern linguistic analyses of Caribbean Creole languages, to treat them as deviant forms of the European languages from which they derived the bulk of their vocabularies. The writers on Guyanese Creole would argue that this is precisely what they were trying *not* to do, but the frequently uncritical acceptance of linguistic categories such as Noun, Verb, Adjective and Preposition would tend to belie any such claim. However suitable these categories may be for describing languages like English, using them without establishing their applicability to Creole assumes that it is similar to such languages. It may be in some respects, but the existence and precise definitions of its linguistic categories must be based only on analysis of Creole language data.

In order to illustrate this, let us examine the area of grammatical morphemes in Guyanese Creole. In Caribbean English-lexicon Creole languages, there is, by comparison with English, a relatively small number of grammatical items performing a wide range of grammatical functions. Thus, *fu* performs the functions of complementiser, modal verb and preposition. The item *dem* operates as a personal pronoun and a plural marker on nominals. And in the case of the item *a* the functions of demonstrative adjective, continuative aspect marker, equational verb and locational preposition are among those performed. There are two possible responses to these examples. The first is to assume that the same form is used in each case to represent a range of functions purely as a result of chance. The second possibility is to hypothesise that the commonality in form might represent some commonality at the semantic level. Were this to turn out to be the case with any of the items, and the distribution of the items in each of its functions was compatible, one could conclude that there is a systematic relation between each of the functions of the item. Any treatment of such grammatical forms in the normative grammar ignoring the significance of shared forms across apparently distinct syntactic functions, runs the risk of going against the intuitions of the native speakers of the language. Only in the absence of any clear semantic link across the various functions performed by a particular language form, can one safely conclude that the formal similarity is of little significance for normative purposes.

This focus on the association of apparently disparate functions of the same form will provide the cohesion necessary for the proposed normative grammar. The major input into such a grammar will be already existing descriptions of specific aspects of the syntactic system. These descriptions, however, were often conceived without reference to other parts of the syntactic system and within widely differing theoretical perspectives. The proposed approach, therefore, with its focus on the overall syntactic system, would provide a framework within which the various descriptions can be integrated.

ON THE APPROPRIATE PRESENTATION OF THE NORMATIVE GRAMMAR

Step (iii) in the previous section refers to the necessity to present the normative grammar in a manner which reflects the way in which native speakers perceive their language operates, and uses Creole terminology for linguistic description within the grammar. The normative grammar can itself promote the use of Creole as a medium of scientific linguistic discourse, even if, to reach a public at present primarily literate in English, it is initially produced in English. In such circumstances, the Creole linguistic terms would be presented alongside their English equivalents in the grammar.

To develop appropriate linguistic terminology in Creole for use in the normative grammar it is not sufficient simply to find, by compounding, borrowing or coining, Creole equivalents of the various terms in English. Rather, a long hard look must be taken at the traditional ways in which language has been perceived by Creole speakers, and how these perceptions have been expressed via Creole. Linguists used to think that traditional perceptions would be loaded with value-judgments favouring the dominant European language and stigmatising Creole. The work of Rickford (1979, 1983), however, has indicated the presence of attitudes of linguistic solidarity and positive linguistic self-identification not previously thought to exist among Guyanese Creole speakers. Against this background it seems worthwhile to explore the kinds of popular perceptions on the linguistic structure of Creole which coexist with these language attitudes.

At the level of phonology, Creole language perceptions are indeed bedevilled by pejorative terms such as *raa* 'raw', or *braalin* 'uncouth', which are used to describe the phonological system of the language. There are, however, certain popular notions which do have some linguistic reality. There exists, for example, popular expressions which oppose speech produced with *yu mout spraal opn* 'one's mouth wide open', to that produced as if the speaker has *bail for example, in ii mout* 'boiled egg in his mouth'. The latter expression, associated with English, or attempts at producing English, implies a popular recognition of the importance of tongue height, backness and lip-rounding in the production of certain sounds, features which are crucial if the boiled egg is to be kept in the mouth. The contrasting expression, associated with Creole, recognises the role played by height, lowness in this case, frontness and lip-spread. Even though both language varieties have high vowels as well as low, front as well as back vowels, popular perception is based on an important difference between the phonemic inventories of Creole and English. In English there is the lower-mid back rounded phoneme /ɔ/ which does not exist in Guyanese Creole. For words of English origin, the English phoneme /ɔ/ is substituted for by the low front unrounded vowel /a/ in Creole. It is this, therefore, which promotes the image of English as a language in which high back rounded vowels predominate, in contrast to Creole in which low front unrounded vowels are dominant. The English vowel /ɔ/ is higher, more back and more rounded that the Creole equivalent /a/.

Further support for the notion that there exists among the mass of Guyanese Creole speakers some very clear ideas about vowel articulation can be seen in the well known expression *shi luk laik shi kyaan se pruunz, bot she kyan se gwaava* 'she looks as if she can't say 'prunes,' but she can say 'guava'. This is used to refer to a deceptively quiet and peaceful individual who is able to react loudly and aggressively when the occasion arises. A speaker who appears so prim and proper that she seems not even able to unpurse her lips and lower her tongue to the minimal degree necessary to produce the bilabial stop /p/ and the high back rounded vowel /uu/, ends up being able to spread her lips and lower the front of her tongue far enough to produce the back velar stop /g/ and the low front vowels /aa/ and /a/.

The proposed normative grammar would require an introduction to the phonology of the language and to the orthography. The traditional native speaker perceptions in the area of phonology should be employed in such an introduction. In the main body of the normative grammar, involving the presentation of syntactic analysis, the exploitation of native speaker perceptions may not be quite such a straightforward proposition. Syntax is a far more abstract area of language than is phonology, particularly for the non-specialist. As a result, there is a preponderance of terms such as *gud* 'good', and *bad* 'bad', *rait* 'right' and *rang* 'wrong', which are applied to syntactic structures based on the degree to which such structures approximate to those of English. One syntactic notion which does, however, seem quite widespread among speakers of Guyanese Creole is that of word order. Thus, when confronted with the speech of Jamaican Creole speakers, one of the common responses of Guyanese Creole speakers is that Jamaican Creole is *bak-to-front* ' back to front'.

Beyond the question of word order there seems little explicit reference to syntactic features within the Guyanese Creole-speaking community. One option which exists, however, is to examine popular expressions which do not make direct reference to language, but exploit particular syntactic features for their idiomatic effect. It could be argued that in fact these expressions become popular because of their skilful exploitation of linguistic features perceived as significant by members of the speech community. There is, for example, a traditional story told in Guyana about a new sugar boiler employed in a factory on a sugar estate. When, during his first day at work, he is asked by the factory manager how he is getting on with the job, he answers, 'Wa don bail don spail. Wa bailin spailin. An wa gon bail gon spail.' 'What has already been boiled has been spoiled. What is being boiled is being spoiled and what will be boiled will be spoiled.' The effect of the sugar boiler's response relies on the sequencing of the completive, progressive and irrealis versions of the same sentence, each version containing a pair of verbs marked for the same aspect/mood and intended to signal that the two actions involved occurred simultaneously. Examples such as this give an indication of what native speakers perceive can possibly be done with the syntactic structure of their language. In addition they provide potential examples for the normative grammar which native speakers would find both relevant and entertaining.

ON IMPLEMENTING THE USE OF THE NORMATIVE GRAMMAR

Devonish (1978) attempted to identify variants with the highest powers of occurrence across the Guyanese Creole continuum, which could constitute the core of the recommended variants within the normative grammar. As stated previously, such variants would be listed alongside other variants of a more restricted usage. Ideally, the normative grammar should list all the variants currently in use. In the interests of practicality, however, and of the urgency with which such a grammar is needed, it may well stop short of satisfying such an ideal. No matter how comprehensive the listing of variants, there are bound be omissions. Such omissions could be due either to a failure to identify forms which are in use, or to language change which is bound to make obsolete particular aspects of the normative grammar from the moment they are written down.

The problem for the community at large is to ensure that they are aware of how it is intended that the grammar be used. They need to be conscious, or course, that the recommended forms are suggested as being appropriate for only a specific group of people operating in a restricted set of circumstances, and that all forms listed are of equal validity. There is, however, another problem: users may assume that forms not present in the normative grammar do not exist in the language and are therefore incorrect. The danger here is that the normative grammar of Guyanese would be introduced into a community used to the prescriptivism of English school grammars. In such circumstances, the Creole normative grammar could be transformed into a dangerous weapon in the hands of new linguistic tyrants wishing to impose a new type of linguistic uniformity in the name of nationalism. In order to counter this, users need to be encouraged to view the normative grammar purely as an aid to their intuitions and as an imperfect point of reference. In circumstances where the normative grammar clashes consistently with native speaker intuitions and day-to-day language usage, it is the latter that must take precedence.

REFERENCES

Bickerton D. (1975) *Dynamics of a Creole System*. CVP, London

Devonish H. (1978) *The Selection and Codification of a Widely Understood and Publicly Usable Language Variety in Guyana to Be Used a Vehicle of National Development*. DPhil Dissertation. University of York

Gibson K. (1982) *Tense and Aspect in Guyanese Creole*. DPhil Dissertation. University of York

Rickford J. (1979) *Variation in a Creole Continuum: Quantitative and Implicational Approaches*. PhD Dissertation, University of Pennsylvania 1983

Rickford J. (1983) *Standard and Non-Standard Language Attitudes in a Creole Continuum*. Occasional Paper 16. Society for Caribbean Linguistics

The Development of Literary Dialects of Romanes, and the Prospects for an International Standard Dialect

Thomas Acton, Vangelis Marselos and Laszlo Szego

When languages have no developed literary tradition, it is only usually when there is a movement to create one that linguists attempt to analyse the possibilities and problems in its development. It is, therefore, often hard to distinguish analysis from, on the one hand, advocacy, and on the other hand, polemical opposition. We do not agree, however, that the only scientifically acceptable task of a scholar is to describe the various dialects without trying to influence their evolution in order to be objective. Of course wishful thinking should not contaminate descriptive linguistics; but equally, the scholar must not oppose the evolution of the language among its native speakers. Both advocacy and opposition, and the educational needs of children must be served best by scholars at least attempting objectivity in disentangling the different questions which must be asked about this process.

The populations of the Middle East, Europe and the European diaspora which are known as 'Gypsy' derive from commercial-nomadic emigrants who left the Indian sub-continent at the end of the first millennium AD. Despite absorption of, or into, local commercial nomadic groups in some cases, many retain varieties of their original mother-tongue, the Indian-derived Romani language. For our purposes we must ask ourselves the following questions: Which Gypsy groups or individuals feel a need for their language to become literary and why? Is it possible for one of the language varieties, or a composite of several to become a standard literary dialect for all or some of the Romani language communities? If so, what will be the form or nature of that standard, and how will it be created?

Controversy dogs all of these questions, both within the World Romani Congress/Romani Union and national Gypsy organisations, and outside. There has been some Romani literary activity in the West, but the main impetus to linguistic development has come from Roma resident in East European countries, where educational levels are higher, enabling a critical approach to history and social identity, and from Indian scholars who have felt an ethnic solidarity with the Romani movement.

One preliminary item of controversy, which we, however, regard as a red herring, is that of the use of theories about the origin of the Romani peoples as justifications for the development of this or that standard. Whether the Indian ancestors of the Rom, Sinti, Kale and Romanichals and other Gypsy groups were of high or low caste, or whether different castes or ethnic groups contributed outside India to the formation of the Romani peoples, has no bearing on what their linguistic or social rights are today. How much Indian blood or vocabulary has been 'inherited' by any particular Gypsy group has nothing to do with the value that their mother tongue has for them and the respect due to it from others.

Equally, it is unimportant whether contemporary Romani varieties derive from two or more Indian languages which have converged outside of India (as Derek Tipler, before his death, speculated to one of the authors) or whether there was a single original ur-Romanes from which all modern varieties are derived. If a standard is to be constructed, it must respond to contemporary needs, not be the artificial reconstruction of some supposed lingua franca of the past.

The first problem, then, that must be faced is the tremendous range of variation among modern dialects of Romanes. Amongst 'European' Romani dialects (that is, those which possess Greek loan words) scholars have usually differentiated first between 'Vlach' and 'non-Vlach' dialects on phonetic, lexical and other grounds; but it is by no means clear that the latter group constitutes a unity. Cutting across these 'original' distinctions, are classifications based on the extent to which local language varieties have been influenced by other languages. Contact languages have been created, such as the English dialect of Romanes, which is largely English in grammar and inflection, and to a considerable extent in lexicon, but is still referred to by its native speakers as Romani, as is the similarly adapted Ròmka dialect in Epirus. Other Gypsy groups, such as the Rudari, Irish Travellers and Jenisch speak well-formed and often secret languages in the derivation of which Romani may be third or even fourth importance after other languages.

It is beyond the scope of this paper to detail such variety. Rather we shall take a couple of examples of literary language-building as a prelude to speculation about the construction of an international standard. We shall first look at an attempt to develop a literary version of one particular dialect, English Romanes, which is so 'creolised' as to be mutually unintelligible with most other Romani dialects, and thus presents very specific problems. Secondly we shall look at the situation in central Europe and the possible development of a regional standard between dialects which, if not always mutually intelligible, do share Indian-derived grammatical structures. Finally we shall make some remarks about the prospects for an overall international standard.

THE DEVELOPMENT OF WRITTEN ENGLISH ROMANES

The conventional wisdom is that the English Romani dialect is in decline. Acton and Kenrick (1984), however, have found current reference for the great majority of the vocabulary found amongst English Gypsies by the early

The Development of Literary Dialects of Romanes

linguists, Borrow, Smart and Crofton. The Romani texts, written rather than recorded by these linguists created a misleading impression and obstructed any development of a literary English Romanes. Current developments of a more viable written Romanes are dependent on a greater realism about how the language is spoken which abandons the hypothesis of decline, and with it any literary imperative to 'improve on' or 'revive' the contemporary vernacular.

Until recently only about 10 per cent of nomadic English Romanies were literate, and most settled Romanies would seek to keep their ethnicity secret. Individuals have used their language for letters, or have written down items to gratify the whims of scholars or evangelists, but they have not hitherto established a literary tradition in Romanes, although Gypsy writers like Wood, Odley and 'Lavengro' have brought occasional Romani words and phrases into books written primarily in English.

Today, however, with increased schooling, the foundations of mass literacy are being laid. Many Gypsy children want or would be prepared to use their own language in school, but do not know where to start. How should Romani words be spelled? Has anyone else ever done such a thing?

The orientalist Gypsylorists who studied Gypsies in the nineteenth century made up texts which sounded as archaic and un-English as possible, illustrating as many Romani words in as short a space as possible. When, however, Gypsies are using Romanes in a book for commercial publication, or an essay for a teacher, they do not approach the language in the same way. They produce something much closer to the vigour of the speech and conversational strategies of Gypsies, in particular their code-switching between English and English Romanes.

Speakers of English Romanes use a mixture of an exotic, largely Romani special vocabulary and English vocabulary within a largely English grammatical setting. Reproducing that mixture in authentic-sounding utterances is notoriously difficult for non-Gypsies. Mastering the special vocabulary is easy enough, but substituting at random (or, worse still, as densely as possible) into standard English will not automatically produce utterances that Gypsies will recognise as 'genuine Romanes', that is, the sort of thing that would occur naturally in conversation.

First of all, it is clear that in producing what we may call the 'Anglo-Romani code' only a limited English vocabulary may be used, although that includes items (for example, 'brazen') which are archaic in standard English. Equally, although the grammar is 'English', it is not the same as that of standard English. Sentences are shorter and subordinate clauses far fewer. The peculiarities of the English of English Romanes have not been systematically explored by linguists.

The Anglo-Romani code, then, is a particular kind of 'mixture' of Romanes and English, which only in extreme cases will produce sentences consisting entirely of 'Romani' vocabulary, but with 'English' grammar. If we actually listen to spontaneous 'Romani' speech by English Gypsies, we often find that only about 20 per cent of the words are from the special Romani vocabulary. That is sufficient, however, to render rapid speech unintelligible to outsiders.

Within one short passage of speech a Gypsy may render an idea at one moment by a Romani term, the next moment by an English term. Which occurs when would seem to depend in some way on context; but again, there has been no serious investigation of this; yet it is not difficult to pick out Romani sentences which sound unnatural and those which sound spontaneous.

Romanes and English, however, are not only mixed within the 'Anglo-Romani code'. There is a second level of mixture. In any extended utterance Gypsies will sooner or later switch into another code, standard English or some other English dialect. In this they will no longer be constrained by the limitations on the use of English that operate within the 'Anglo-Romani code'. Once they have switched into the 'English code', neologisms, Latinisms, mimicry of the upper classes and of television performers can all abound. Let us represent these levels of mixing diagrammatically:

Table: Levels of Mixing in English Gypsy Speech

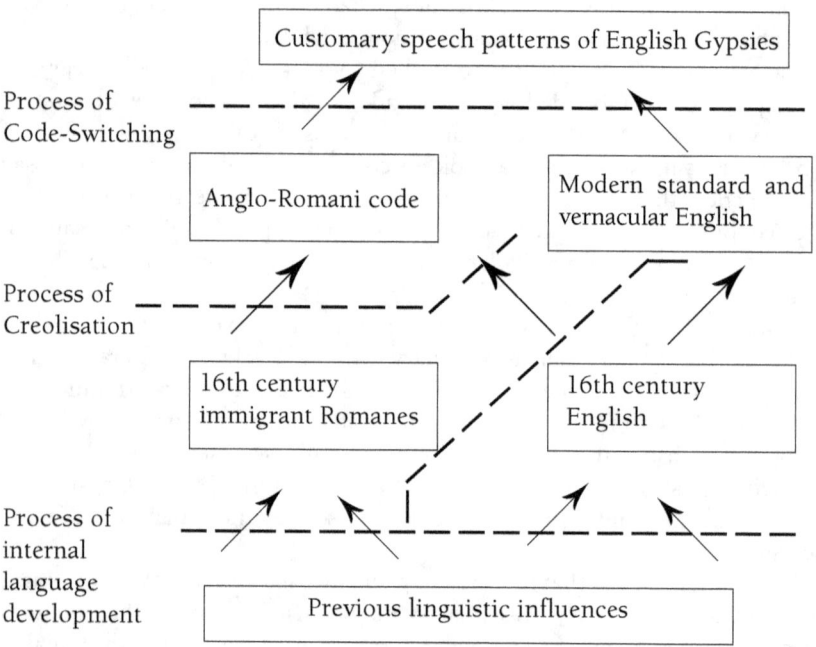

The 'mixture' that results from creolisation occurs within sentences; code-switching occurs from one sentence to another.

Linguists have only recently begun to pay attention to the phenomenon of code-switching with any degree of seriousness (Gumperz, 1982), but it seems that it is also rule-governed behaviour, not mere random whimsy. The rules, however, are not purely linguistic or grammatical; they relate to 'conventional strategies' which are also influenced by the environmental and social causes. By their choice of code the speakers make signals to their listeners about their status and about the status of the conversation or part of it, and erect boundaries to keep their listeners at bay or to draw them into a closer intimacy.

We can find an interesting example of code-switching in one of the songs which is known to practically every Gypsy child in London. It uses both 'Anglo-Romani code' (AR) and a standard, very un-Romani English (E); and also an intermediate code, which is virtually standard English but occasionally quotes a Romani word (EQR). We mark the code at the beginning of each line:

EQR:		I'm the Romani rai,
EQR:		Just an old didikai,
E:		My home is a mansion beneath the blue sky.
E:		I was born in a ditch, that's why I'll never grow rich,
EQR:		And that's why they call me... the Romani rai.
AR:		Kakka chavvi, dik akai,
AR:		Father's gone to sell a mush a kushti grai,
EQR:		And that's why they call him... the Romani rai.
EQR:		I'm the Romani rai,
EQR:		I'm a true didikai,
E:		My home is a mansion beneath the blue sky.
E:		I live in a tent, but I don't pay no rent,
EQR:		And that's why they call me... the Romani rai.

There is in this song a complex and multi-faceted irony about the nature of wealth and social pretension (Acton and Kenrick 1984, pp.132-33) which turns on the contrast between the words rai 'gentleman' and didikai 'rough Gypsy'. This ironic tension is heightened by the switching between codes which have their social status and associations.

The EQR passages are fairly standard English in which three Romani items, 'Romani', 'rai', and 'didikai' all of which are common in popular English writing about Gypsies, are quoted. This part is sung slowly and should be intelligible to a non-Romani speaker. The E passages, also sung slowly, are flowery, almost pretentious, and with the exception of one double negative, in standard English.

The AR passage, however, is sung very fast, even gabbled, and although it is still a mixture of Romani and English, using English words ('father', 'gone' and 'sell') for which common Romani words are available, it will be unintelligible to anyone not habituated to fast English Romanes. This passage will exclude the non-Gypsy listener - exactly as two Gypsies standing in a market might wish to exclude on-lookers from information about a father's business.

This little song, then, might serve as a paradigm of Anglo-Romani verbal strategies. As a text, it presents two possible patterns, AR and EQR for the writing of Romanes - which it balances with English. This balance of vocabulary and codes, in which the 'Romanes' and the 'English' make points at each other, is the hardest thing for a non-native speaker. They can be picked out precisely because they seem to be 'trying too hard'.

When Gypsies or friends of Gypsies sit down to write original Romani prose, however, these unconscious mechanisms may not operate. The convention is that Romanes is declining, that old people speak it better than the young (in fact, it is appalling bad manners for young people to claim to be good at speaking Romanes). The tendency may be, therefore, to try to make the text as pseudo-archaic as possible by cramming as much of the Romanes-derived lexicon in as possible. It is clear that Smart and Crofton (1875) worked over their long prose texts intensively with their informants, 'improving' them - that is, making them more 'Romani' - at each revision. Small wonder, then, that if these texts are compared with spontaneous modern English Romani speech, there is a misleading impression that the Romani flavour has become more dilute in the past century. A better comparison might be with the first modern English Romani scripture translation. 'Shavved then got latchered', the text of which is as dense with Romani words as anything of Borrow or Smart and Crofton, but was generally found extremely difficult even by close friends of those Gypsies who actually worked on the translation.

This self-consciously Romani literary style cannot be a useful example for young English Gypsies of today. In fact even in Borrow and Smart and Crofton there are directly quoted songs and proverbs which do sound as though they are taken from actual Gypsies, and are easily understandable still today. A successful literary Romanes must try to capture the living power of the rhythms and vocabulary of ordinary speech. This is in fact what emerges in some of the entries to the National Gypsy Education Councils' children's writing competition, as for example in this story by Sandra Price (*Traveller Education*, 15, 1980, p.10):

Joey, Mary and the Matchiko Chorers

> Mary and Joey were atching with their dadrus and dai by Shrewsbury in the puro drom. At a rarti they dikked a drag vel in the drom, and shunned a lot of matchikos moving in the drag, and dikked two mushes counting a lot of lovva, and the one mush penned to other as they had chored sor the matchikos from the gav.
>
> Then the mushes walked off to the kitchema. Mary opened the jigger and loosed sor the matchikos out, and they prastered over the pubs.
>
> When the mushes vel palé to the drag, dordi! They velled to the trailer and putched Joey's dadrus if he had loosed the matchikos out, and wanted to kor him. Joey's dadrus delled the one matchiko-chorer between the two yoks, and stretched him. The vavver mush pulls out a chiv and penned he would mor Joey's dadrus, but his dai got the yogger out and shot the mush in one leg. The dui mushes prasters off in the drag and poggers it up against a rooker and they were lifted to stiraben by the musgros for drunk.
>
> Joey's dadrus had to shift from the puv, as there was hundreds of matchikos what the mushes had brung to the tan, mullering for hobben, and they was mewing all the rarti, so you could not sutti.
>
> What they suffered!

The style of competitors like Sandra Price has clearly influenced that of more recent scripture translations, such as 'A kushti lav' and 'More kushti lavs'.

There exists, however, an alternative style, aimed at a different audience, for the utilisation of English Romanes, which we can see in some of the poems of 'Lavengro' and of Tom Odley. These are primarily works in English about Gypsies, which quote from Romanes, but expect a primarily Gaujo readership (otherwise they would not be commercially publishable). The demand is that ordinary English readers should accept (perhaps with the help of a brief glossary) the added Romani vocabulary. In this passage from Odley (p.36) a child's birth is announced:

> A call from the wagon by the two men is heard,
> Which raises their spirits, for 'chal' is the word.
> To the wagon they turn and listen for more
> From the woman a-standing at the wagon half-door.
> 'Your rovval's a'mishto,' she says with a smile,
> 'You can wel in and dik her after a while.
> The chavvi's tudding just now; he's filling his per,
> And Genti's a-sutti, so don't disturb her.

Such a style is not a new tactic in the utilisation of ethnic languages. There is a great mass of Scots and regional English dialect used in books whose authors have carefully kept just the right side of intelligibility for readers in South east England.

Sometimes this tactic is a deliberate part of a political statement as in the banned work of the Angolan José Luandino Viera, which was deliberately presented to a Portuguese public 'written in the mixture of Kimbundu and Portuguese spoken in Luanda's musseques' (Viera/Bender, p.vii). Similarly Roumain's famous Haitian novel *Gouverneurs de la Rosée* was written not in Creole, but in standard French, quoting Creole. In both the rulers were faced with the realities of colonialism at least partly be being made to sample the languages of the oppressed themselves.

This strategy may, on occasion, represent a toning down of political content. For example, compared with the Jamaican Creole of Bob Marley, the 'Black English' lyrics of the pop group 'Musical Youth', whose record was such a hit with ordinary English youth, are about as political as putting 'Merched' and 'Dynion' on Welsh public toilets. The infused flavour can be one of exoticism rather than of resistance to oppression.

No matter. Whatever the form is used for, the point is that this is also a strategy which utilises the power of vernaculars and gives respect to their speakers. Where Sandra Price is writing a dialect of Romanes naively, as she would speak it, without reference to any literary tradition, Odley and 'Lavengro' use different branches of the English literary tradition and graft onto it some Romani language and experience. Both of these seem viable literary enterprises to us. In the end literature is justified by its effect on the reader, not by its grammatical correctness. It is successful literature that creates linguistic precedent, not the other way round.

POSSIBILITIES FOR THE DEVELOPMENT OF A CENTRAL EUROPEAN INTER-DIALECTAL ROMANI LITERARY LANGUAGE

While we have been talking about Britain, the main practical question about writing Romanes, are questions about adaptation of Romanes to the host language. When, on the other hand we come to the much larger Romani communities of Central Europe, the practical question is that of accommodation between varieties of Romanes, each of which has been less influenced by a host language.

Proponents of the development of an inter-dialectal standard tend to claim that the differences between dialects of varieties or dialects of Romanes are mostly created by host language interference. Opponents stress other grammatical and phonetical differences. It is vital, therefore to commence with a clear over-view of the differences.

The facts of nomadism and migration have created a patchwork of local variations and adaptations and have left the broader dialect groups without clear geographical boundaries. Nevertheless we can trace three broad categories in Central Europe which must date at least to medieval times. For the purposes of this paper we will call these Sinti, Paibano (or Carpathian), and Vlach (or Vlashiko).

Sinti

The majority of Central European Sinti speakers live in the German-speaking territories. Dialects in this group tend to be everywhere adapted to the host language. It is relatively rich in loan-words of German origin, and its grammar is very similar to that of Paibano. Its speakers tend to use the articulation of the environmental host language; in Germany they speak like Germans, in Hungary like Hungarians.

In Hungary there are some very small Sinto communities living alongside the lower course of the Danube, but there are only a few old people in them who know some words of Sinti. In everyday life they also speak Hungarian, while some of the younger generation, especially those active in the Romani civil rights movement, learn Vlach Romanes as the most widespread variety in neighbouring countries.

Paibano

Paibano is spoken in almost all Slavonic countries, and is the commonest variety of Romanes in Czechoslovakia and Poland. It is rich in Slav loan-words and its grammar has some characteristically 'archaic' features. Its phonetics differ from those of other Central European languages and give it, like Vlach, a

'Romani tone'. It is very probable that the first Romani immigrants to Central Europe spoke Paibano.

In Hungary there are few fluent speakers of Paibano left, and the language as they speak it is also full of Hungarian loan-words. Up to the nineteenth century it was the language of the majority of Hungarian Roma; for the most part it is now either 'creolised' or lost. Nonetheless there were in the last century collections of poems in Paibano published in Hungary, and there are still good authors in Czechoslovakia, Poland and the Soviet Union writing in Paibano. In the latter two countries dialects of this group are referred to as 'Baltic'.

Vlach

Vlach Romanes developed on Romanian territory. Before and after the liberation of Gypsy slaves in the nineteenth century great masses of Vlach speakers emigrated all over the world, including substantial colonies all over North and South America. There can be very few countries without a colony of at least some Vlach Romanes-speaking Roma.

Where Paibano has Slavonic loan-words, Vlach has Romanian loan-words in great numbers. Its grammar shows some interesting developments in comparison with Paibano or Sinti, and its articulation is similar to that of Paibano though in places it is also influenced by host languages. Internationally, more literature has been produced in Vlach dialects than in any others.

Romani Writing in Central Europe

Written literature dates from at least the middle of the last century. For example, in Hungary Nagy-Idai Sztojka Ferenc had published in Vlach, and Ipolysághy Balogh János and Boldizsár József had published in Paibano. There has not, however, been any significant development of the literature over the past hundred years. Since Romani is not taught in schools, young Roma who are interested in literary activity or in the development of their own mother tongue have had, again and again, to make a fresh start.

In some Central European states there is currently a tendency to give the Romani language status in education. The strength of this tendency varies between countries, but overall it is increasing. Romani books, periodicals and brochures have been published occasionally, chiefly in Hungary, Czechoslovakia, the Soviet Union and Jugoslavia. Laszlo Szego (1983) has discussed this literature in some detail; nevertheless it may be worthwhile to list here some of the more significant twentieth century Central European Romani writers to indicate how firm a foundation there could be for a Romani literature.

In Hungary Bari Károly has written in Paibano, while Vlach writers include Daróczi József, Rostás György, Andro Loshtye and Karsai Ervin.

In the Soviet Union Paibano writers include Mihailo Bezludsko, Nikolai Pankov, Rom Lebedev, Nina Dudarova, Vano Hrustalyo Timofeyevo, Leksa Manush and Karlis Rudevichos, while Romka Demeter and Gyordyis Kantya have published in Vlach and Nikolai Satkevich in Sinti.

In Czechoslovakia Paibano authors include Bartolomei Daniel, Frantishek Demeter, Voyta Fabián, Tera Fabianová and Ondréi Peshta.

In Bulgaria there is Mitko Golemanov (Vlach), and Paibano writers in Jugoslavia include Raiko Durich, Tomalo Randarimasko and Jusuf Shaip. In Poland there is the Paibano poetess Papusza (Bronislawa Wajs) and in West Germany the Vlach writer Vittorio Mayer.

It is notable, and rather sad that until the 1990s we do not hear about Romani writers from Romania or the German Democratic Republic. We fear this regrettable phenomenon must be attributed to the cultural policy of the states in question.

There must be real fears that if the process of social integration of Roma in the Central European States proceeds without the establishment of the necessary cultural institutions, then the language may eventually become extinct.

Within Hungary, however, it is possible to see some progress towards the creation of an inter-dialectal literary standard which is not the result of any conscious policy.

With the improvement of the living standards of Roma since 1945, there has been a dynamic development of the Vlach-speaking Lovari group. This was originally a horse-dealing and trading group living in Northern Jugoslavia and Southern Hungary. As they have spread more broadly in Hungary and other countries, and as communications between Romani groups have improved, so a popularised Lovari dialect, which has taken up various elements of other dialects, has tended to become a Vlach Romani 'standard language', providing a basis for several independent projects for creating dictionaries and normative grammars. With only a few problems (relating to the phoneme dj, and palatalised versions of s' and z') this dialect can be rendered phonetically in the orthography adopted by the first World Romani Congress in London, 1971, which has the advantage of not using any diacritical marks. The fact that most Romani dialects can be written in this orthography makes comparison easier.

The question then remains to what extent such a process of the emergence of an interdialectal literary standard can, or should occur or be encouraged within Central Europe as a whole, and, beyond that, internationally.

TOWARDS A WORLD STANDARD ROMANES

In a seminal paper, 'Problems in the Creation of a Standard Dialect of Romanes' Hancock (1975) presented an account of the political difficulties a non-Gypsy world presents to Romani organisational unity, and drawing on the earlier work of Kochanowski, initiated a technical debate comparing different Romani dialects. Our intention here is not so much to intervene in that debate as to comment on what is necessary to carry that debate on and bring it to fruitful and widely acceptable conclusions.

It is all too easy for intellectuals to sit in armchairs and devise an ideal standard, reconstructing an archaic deep structure, enriching vocabulary by giving different meanings to equivalents from different dialects (galbeno, yellow in Vlach, could be assigned to mean 'ochre', while zhoto, yellow in Paibano, could be assigned to mean 'lemon-coloured', or so it has been proposed). It is much harder to turn these into mass usage. Are we to work on the adaptation of some one numerically large dialect to a standard - thereby making other dialects under-privileged, or are we to try to create some averaged-out inter-dialectal standard with the dubious advantage of being no-one's mother-tongue? May we even see the development of main and subsidiary standards?

Once we have general literacy, and Roma can appreciate from the written version the common structures of many Romani dialect, then many Romani dialects, such as the Vlach and Piabano families discussed above, are likely to be mutually comprehensible with any international standard. On the other hand, the English Romani dialect discussed above will most certainly not be. The development of a standard dialect would not lessen the need for every dialect group to make the most of its own language. Equally, however, the development of a literary English Romanes would not lessen the advantages to English Gypsies of also learning and appreciating an international dialect. Romani intellectuals should strive to master as many Romani language varieties as possible and encourage publications by members of the less well-known and less cultivated dialect communities.

Instead of prescribing the form of an international standard, intellectuals should provide the medium for a free fermentation in which common experience can lead to a common literature. There should be more literary journals actually in Romanes like *Loli Phabai* which should also deal with theoretical problems of language development. Also, of course every channel of private correspondence and association at conferences, festivals and cultural exchanges should be encouraged.

Institutions should enable, rather than constrain this process. An international Romani Academy or Language Committee should create a library which as well as containing printed literature, should archive tape-recordings and correspondence between specialists. This should not be like existing collections, geared to academic work by non-Gypsies on Gypsies, but should be designed to assist creative work by Romani people themselves. Under such conditions a corpus of material might be built up which will enable the international Romani consciousness to express itself in a common tongue without in any way detracting from the local and specific development of particular language varieties.

REFERENCES

Acton, T. and Kenrick D. (eds.) (1984) *Romani Rokkeripen Todivvus*. Romanestan Publications, London

Borrow, G. (1874) *Romano-Lavo-Lil*. Murray, London

Gumper, Z. and Gumper, J.J. (1982) *Discourse Strategies*. CUP, London

Hancock, I. (1975) *Problems in the Creation of a Standard Dialect of Romanes*. Southwest Educational Development Laboratory Working Papers in Sociolinguistics No. 25. Austin, Tx

Kochanowski, J. (1963) *Gypsy Studies*. International Academy of Indian Culture, New Delhi

'Lavengro' (pseud) (1973) *The Gypsy Poems and Ballads*. Midas, Tunbridge Wells

Odley, T. (1983) *Dirty Gyppo*. Stockwell, Ilfracombe

Roumain, J. (1944) *Gouverneurs de la Rosée*. Tr. Hughes, L. and Cook, M. (1978) *Masters of the Dew*. Heinemann, London

Smart, B.C. and Crofton, H.T. (1875) *The Dialect of the English Gypsies*. Asher, London

Szego, Laszlo (1983) *Cigányok-honnét jöttek, merre tartanak*. Kozmosz Könyvek, Budapest

Viera, José Luandino (1980) *Luuanda*. Tr. Bender, E. Heinemann, London

GLOSSARY FOR ENGLISH ROMANI TEXTS

Shavved: ran off; *latchered*: found; *atching*: stopping; *dadrus*: father; *dai*: mother; *puro*: old; *drom*: road; *rarti*: night; *dikked*: saw; *drag*: vehicle; *vel*: welcome; *shunned*: heard; *matchiko*: cat; *mush*: man; *lovva*: money; *penned*: said; *chored*: stolen; *gav*: town; *kitchema*: pub; *jigger*: door; *prastered*: ran; *puvs*: fields; *palé*: back; *dordi!*: (expletive); *kor*: fight; *delled*: gave, hit; *yoks*: eyes; *vavver*: other; *chiv*: knife; *mor*: kill; *yogger*: gun; *dui*: two; *rooker*: tree; *stiraben*: prison; *musgros*: police; *tan*: place; *mullering*: dying; *hobben*: food; *sutti*: sleep; *kushti*: good; *lav*: word; *chal*: son; *rovval*, *romni*: wife; *aimishto*: OK; *chavvi*: boy, child; *tudding*: taking milk; *per*: stomach; *a-sutti*: asleep.

The Development of Literary Cypriot Greek: Has It Any Educational Relevance?

Maria Roussou

Cypriot Greek, or the Cypriot dialect, is the form of the Greek language spoken in Cyprus by about 500,000 Greek Cypriots in Cyprus, and 250,000 Greek Cypriots who from the beginning of this century emigrated to mainland Greece, the United Kingdom, the U.S.A., Australia and other countries.

According to Christodoulou (1982), it is not an independent Cypriot language, but a dialect of Greek which has its own strong characteristic lexical, grammatical, syntactical and phonological features, which are quite distinct from other dialects of Greek; nonetheless, it is still considered a member of the group of Southern Greek dialects spoken in the islands of Chios, the Dodecanese and Crete, with which it shares a number of common elements.

It is widely believed that it is a 'Homeric' dialect. By that it is not meant that it is a form of classical Greek, but that during the struggle of the Cypriots against various conquerors who have passed through the island, the dialect has preserved elements of Homeric and ancient Greek. Christodoulou, however, comments that all contemporary forms of Greek contain elements of ancient Greek, but notes that the Cypriot dialect, by virtue of its isolation in the eastern Mediterranean basin has retained more.

Katsouris (1983) argues that Cypriot literature was developed from the oral traditions of naive poets and wandering singers, and flourished in some periods; nonetheless it was far less developed than on the mainland. Since Greek spoken in Cyprus was thus less affected by literary Greek, but retained more elements of the Homeric language, but was also affected by the language of the Hellenistic, Roman and Byzantine periods, and by Venetian and Ottoman influences. Cypriot writings of the Ottoman period contain a number of Turkish loanwords, which have been given a Greek form following the rules of the Cypriot dialect.

During the British colonial period (1878-1960), the Cypriot dialect was further influenced by English, and, at the same time, through limited but highly valued educational and literary contact with mainland Greece, was also affected by Katharevousa, the 'pure Greek' of the period between 1878 and 1960 used by various writers of the Athenian literary schools (Katsouris 1983).

There are three main stages in the historical evolution of Cypriot Greek: the dialect of antiquity (c300BC-300AD), the dialect of the middle ages, and the contemporary dialect. The 'new ' Cypriot dialect may be said to begin with pieces of literature dated by researchers to the Frankish period of Cypriot history in the 13th century. In view of this it could be argued that the Cypriot dialect is the first modern Greek dialect to be preserved through written texts.

The 'Assizes', the laws of the Frankish Kingdom of Cyprus translated into Greek for the literate bourgeois Cypriots, is the oldest surviving text. It was followed by other official documents, and by the Chronicles of Leontias Mahairas and Georgios Voustronios, and a set of 'Cypriot Love Poems' by an unknown Cypriot writer who copied Petrarch.

From the Ottoman period (1572-1878) have survived the 'Lamentation for the Conquest of Cyprus by the Ottomans', and a number of narrative poems or ballads, such as that concerning the hanging of Archbishop Kyprianos in 1821. These constitute valuable documentation of the literary language of the time. Church services and litanies survive in the handwriting of monks. Monasteries acted as schools (often in secrecy from the Ottomans) and as small publishing houses using scribes to copy ecclesiastical documents. There were also in the 19th century some books of information written by Cypriots like Neofytos Rodinos and Archbishop Kyprianos, which were affected by standard modern Greek.

In contemporary Cyprus we have the tradition of the poietarides, the wandering poets who improvise and compose poetic dialogues, often in competitions, during various cultural festivals. Although till lately this was an oral tradition, some have published their work. The series 'Library of Greek Poets' founded by Dr.Yiagoulis had by 1983 published 10 books covering the main folk poets residing in Cyprus, and is expanding to publish works by Cypriot poets living abroad.

Pantelis Kakolis from the Famagusta district, is an immigrant owner of a take-away foodshop in Manchester. His life and creative work were presented by Channel 4 in 1983 under the title 'Landscapes of Childhood', which illustrated his poetic talent and literary use of the Cypriot dialect. He is the first Cypriot abroad to consider publishing a bilingual book of poetry to help second generation Cypriots in English-speaking countries to understand poetry in their dialect. This poem, perhaps, embodies his purpose:

> My village, I carry you with me, wherever I go
> If I am lost, you come and find me,
> You are my bread and my sleep.
> I took you with me,
> And now we live together in a foreign land.
> We don't argue or quarrel,
> We don't take sides.
> I build a wall around you to protect you.

Christodoulou argues that Cypriots today use two phonological (phonetic) systems, if not three, if we include the way they pronounce English words and they switch from one to the other very easily. The first one has [tʃ] and [ʃ] the second [k] and [χ]. These two separate systems are used by Cypriots according to circumstances; for example on TV and radio, in the schools, in government speeches and on other formal occasions a conscious attempt is made to use [k] and [χ] in imitation of the standard Greek pronunciation, while in their everyday lives they mix the two systems. This is related to the fact that Cypriots themselves do not have a great esteem for their dialect, and prefer to conduct formal interactions in the 'pure' language of the Athenian Academia. This is an important conflict in the lives of Cypriots, because on the one hand they are struggling to respect a culture called Cypriot, which has its own state, traditions and language, and on the other hand, as Dalphinis (1998) argues:

> A view of education as a methodology for colonial purposes would indicate that the oral societies, in their search for literacy, are by definition involved in the self-destructive practice of placing less importance upon the oral basis of the cultures they hope to represent.

The Cypriot educational system has been greatly affected in its organisation and curriculum content by the British system, especially in the primary sector, while secondary education has, for socio-political reasons, been more affected by the mainstream Greek tradition until after 1960. Both primary and secondary schools offer, through an agreement between the Ministries of Education of Greece and Cyprus, free textbooks which are prepared by a government body for curriculum and examinations called KEME.

Since the educational systems of both countries are highly centralised and since circulars from the ministries forbid the use of any text books other than the ones approved by them for teachers and government employees at all levels of education, the standard language of books prepared in Athens enters every classroom throughout Greece and Cyprus. The teaching of oral communication, as well as the introduction of reading and writing, aims at the acquisition of Standard Greek. For rural Greek Cypriot children standard Greek was almost a second language before the 1970s when the widespread use of standard Greek made the language as familiar to Cypriot peasants as it was already to urban Cypriots through secondary and further education. The problem of 'free talk' in the playgrounds of the village school, and to some degree, the urban school, was that children used to express themselves in dialect, sometimes very heavy dialect, and the teachers were required like policemen to correct the first time and punish the second, giving examples of what was acceptable inside school premises. Attempts to discuss the child-centred approach, and the need to accept the children's first language, i.e. the vernacular of the home, especially at the reception stage of a child's education, have proceeded very slowly because they have been hampered, mainly by political arguments based on nationalist ideologies that 'to survive as an ethnic group we have to be more Athenian than the Athenians themselves' and that standard Greek should be enforced at all state-initiated interaction. Nonetheless, some enlightened educationalists, such as the EMOK Association for Educational Reform, have taken some initiatives in organising discussions to encourage teachers to accept the dialect, or the form of the dialect that children bring with them at the age of five and a half when they enter primary school.

Since the Cypriot dialect is considered by the educational system as a marginal language, the perspective of policy makers and teachers is to abolish it gradually by not recognising it in the classroom. The language that most children bring to the classroom is not seen as part of the pupil's developmental process, so that in some cases, especially in rural schools, teachers classify those 5 year olds who do not react to their standard language as 'too shy' or 'unable to speak' or 'not clever enough to interact in the classroom' (Roussou, 1984a).

In 1982 EMOK organised a conference with the title 'Language and Education' at which the learned Greek professor of Education Yiannis Kakrides was the guest speaker. He said:

> The good teacher, to whatever educational level he may belong, we shall call a philologist, a term first coined in the 4th century BC to denote a man who is in love with words ...... He is the one who can separate those words which are emotionally charged and which fill one's fantasy with colours and shapes.

According to his thinking the teacher could bring into the classroom, or at least allow, those words that have meaning and emotion for children. He was reading one of the early texts in the dialect with the help of a glossary, when he had suddenly realised how important it must be for both young and adult speakers of the dialect to be able to write and express themselves in their dialect. Kakrides recommends that all teachers enrich their lessons (which are usually full of new concepts and knowledge) with words which are full of emotions and excitement. He says:

> The child's world extends to where his/her language extends. Enrich the language, use all forms that s/he is familiar with... The child's creativity will flourish.

Education in general, and mother tongue teaching in particular should put into practice some of these ideas. But many practical problems remain. Do parents need to be informed about these discussions and valid arguments for accepting children's vernacular? Do teachers need to be informed and trained in ways of proceeding in practical classroom situations about these issues? Who will take the responsibility of discussing the dialect/standard question with the states of Greece and Cyprus and their educational representatives in Britain (Roussou, 1987)?

It has to be done some time in the very near future. Materials for teaching Greek as a mother tongue or community language are now produced by various agencies involved in the education of Greek/Cypriot bilingual children.

The principles and educational arguments on which the introduction of mother tongue is based should also be reflected in the choices made concerning the use and/or acceptance of the children's vernacular.

REFERENCES

Anthias, Floya (1984) 'Some Issues Affecting Greek-Speaking Migrants in Britain: An Ethnic Profile' in Roussou, Maria (ed.) *Greek outside Greece*, National Council for Mother-Tongue Teaching, Stamford, Lincs

Christodoulou, Menelaos (1982) *The Cypriot Dialect and Its Development Throughout the Centuries,* Centre for Sociological Research, Nicosia

Cristofides A. and Montis C. (1974) *Anthology of Cypriot Poetry*, Nicosia

Dalphinis, M. (forthcoming) *Caribbean and African Languages: Social History, Language, Literature and Education,* Whiting & Birch Ltd, London

Kakridis, Yannis (1983) *Language and Education*, EMOK Publications, Nicosia

Katsouris, Yannis (1983) *Greek Cypriot Literature*, Popular University of Nicosia Seminar Series, Nicosia

Roussou, Maria (1984a) *Teaching Greek as a Mother Tongue in Britain*, Schools Council Publications, London

Roussou, Maria (1984b) *The Linguistic and Cultural Background : Greek*, delivered at EEC London Colloquium), Schools Council Publication, London

Roussou, Maria (1987) *An Introduction to Community Languages in Britain: Greek*, Cilt Information, 43

The United Bible Societies Romani Scriptures Programme

Paul Ellingworth

The main motive of Bible translation is usually the desire to communicate what is believed to be a message of universal significance. Nonetheless, from at least the time of St. Mesrob of Armenia, (around 335-440 AD) it has frequently played a part in the creation and development of a literary tradition. Today scripture translation and literacy programmes often go hand in hand, and special simplified translations, known as new reader selections, are available in many languages. The translation of scriptures into a hitherto entirely oral language, however, does not ipso facto create a literary tradition - even if, in accordance with the best translation practice, the work is done by mother tongue speakers of the receptor language.

This paper cannot trace the role of scripture in the creation of a Romani literary tradition; it is, rather, a cry for help from a United Bible Societies (UBS) consultant more in need of advice than able to offer it.

I approach the question of Romani scriptures with certain presuppositions open, of course, to modification as data accumulate and are evaluated. These emerge from the corporate experience of almost fifty UBS colleagues engaged in similar work, complemented and sometimes challenged by the work of friends in the Sumner Institute of Linguistics/Wycliffe Bible Translators and similar agencies, and less directly from the insights of general linguistics. UBS consultants are in touch with over 700 scripture translation projects.

One of these presuppositions has already been mentioned in passing. This is that translations made by mother tongue speakers of the receptor/target language are to be preferred, though in many situations, translators may need and request expatriate help where their knowledge of the original languages is limited.

This already implies a second principle, that translations of the Bible, as of any other book, should be based on the original texts. To translate a translation inevitably doubles the potential distortion.

A third, somewhat remoter, principle relates to the nature of language itself, and thus of translation. It is that although languages differ in an indefinite number of ways, and the genius of each language must be unreservedly respected in translation, there is, underlying all natural languages, a linguistic faculty common, with marginal exceptions, to all human beings, and shared, as far as we know, by no other species. This means that any talk of "primitive" and "developed" languages is likely to focus attention on inessentials, and so prove misleading. Such talk is in any case in conflict with the mass of the evidence. To mention only the lexical level, English, which a native speaker may arrogantly assume to be the classic example of a "developed" language, is primitive compared with Greenlandic in its vocabulary for snow, and with Arabic in its vocabulary for horses.

The consultant therefore approaches Romanes with the assumption that it will not be fundamentally different from any other language. This initial assumption is rigorously tested by the problems listed, but so far, these problems, whether linguistic or extra-linguistic, have not individually proved to be peculiar to Romanes, even though they rarely if ever occur in combination in any other language community or group of language communities.

Even before the process of translation begins, it is wise to anticipate that of distribution. Assuming there will one day be stacks of printed books in a storeroom and an equal number of people able and willing to read them, how does one get the books into the people's hands ? Or, conversely, how do the people get to know that the books are available ?

For most languages, at least in the case of the Bible, the problem is in principle simple to resolve. There is a national Bible Society; there is a language community located largely or wholly within the country; there is a ready-made infrastructure on which lines of communication can be set up. There is even a recognized procedure for dealing with exceptional cases. If, for example, someone in Norway writes to the Bible Society in Greece for a Greek Bible, the order will be referred back to the Norwegian Bible Society. In the case of international languages such as French, the complications are greater; but they can in principle be resolved by consultation among the French-speaking Bible societies. The same is doubtless true, *mutatis mutandis*, for any other international publisher.

In the case of Romanes, to put it bluntly, the system does not work. The structures of national Bible societies have to be bent before they can handle Romanes. I emphasize that this is the publisher's problem, not the customer's; but unless it is solved, the entire Romani scripture translation programme is doomed to futility. It is not so much nomadism that causes the problem here; it is rather the low correlation between national boundaries and concentrations of speakers of particular varieties of Romanes.

The least unsatisfactory solution found to date is twofold. First, the normal Bible society policy of consultation and co-operation with groups of potential users, such as churches and key groups within them, needs to be extended beyond initial consultation about the need for a translation to the entire distribution process. Effective distribution must be done predominantly by Romani people themselves. The heart of the problem, and at the same time the key to its solution, lies in the interface between the static, national structures of Bible societies, and the more flexible structures of Romani (including Romani Christian) society.

Secondly, a willing national Bible society must undertake the task of publishing scriptures in a dialect of which there may be many more speakers outside the country than within it. For example, *Ruth*, in Mateo Maximoff's

Kalderash translation, was published by the Swedish Board of Education in association with the Swedish Bible Society, whereas the Psalms and the New Testament in the same translation were published by the French Bible Society. The UBS does not itself publish scripture translations. Its Europe and Middle East Region, however, attempts to maintain communication between the various interested groups.

Closely related to the question of distribution is that of assessing the potential market, and whether the translations are to be bought individually by speakers of the language, or by churches or other groups for free distribution. Bible societies have limited free distribution programmes of their own, and their general policy is to provide scriptures at a price which the intended users can afford. In recent years, small pilot editions, usually of a single Gospel, have been successfully distributed, together with a questionnaire, to obtain readers' reactions and thus help to assess the potential market.

The first task is to assess the total number of speakers of a given language. Reliable answers are difficult to obtain. From time to time various groups, including the UBS, have issued surveys of Romani dialects, including estimated numbers of speakers, and sometimes information about literature available. Different experts may criticise the figures as over- or under-estimates. But even had we accurate demographic statistics, there are other factors, also difficult to quantify. What proportion of the speakers are functionally literate in the dialect in question? In other words, how many of them are able to read a text in the dialect so fluently that they are not discouraged after a couple of pages? - assuming that the text itself is clearly written, stylistically pleasing, and not unduly complicated. The answer to this question varies widely from one area to another, even among speakers of the same dialect.

Furthermore, it still has to be ascertained how many of the functional literates are likely to be interested in reading parts of the Bible. This question requires careful research, and probably a pilot publication. Analogies from one language to another, and especially from literary to predominantly oral languages, can be completely misleading. It may, for example, be safe to assume that in a large, stable, literate and secularised language community, such as the speakers of German, almost everyone will be functionally literate, but only a small proportion will be interested in reading the Bible. By contrast it may well be that in some smaller, closely knit and predominantly oral communities, such as the speakers of most Romani dialects, interest in the language will be so great that functionally literate members of the community, whether Christian or not, will be anxious to lay their hands on any literature in it they can find; furthermore that they will read it aloud to other members of the community. This certainly cannot be assumed in advance, but there is evidence it happens in some communities.

Already we have crossed the border between written and oral communication. Bible societies now routinely consider the publication of scriptures in oral as well as written media, especially on cassette. At least in predominantly oral language communities, oral presentation should have priority, and it should not be assumed without evidence that the recording ought to be a simple reading of the printed text. In the case of Romani scriptures published by the French Bible Society, for use mainly by the Eglise Evangélique Tzigane, the translation was prepared primarily for oral presentation, and transcripts of the tapes have been made available for literates. In the case of the Kalderash *Ruth*, the recording was prepared after publication of the written text; it includes not only the biblical material, but also specially composed music in the Jewish tradition, sung and played by musicians of national reputation. In such situations the use of both oral and written media may be more effective than either alone. The educational implications of this procedure are clear.

In addition to the current situation we must also consider the possible growth or decline of the numbers of speakers, literates and Christians over a five or ten year period. Predictions about the "decline of Romanes" tend to be based on the psychology of the predictor rather than on observable phenomena in the outside world. Nevertheless, if reliable figures are available for earlier dates, it makes sense to take them into account, and even, with the greatest possible caution, to extrapolate from them.

A Bible society must then normally tread a careful path between two extremes. On the one hand it certainly does not operate with any rigid rule, such as refusing to publish an edition of less than so many thousand copies. On the other hand its resources, and those of the UBS as a whole, are limited and subject to many claims. It is quite understandable if general secretaries of national Bible societies spend almost all their time on the national language(s), and for Romani speakers who form a small minority in their countries to be largely neglected. The UBS can do something to encourage national Bible societies to see the whole picture, but the problem is constantly present.

There are other problems. Although translations have until recently appeared in a baffling variety of orthographies, the question of a standard Romanes orthography for international use has (as far as a bystander can judge) largely been resolved with a broad phonemic transcription.

Sometimes the question of the very necessity of any Romani translation of the scriptures is raised, since most Gypsies speak the language of the host society. The answer is that scripture, or anything else, is more effectively communicated in the mother tongue of the community. Nonetheless, the golden rule is that scripture translations, like anything else, will not be effective unless in some way they grow out of a felt and expressed need within the language community itself: they cannot be imposed from outside. It is possible that in some situations an oral presentation may be preferable to a printed text.

There is also a personal element in the organisation of scripture translation. This is by no means peculiar to Romanes: there are Einzelgänger in any community. But it may be that my limited observations indicate a wider tendency. Where, within a predominantly oral community, individuals appear who have not only reached the stage of passive, receptive functional literacy but have also become creative writers, and therefore potentially excellent translators of scripture, they tend to have done so by virtue of strong qualities of character and temperament which make them perhaps less happy as members of a team of translators.

The Bible, however, is the book of a community; only in a secondary sense can it be viewed as a collection of individual literary products. The experience of the UBS and other agencies is that the best scripture translations are made not by individuals but by small groups, often of three or five members, working together. This observation is intended simply as a statement of observed fact, not as a criticism of individuals. One-person translations are not ideal. But in real life, the choice is most often between the less than ideal, and nothing at all.

Problems of scripture translation and distribution remain in 1998. Indeed, it is not unknown for prejudice against Roma to influence Christian organisations. Yet three related developments have considerably changed the situation for the better.

The first was the collapse of communism in central and eastern Europe and the consequent opening of vast Romani-speaking areas to scripture distribution unlimited by political constraints.

This development led directly, in the second place, to new opportunities for Roma scripture translators to meet, often for the first time, and share their experiences. The UBS has sponsored two such meetings, both in Wiener Neustadt, Austria. The first, in April 1994, was mainly concerned with the exchange of information, though there was also some discussion of modern translation principles. The second, in April 1997, was a workshop more strongly oriented to practical work. It is hoped that a further such workshop may be held in 1999.

A third development is what is sometimes described at 'networking'; in this context, sustained cooperation between the UBS and its member societies on the one hand, and other organisations on the other. Such cooperation was not unknown in earlier years: for example, with the Scripture Gift Mission (now SGM International) in preparing biblical selections in Anglo-Romani. It has now extended to include, among others, the Cooperative Baptist Fellowship, which sponsored publication of Mateo Maximoff's Kalderash New Testament, and continues to offer generous support to other Romani scripture projects; Trans World Radio, responsible for a Romani Bible correspondence course which will soon require the Maximoff translation of the Old Testament; and Language Recordings, with whom it is hoped to develop audio recordings in Romani dialects.

Details of scriptures available in Romani dialects may be obtained from the United Bible Societies, Allied Dunbar House, East Park, Crawley RH10 6AS, UK.

SECTION THREE

Language in Society

Introduction

This section highlights aspects of the relationship between linguistic change and social pressures in the Caribbean, England, Germany and Ireland. In each case study the issue arises of the survival of a linguistic group's traditional forms under pressure to assimilate to those of other linguistic groups with greater political power.

In Barbados a positive use of Creole is emerging at the same time as the increasing use of standard English by upper-class groups seeking a kind of 'assimilado' status within English/American cultural, economic and political value systems. But sound changes within Caribbean English reflect historical as well as contemporary sociolinguistic interaction between Creole and standard English. In Britain such assimilation is marked by the decreasing fluency of Black youth in the Creole of their Caribbean parents, although symbolic use of some Creole forms by Black youth is a gesture of group solidarity.

Historical and political dimensions are called into play, however, by Creole/African nationalism among speakers in Britain, Jamaica and elsewhere, who positively value Creole as providing an alternative communal culture and political direction to domination by speakers of English. Yekwai's paper expresses this ideology.

This theme of distrust of the dominant community is echoed in the experience of the Sinti in Germany, whose language, culture and genealogies were researched in the 1930s by German scholars who passed their findings to the Nazi administrators. They used them to find and exterminate tens of thousands of Sinti (and hundreds of thousands of other Gypsies), including many who had disguised their Sinti origins and 'passed' as Germans. The present day Sinti, therefore, try to keep their language secret, and do not encourage research into their language, especially by outsiders (see also the paper by Müller and Szabo). Persecution of the Irish Travellers, the speakers of Gammon/Shelta in Ireland, may also have contributed to its present 'underground' status and use.

Societal perceptions of such linguistic groups, which lack a written tradition and face the dilemmas of assimilation by literate majorities, resemble to a certain extent the educational establishment's perception of the situation of English working-class non-literates. There has been an attempt to remedy their alienation from writing by approaches to literacy which value the oral dimension of their lives, and present writing as an instrument which can assist this.

In cases where the political control of linguistic change by the dominant group is uncontested, the following model of societal/linguistic assimilation seems to emerge as the establishment's image of the situations discussed in this section:

| Non-assimilated oral culture | → | Partially assimilated oral culture | → | Extinction of distinct separate culture with oral acquisition of literate culture | → | Assimilation into literate culture |

The question is: is this process inevitable? Or, can it be contested through the simultaneous continuance of both oral and written cultures on an equal footing?

Language Variation in Barbados

Ivy Devonish

INTRODUCTION

The indigenous population of Barbados is composed of a large majority of people of African descent and minorities of people of European, Indian, Jewish and Chinese descent.

Officially the indigenous population speak English and many Barbadians, especially those of the 'old school' would not admit to speaking anything else. Within Barbados, however, there is a variety of English referred to by the inhabitants as varying from Bajan to Raw Bajan. The term Bajan is generally used as a noun to refer to a native of Barbados, or linguistically to refer to the Creole spoken by Barbadians. Raw Bajan is the variant closest to the basilectal form of the Creole. Examples of these are:

Raw Bajan
(1) Garfield tek-off lik bul kôw du behin é an é lehgo de fus bal.
(2) Garfield ron down like a bul kow du behind hi an é lehgo de fus bal.

Bajan
(3) Garfield ron down like a bull-cow does behind him an hi let go de firs ball.
(4) Garfield run down like a bull behind him and he bowl de first ball.

Standard English
(5) Jack ran like a bull when he bowled the first ball.

One can, therefore, describe the language situation as a continuum; at one end there is something similar in grammar to Standard English, which is the socially preferred high status dialect (or acrolect), and at the other end, a low status dialect (or basilect), with a central span between them (conveniently referred to as the mesolect). Linguists have described many Caribbean communities in these terms (Carrington, 1974, p.62).

An important social fact associated with this continuum is that Barbadians, like other islanders in the Caribbean, are not restricted in their competence to one variety in the range. Each speaker commands not a point but a span of the continuum. What they use in conversation depends on the audience and situation. The more informal a conversation, the nearer to example (1) above (or the basilectal end of the continuum) it will be.

Which spans and which varieties different persons control is influenced by their social class, education, occupation, district (village), age, sex, peer group, ethnic group and whether they live in an urban or rural area, as I will illustrate.

THE HISTORICAL BACKGROUND OF BARBADIAN CREOLE

The origin of Barbadian Creole, as of all Creoles in the Caribbean, is not definitely known, but there are several theories. That most favoured by linguists is the 'pidginisation and creolisation' theory proposed by Stewart (1962). The evidence is said to point to the prior existence in Africa of some established Pidgin/Creole based on the Portuguese language spoken by groups who established trading posts along the Gold Coast. It has been suggested that this Afro-Portuguese based pidgin 'yielded its place to, or set the pattern for,' English, Dutch and French pidgins, all of which were then transported to the Caribbean islands and flourished amongst the slave population there.

Indeed, if this is so, little or no evidence exists in the language of Barbados to show any Portuguese pidgin influence from Africa. The only Portuguese word in Barbados is the word 'Barbados' itself, which comes from an entirely different source. The Portuguese gave the island its name when they landed in 1536; the traditional explanation is that it is a reference to the 'bearded' fig trees of the island.

Bajan has basically a West African syntax and no evidence of the influence of any other languages other than English, unlike other Caribbean islands which have French, Dutch, Carib, Spanish, Hindi, Bengali, Tamil, Chinese and other influences. For example, in St Lucia and Dominica the formal language is English, but French Patwa is the mother-tongue of 90% of the population. One reason why Bajan shows no other foreign language influence is pointed out by Leitch (1980):

> ...the one territory where an English Creole developed not subject to the influences of other languages is Barbados, which never belonged to any other colonial power, and had few migrants from other groups such as Chinese.

In 1625 the English contact began when a small group of Englishmen landed on the now deserted island of Barbados, the Portuguese having named it and left. They were followed later by indentured servants from Ireland and the West of England, and Royalist captives sent by Cromwell; eventually Barbados became an outpost to which the rulers of England sent rebellious Scots, Irish Presbyterians, Quakers and others. English had been established on the island for five years when in 1630 African slaves began to arrive, speaking one of the Sudanic languages - Ewe, Ga, Twi, Fanti etc., or, if we are to believe it, an Afro- Portuguese Pidgin.

Thus in Barbados, as in other islands of the Caribbean, a Creole emerged out of a colonial situation or in a context of the domination of one linguistic group by another. Plantation slavery and its hierarchical system may be assumed to have been the instigator of the varieties of language spoken in Barbados. The house servants heard the most English, and probably spoke a variety of English different to that of the servants who worked in the 'yard', who again would speak a variety different from that of the slaves working in the fields, who had less contact with formal English. But, as Leitch points out, house servants still had the capacity to understand and speak the variety of the slaves working in the cane fields. Today in Barbados we still find the most educated person, (who will normally speak standard Caribbean English) will be able to understand and speak the variety of, for example, a sugar cane worker in Barbados.

In the Caribbean, then, African (unwritten) languages were brought into contact with European (written) languages. In Barbados, English dominated and suppressed the African languages because:

1. The slaves were forcibly discouraged from using their own language, because they outnumbered their white masters who feared plots and revolts if they adopted their own languages.
2. There was a deliberate mixing of African language groups in Barbados as in the rest of the Caribbean, to protect the slave masters by producing confusion and diminishing the threat of group resistance to the English language and cultural heritage.

Although, however, English was considered the predominant language, it was not taught; many of the plantocracy were illiterate. If the planters had taught the Africans to read and write English, there would have been some form of standardisation and the slaves would have known exactly what sounds or grammatical structures they were trying to reproduce. In the absence of this the Africans were left to understand their masters and communicate amongst themselves as they wished.

Creole resulted, possibly starting as a pidgin for the Africans to communicate amongst themselves and (although it may also have been used to communicate with white people on occasion) as a means of solidarity to exclude the plantocracy. One notices in Creole certain words of English origin that have an entirely different meaning from the original words:

Word	Bajan Meaning	Standard English Meaning
Cute	ridiculous	clever, attractive
Fresh	high-smelling	new, novel
Bad (pronounced baad)	very good, excellent	worthless

Mean	fine, attractive satisfying	vicious, malicious, small-minded
Wicked	excellent, capable	sinful, roguish
Tea	any hot drink e.g. lime tea, cocoa tea, green tea (ordinary tea)	drink made from Tea plant leaves

Thus one can see the Creole developing with an extensive vocabulary and much of the grammar of the culturally dominant English, but re-shaped in terms of pronunciation habits and the grammatical preferences of the submerged African languages - Ibo, Ga, Fanti, Twi, etc. If and when the dominant language is removed, as it was in Haiti after the Toussaint L'Overture rebellion, the Creole lives on. If the prestigious influence of the dominant language remains as a cultural factor, the Creole will gradually move towards that language, gradually losing more and more of the grammar etc., of the submerged African languages. This is in fact what is happening in Barbados, where there remain few known African words. Colleymore's (1970) vocabulary lists only ten: these include nyam (common in all Caribbean islands, wunnah, cou-cou, yam and others. There are also English items in Bajan which are 'word-for-word' translations of African structures into English, leading to compounding and idiomatic frames which are not characteristic of English, but structurally African, for example:

Hard-ears (adj.), stubborn, disobedient	Bajan
N 'aso ye den, he/his ears he hard	Twi
God-horse (n), praying mantis, stick insect	Bajan
Dokin Allah, horse of Allah	Hausa

VARIATION FROM PARISH TO PARISH

In Barbados there is little variation of dialect from parish to parish. The island has only 166 square miles, and a person in St. Lucy may often socialise with an individual from Christ Church in the office or at school. Advances in transport and socio-economic and political changes, the relatively low cost of telephones, and the media have drastically diminished the few differences there were. The period of adjustment required, for example before a standard English speaker can understand a Cockney, or a Barbadian a rural Jamaican, is not needed in Barbados.

Nonetheless, some parishes are notable for certain grammatical forms, intonation and high percentage of basilectal forms, and observers may seek to identify localised vocabulary. For example one teacher who I interviewed (during fieldwork in 1981-82) commented that when she taught at a local school in St. George, children would refer to a new strain of influenza as the *new sick*. Although I am myself a St. Georgian, I was not familiar with this phrase; I was, however, with another example she quoted, which was used considerably by the adolescent peer group in the 1960s when the 'in thing' was to create nonsense verses:

We were fighting with we one another.
(We were fighting with each other.)

One can call this a peer group phrase since it is not used by the adults in the village.

Again, many of the individuals I interviewed commented about the dialect of St. Philip as 'different'. Their accent varies from that of other parishes. One teacher commented that they tend to put an 'o' in words; another, an English teacher, claimed that they sound like people from Somerset. A teacher from a St. Michael school specified these as oral grammatical usages of students from St. Philip:

I had to went to town. I had to go to town.
I ain't going now. I am not going now.
What yu want fu do? What would you like to do?

The forms above, however, would not be used in the classroom by children to their teachers, but rather by individuals in their peer groups.

Another parish well-known for its accent, and characterised by a higher raised larynx voice than the other parishes is St. Lucy. They use the personal pronoun *me* more often than any other islanders.

The last parish on which I will comment is St. Michael's. The commercial capital is Bridgetown situated in St. Michael. Its inhabitants are now mostly a mixture of working class and middle-class, who would be lost in the rural areas of the plantation. It is notable as the area which leads in language, as the area which speaks standard Caribbean English. It is easy for a person from the rural area to recognise the 'highly influential acrolect' speech of a resident of St. Michael, and vice versa.

The example below illustrates this and also poses the pedagogical questions. It is an extract from an interview with a Barbadian teacher:

Interviewer: So how do the people of St. Michael speak?
Teacher: All right, generally. If you hear them dem in class, they speak standard English. I don't know if you hear two girls when you were coming along there... One said *'But wha we gine?'* (where are we going?) and the other one say *'Man we lookin' fa somb'dy'*.

The reported dialogue between the two girls not only highlights the variety of language used outside the classroom as totally different from what the teacher is trying to teach the pupil; it also shows the need for a special approach to the West Indian language situation as the traditional methods of teaching English are inappropriate. The example also shows the capacity of children to switch at an early age between Bajan and something close to standard Caribbean English for the classroom.

Finally, a remark made to me by Dr Derek Griffith, a Barbadian postgraduate student studying in London, sums up the relative lack of importance of these perceptions of geographical variation:

> At school, I presume that I met students from most parts of Barbados, although the majority would no doubt have been from the environment of St. Michael. I did not notice any difference in speech in my classmates except for some variation in ability to speak 'nice'.

VARIATION BY SOCIAL SITUATION

Where speakers operate on the continuum tends to be related to social class and rural-urban factors. Older rural working-class speakers will tend to operate closer to the basilectal end of the spectrum, while the younger urban middle class tend to operate closer to the acrolectal end. All middle-class speakers, however, whether in St. George, St. Andrew, St. Joseph or St. Michael would have a command of the whole range of varieties, but many would not admit the ability to speak Raw Bajan, especially the older middle-class, because it is seen as inferior. I have noticed, however, the ability of the middle-class to switch according to the topic of conversation and relationship to individuals around. By contrast, a working-class person from a rural area might only be able to command one variety of Bajan speech, depending on education.

Nevertheless, both Raw Bajan, and the middle-class or standard variants operate as stylistic types. A language form is chosen for particular purposes and situations. Thus, MPs addressing a Barbados Labour Party meeting will phrase their speech in a language quite unlike that used when addressing a village gathering or that used among friends at an informal gathering. The diagram below, based on Hughes (1981), illustrates this:

Social Situation	Standard English	Bajan
MP in parliament	x	
MP's political speech to villagers*	x	x
Talking to friends	x	
Sermon in church		x
Instructions to waiter		x
Personal letter	x	
Speech in political context	x	

University lecture	x	
Family conversation		x
News broadcast	x	
Radio 'soap opera'		x
Newspaper editorial	x	
Caption on cartoon		x
Poetry	x	(x)
Folk literature		x

*political speech to villagers - There would be code-switching according to social purpose; standard Caribbean English would be used to impress villagers, and Bajan to show acceptance of their variety and communicate more easily.

The importance of using the right variety in the right social situation is difficult to overestimate. An outsider who accurately learnt to speak Bajan would be ostracised if he used it in formal speech, but it is common to have someone read aloud from a newspaper in standard English and then discuss the topic in Bajan. The degree of overlapping of language contexts would be a fruitful subject of research in socio-linguistics. Recordings I made of church services illustrate the variation.

Thus, in an Anglican Parish Church where the audience tends to include a few Europeans, together with both Barbadians from the village speaking Raw Bajan and educated upper-class and middle-class Barbadians, the rector, of English ancestry, spoke standard Barbadian English. In a village Pentecostal church, however, with a local pastor and congregation, a variety of speech much closer to the basilect will be spoken, characterised by a strongly Bajan phonology, grammar and lexis. African features in language, singing, non-verbal expressions and movement of the body can be observed.

In another local church that I visited, however, the variety of speech utilised varied from basilect to acrolect with the idiolect of the individual preaching. Preachers included a local teacher, a local university lecturer, a local mechanic and a local accountant. In this church there was also a Canadian influence, as its leader for the past twenty years has been a naturalised Bajan of Canadian origin. Its Sunday school also has an Irish teacher, and I found that the Sunday school children have adjusted linguistically and phonetically to his Irish variety of English. This was in contrast with their parents who had not socialised with him, and found it difficult to understand his variety of English.

Linguistic adjustment can work both ways. Alleyne (1981, p.47) comments that: 'although there remains so marked a phonological divergence between what is known in Barbados as 'Raw Bajan' and English, that it amounts to incomprehensibility for a monolingual speaker of English, the simple device of slowing down the 'Raw Bajan' speaker will probably have the effect of making him comprehensible to a speaker of English and this is because the syntactic structure and also the morphology of present-day Bajan have, in historical circumstances ... developed further away from the field-slaves than in other Caribbean colonies'.

The linguistic development which Barbados has undergone resulted in the elimination of what was in the 16th century, a dialect analogous to the Jamaican dialect. Texts from Barbados containing small amounts of speech, by historians who visited Barbados in the 18th and 19th centuries demonstrate that there existed such a dialect. In fact it is clear that the two dialects are closely connected historically, but only a few traces, such as unu (second person plural pronoun) used in Barbados and Jamaica remain as evidence of this connection.

> *wunu(h), unu, unuh, you* (pl), all of you Bajan
> *unu,* you (pl), all of you Igbo

Allsopp (1980) asserts that a secondary diaspora of Black groups from Barbados carried this pronoun to Jamaica and Belize, where it remains entrenched in their Creoles. Phonetically, however, Bajan differs from Jamaican Creole, as indeed it does in grammar. For example, Jamaican Creole shows the noun plural by using dem, for example:

> *De girl dem play.*
> There is no noun-verb agreement. Barbadians would say:
> *De girls de play.*

The differences seem little, but speed, pitch or tone of the voice, sometimes with particular types of stresses to signal certain meanings, play a large part.

THE WHITE POPULATION

These can be divided into two groups:

1. The descendants of the old plantocracy and recent immigrants who use standard English, though influenced by Bajan style. Many are familiar with and can speak Bajan, though not fluently. Within a relatively small span of variation they tend towards acrolectal variants.
2. The poor Whites, who are descendants of indentured servants, and prisoners deported by Cromwell. After expiry of their indentures, many settled in St. John, Bath, Martin's Bay and Newcastle, many near the plantation where their descendants are still living. They are often referred to as *Red Legs* (supposedly referring to the effect of the sun on their skin) or *Bakra Johnny*. (Red as noun and adjective, is also applied pejoratively to 'coloured' Negroes, in reference to their skin colour.)

Both ethnic groups, especially the latter, are referred to as bakra or buckra, a white person (cf. Efik mbakara (n.pl.) those who rule).

The poor whites operate mainly in the basilectal and mesolectal spans. In

Hymes (1971), Alleyne comments: 'Another fact that has not been given sufficient importance by Creolists is that Creole served as a means of communication among segments of the White population of the West Indian colonies. Still in Barbados one finds White groups speaking Creole'. He goes on to comment that in Reunion Island off the coast of East Africa, the only monolingual speakers of Creole are poor Whites in the island's highlands. In Barbados the majority of poor Whites operate on the Basilect spectrum because the community is small, and there is little socialisation or intermarriage outside it. If outside socialisation does take place it is sometimes within the rural community.

THE PHONOLOGY OF BAJAN

Many words come from English but sound different, sometimes very different. For example in the sentence *The cake will burn in the oven if you do not turn it off now* every word could be said as a Bajan word: *De cake will bun in de ooven eef ya don't/[kyan] tun it offe.*

Historically many sounds present in 17th and 18th century regional English usage are still preserved within Barbados. Le Page and Cassidy (1967) and Willeford (1977) suggest that early English phonetic structure was reinterpreted through the matrix of a phonemic structure either of West African languages or of a Portuguese West African pidgin. The resultant pidgin was creolised, becoming the native languages of the Caribbean. Subsequently Scottish and 19th century educated southern British English have acted as models for the Creole-speakers. The educated version of Creole, as used by the middle-class, has acted in turn as a model language for the educated version of Bajan.

In Bajan, compared with standard English, final consonantal sounds, particularly ts and ds are often completely ignored phonetically. The y in, for example, a word like *every* tends to disappear, as does the u in *you* (unless the word is used emphatically) and the r in *for*. The last two words, rendered phonetically in standard English as /juː/ (you) and /fà(r)/ or /fo!(r)/ (for) become /jnh/ (yuh) and /fnh/ (fo) respectively. Also /breik/ (break), /meik/ (make), and /teik/ (take) become *brek, mek,* and *tek,* relics of 17th century pronunciation. The phonetic pronunciation of *cyan* (or *kyan*) for *can't* is prevalent throughout the Caribbean. If the final t is dropped, it becomes difficult to distinguish from its opposite, the affirmative *can,* although this word is often pronounced *kin. Cyan* is generally preferred to the more exact dissyllable *kee-ahn* (Colleymore, 1970).

Another sound present in all the Caribbean islands is the pronunciation of [θ] as in *thin* and [θ] as in *this* as *dis*. The aspirate is frequently omitted, and the sound *th* is usually rendered by *d* as in *de, dis,* and *dat,* for *the, this,* and *that. Mother* becomes *moder* and *father* becomes *fader*. It is noticeable, however, that the final *th* does not follow this rule; dental *teeth* becomes palatal *teet* (both singular and plural).

Some vowel sounds are lengthened so than *man* becomes *maan, in* becomes *iin*, and *jaw* becomes *jaa*. *Gordon* becomes *Gaadn* and *garden* becomes *gyaadn*. Sometimes initial, medial and final consonants are dropped; thus one often hears *uman* for *woman*, *smadi* for *somebody* and *yeside* for *yesterday*.

The auxiliary *does* in the present tense of the verb does not denote emphasis, but expresses habitual action, e.g. in *He does write well*, no stress is placed upon the word *does*. Differences in stress also contribute to phonetic structure; they create what the British call a 'sing song' tone. For example, *I kin do it* in Creole represents both of the forms *I can do it* (statement) and *Can I do it?* (question) in Standard English.

NON-VERBAL COMMUNICATION

Gesture is used to complement, extend enforce and emphasise or reinforce meaning. Thus the continual waving of the finger might be used by an adult when reprimanding a child to enforce a warning.

'Hands' is used during a quarrel mainly by women to extend or enforce a threat.

The arms crossed demonstrate determination or even sarcasm. A 'cut eye', when one cuts one's eyes at an acquaintance, leaves him under no misapprehension; the eyes are fixed on him in a stony glare. A shrug of the shoulder, a wave of the hand, a nod of the head and nasal sounds such as *uh hum* (yes), *un un* (no) or *unun* (nice) are all used also to extend or emphasise meaning, especially in rural areas, by Bajan speakers.

In the plantation culture of Barbados and other Caribbean islands, the use of the body during oral communication continued to the extent that it should be seen as an extension of the West African cultural admixture. In Barbados gesture is not merely a complement of vocalisation or oral expression but can be a totally independent communication device, such as 'cutting one's eye' (mentioned above). This has a distinct significance; once this action has been completed there is absolutely no need for any further verbal communication.

Another gesture used in the Caribbean that has distinct and definite African links is the *stupes* or *suck teeth*. This is done to convey disgust, contempt, defiance and annoyance, as by elders to younger children or within one's peer group. A child using this form of communication to an adult is seen as impertinent. In Africa any kind of *stupes* is considered unaesthetic, as my Ghanaian and Ugandan friends have pointed out to me. Nigerian usage of the *stupes* correlates to the Caribbean usage; it can be utilised stylistically within one's peer group and not be offensive, or on an individual level to show annoyance when you make a mistake. This is usually a quick sharp *stupes*.

A further type of gesture is the use of hands instead of words. For example, men (who seem to use more of this type of non-verbal communication as opposed to women who use the stupes more regularly) might use this type when describing an event, for example, *He see de dog and went like dis* (hands hit together moving fast). The speaker does not need to convey verbally that the person described ran away quickly; the action speaks for itself.

The Caribbean country women laugh, move and wail with their entire body. One only needs to attend a country funeral or local Evangelical church to observe this type of communication. The gestural forms clearly draw on an African heritage. For example the wailing ceremony at a Ghanaian funeral resembles the practice of *going into the spirit* - a non-verbal spiritual religious dance associated with local churches in Barbados. This is similar to an African 'possession' dance, when the spirit of an ancestor actually takes control of the dancer's body and he loses control of speech and faculties. This is very unEuropean, and is seen in many Black churches in England. Religion seems an area fit for serious and respectful anthropological investigation, if only for the insight on the mechanism of a philosophy that motivates some lifestyles and attitudes not yet nationally understood and respected.

THE ORAL MODE OF COMMUNICATION

Creole is essentially and traditionally an oral vernacular, as are numerous African languages and dialects. Folkculture, family history, village tales etc. are handed down from one generation to the other orally. Interviews I conducted with a number of Barbadians illustrated the phonological variety and attitudes to it.

EXAMPLE I: A female teacher aged 34
Extract from an interview on children's linguistic needs recorded in a school staff room, January 1982.

Teacher: ...and they will tell you, if they speak like that at home, they will be ostracised; but their family will tell him, 'Why are you speaking so poor, great?' So that I think these children have a - they are like - At home they have to revert to the dialect.
Interviewer: So they are bi-dialectal?
Teacher: They are attempting to be bilingual. De problem comes that some, I think, honestly do not understand certain standard English forms so that you get them, well, the hypercorrection and 'bad' standard English grammar because they do not understand the standard grammar. So we gone back to teaching the formal in the hope that...
Interviewer: So how do the people of St. Michael speak?
Teacher: All right. Generally if you hear dem in class they speak standard English. I don't know if you hear two girls when you were coming along there, de ones that come in holding each other?
Interviewer: No
Teacher: One said 'But wha we gine?' (where are we going?) and the other one say, 'Man we lookin' fa somb'dy' but they would not say that in a classroom, with a teacher there...
Miss X had mentioned something about 'recognise', but we use it in a

peculiar way, I don't remember, we use it slightly different in that, I would have to get her on that, she told me, 'Ol' people use it .. Miss, Y, you will remember this, how ol' people here use 'recognise'?'

It is difficult to pinpoint the social class of this interviewee. Although she is undoubtedly middle-class by profession, there are lexical and syntactic items drawn from folk-speech. Specifically Barbadian features occur throughout; sometimes she is using a broad band of the spectrum, at other times only a narrow one.

The interviewee is the head of the English Department. Traditionally all girls from her school had to speak the prestigious mode of speech. Most had had to pass the 11+, so that every pupil in the school had a high IQ.

Language plays a very important role in this type of government school. The interviewee belongs to the new school of thought in the Caribbean concerning language. Creole is no longer condemned as ardently as before; the interviewee does not hesitate to use Bajan to illustrate a point, nor refuse to admit that she speaks it as did the interviewee in the next example. She illustrates the capacity of most Barbadians to understand Bajan regardless of class. She switches from one mode to another depending on the tenor, field and mode of discourse. The style used to communicate in a formal situation with the interviewer is noticeably closer to Standard English than that used informally to communicate with a colleague.

EXAMPLE II: A senior female teacher aged 50.
Extract from an interview recorded in her office in January 1982.

Teacher: Nowadays, with many Caribbean countries becoming independent and with an upsurge in national feeling, they are so many people who feel that dialect should be exalted and I have no quarrel with that, but not exalted to the extent that they do not recognise the importance of I.A.E. ...

...Well, Internationally Accepted English because - and that it - I think it is better to stress that if it is used as an international linguistic medium and - You know our dialect has no alphabet and de vocabulary I find, although very expressive, to a certain extent limited. I know that's an opinion that some of my colleagues do not share, but, um, there has to be a standard...

...Well, there always have been - they - For instance, our closeness to the United States where um 'OK' is almost spoken internationally now, and as much used as the word 'Coca-cola' and with the University of the West Indies you will find that um there is almost in some instances - what should I call it - a Caribbeanisation of de language to a certain extent.

This interviewee is upper-middle-class and from an affluent Afro-Caribbean Barbadian family from the capital, where prestigious norms of speech are utilised. She stresses every letter in a sentence and is conscious of the effect produced. She later remarked that in her age-group 'the importance of girls speaking 'properly' purely for marriage and social reasons was greatly stressed by parents'. She saw herself as a traditionalist and spoke standard English throughout the interview, but there was still a Barbadian tone.

EXAMPLE III: A male middle-class Barbadian Rastafarian in his 30s. Extract recorded at a meeting in the 'Barbados Cultural Heritage' Series

Most brethren suppose to recognise and know the Brother Analisha. So, um, as I say, it was plan tonight for a lecture, but I and I were saying that a family occasion like this here call fe something probably closer than jus' a lecture where each and ever one 'ave could come into one and let ever man get an opportunity to say his portion. De topic of I and I conversation is pertaining to Ethiopia but before I and I actually began we would like just to say a short word historically and prophetically, um, fu dis occasion, which is to speak of Psalms 87, where it is written that God foundation is in de holy mountains for Jah love de gate of Zion, more than all de dwelling place of Jacob...

O thou most high Jah RastafarI, de house of David and de throne of David stand forever.

The speaker was speaking to an audience of 300, most of whom were Rasta. It was supposed to be a poetry reading, but when the speaker saw the large Rasta representation, he decided to turn it into a *family occasion*. Apart from the non-Rasta 5 per cent of the audience, language used was therefore influenced by Rastafarian usages; it is Bajan/standard Caribbean with Rasta terms. It may not always be possible to tell a Rasta by his appearance but, in the absence of other signs, his speech may reveal his identity. In Barbados the Rasta religion from Jamaica began creeping in in the 70s. Today many young men have joined the movement and adopted Rasta language, and one can hear speech with many Jamaican characteristics but Barbadian phonology.

The mi of Jamaican Creole speech as in *Mi have mi book* (I have my book) is perceived by Rastafarians as expressive of subservience and therefore the pronoun I not only replaces it but takes on a special significance in Rasta utterances, giving the language many I words like *Ital, TafarI* and *Sailassia I*. The speaker uses I as singular and I and I as plural, and uses many biblical phrases. Syntax, grammatical construction, tone, pitch and inflexion are all used by the Rasta to create a new image, a new perception of self as man. These usages, however, have had little impact on the language of the community, possibly because of the negative reception Rastafarianism has received from middle-class and other Barbadians. During the meeting Creole became more prominent as the atmosphere, - music, drumming etc. - became more intense.

THE WRITTEN MODE OF COMMUNICATION

Officially and traditionally all written material in Barbados is in standard English, and only recently have local writers begun to assimilate the rich oral tradition of Bajan by writing it.

The elite and the bureaucrats still object to it being written, mainly because people feel Creole is unstructured and unsuitable for communication, and because its written mode has no established phonemic orthography and lacks uniformity.

Those who venture into writing Bajan, such as Edward Kumanu Braithwaite, poets like Bruce St. John and Margot Blackman in her collection of proverbs, all seem to use a different system of orthography. Thus, for example, these proverbs appear variously as:

Ev'ry skin teet' ent a laugh. (Blackman 1982)
Evah skin teet en a laugh. (St. John 1974)
(Every smile is not a laugh.)

Do fuh do ent nuh obeah. (Blackman 1982)
Do fo' do ain' no obeah. (Allsopp 1980)
(If witchcraft is performed simultaneously by two individuals against each other the result is negative.)

Many critics object to the recognition of the validity of the vernacular as a medium of expression since it is rarely written and this accentuates distinctions between the literate and unlettered. There is also an absence of popular, readable and acceptable grammatical studies.

Despite these negative feelings, however, the rise of nationalist sentiments seen in the poetry of Bruce St. John and Glyne Walrond, under the influence of other Caribbean poets like Louise Bennett, has led to a conscious re-evaluation of Creole. Many people here and in the Caribbean feel proud to produce something that is *ours*; pride which was until recently never expressed openly and never to strangers. There is also a feeling that intimate jokes, stories, folk art, humour, proverbs, and folktales cannot be communicated effectively in standard English.

I analyse a example of such humorous writing below. But in Barbados today one can observe an increasing use of Bajan Creole in serious writing in two distinct areas:

1. The utilisation of semi-folk language technique for the debate of serious public and political topics in the local press. This is not the kind of popular dialect column illustrated below, but rather a sort of linguistic compromise, as in the writings of Austin Tom Clarke and Timothy Callender, which are full of Creole idioms, within standard English forms, used to give an effect of 'serious' informality.

2. What is popularly known as 'dialect poetry', but of a more serious nature than amusing 'dialect verse', which has a long traditional history in both the Anglophone and the Francophone Caribbean.

EXAMPLE IV: A humorous newspaper column
Extract from a story 'Winken vs Gertrude', in *The Pelican*, 18 December 1981

Winken: I name Winken. I does live in the back o' Cave Hill in a wall-house that I get a mortgage offa the Development Bank to buy, plus a lil second-hand motto-car. I telling you all this, sir, just to show you, that I is a staple, reliable man in the community, and that if um wasn't through the tender mercies of one gentleman living-'bout-here, by which I mean Mr. Jackdear, I would still, all-this-time-so, be catching a lotta night-dew in my chest, out fishing every night, and can't sell none. I is a fisherman by profession.

But, as I say just-now, through Mr. Jackdear, I is a depitty chief of security by vocation, meaning that I does-be-responsible for patrolling the stretch o' beach-front from Paradise Hotel all the way down by Southern Palms Hotel. That is my name and address, sir.

Sargeant: Tell the court what happened to you on Friday night gone, after you knock-off?

Winken: Before I knock-off round midnight,, on the night in question, which as you mention was a Friday, I did-just patrol my beat two times. I decide to patrol the beach-front two times because on one previous occasion in the past, minute I pass Pardise going north and heading for Southern Palms, two beach-bums jump me from hiding under a corrdear tree. So, that is why I patrols two times instead o' one. So, 'pon the night in question, I did-just get back to Pardise whiching is my clocking-out control headquarters, when I say goodnight to nightwatchman, and the cook who having a thing with the night-watchman. I get in my car, And I climb Cave Hill. I did just put she in second gear to climb the hill more easier when out o' the bushes, just there by the bus stop, I see this big big thing, a thing looking like a crocus bag. The thing rush-out in the middle o' the road. Well, I had was to stop.

Screech! I put on my brakes. 'Cause I believes in law and order, being as how I is a security-guard. I get out now. I walk-round to the front o' the car, and feel the crocus-bag, thinking um was a bag o' potatoes, or a bag o' cabbage that drop-off a lorry heading for the BMC. The minute my hand touch the thing, the bag, Wop!

A lash in my backbone! I get frighten now. 'Cause, as I give evidence when the constable come later that night to my house, I couldn't believe that a crocus bag have hands.

Wop! The second blow benn-me-up. I now flat on my back in the middle o' the road, side o' my motto car. And standing up over me is this big big crocus-bag, and a woman inside-up saying, all the time, 'You is a mah-guffy? You is a gorilliphant? You is somebody too?' Um was only then, when the stars went outta my head, and when my head stop spinning from the blows, that I recognise the voice. Um was Gertrude, Gertrude who does-sell cloth and straw-hats behind Southern Palms.

Sargeant: What made you know the person in question aforemention', was the accuse, named in this docket?

Winken: Well, sir, I had was to chase-she-'way from 'pon the beach by Southern Palms humbugging the tourisses the previous Wednesday, the previous Thursday and the previous afternoon, whereby I referring to the night in question. And the voice she use the night in question, being the night she lick-me-down with the pestle, was the ellsame voice she use when I race-she-way from selling without a legal permit.

Sargeant: On the three previous occasions when you race-'way Gertrude from offa the beach, what did Gertrude tell you?

Winken: You really want me to say wha' she tell me? In her own- own words? Or in my own-own words?

Sargeant: To the best of your knowledge and recollection.

Winken: Well, first of all. Before the accuse even open she mouth, she stannup so, look! She stannup with she hands akimbo. She had-on a red thing 'pon she head. She liff-up she dress over she behind. And she skin-round so, look! And when I see what I see, after she raise-up she dress, what my eyes rested on, sir, isn't nothing that I could relate inside this court. Gertrude didn't had-on nothing undernest, nothing at all sir. 'You could kiss this!' she tell me. When she tell me so, I look off. 'Cause, being a believer in law and order, I don't like to look at no lawlessness, like the lawlessness that does go-on 'bout here.

All the waiters was looking and laughing. And I did feel shame-shame. 'Cause Mr. Jackdear get me this job, and um is a job of responsibilities. And for a beach-seller to do so and affronts me so...

Analysis of the syntax and morphology of Example IV

1. There is a mixture of Creole and standard English, and their grammatical rules; thus one finds noun-verb agreement in some cases and subject-verb concord is prevalent also, e.g. . *I believes, she tell, eyes rested, beach-seller to do so, and affronts me.*
2. One can see the lexicon has undergone extensive development through reduplication to extend and intensify meaning. Thus one finds, in the passage, words like *big big thing* (large), *own-own* (her own, individual), *shame-shame* (embarrassed, ashamed). Colleymore (1970) terms these 'compound redundants' and comments that there are numerous examples in Barbadian Creole, such as *play-play* (make-believe), *wee-wee* (tiny), *back-back* (return, go back), *rock-stone* (stone). There are also instances

where two different nouns come together, as in *boar-hog* (male pig), *ram-goat* (male ram), *boy-child* (male child), and finally a reduplicated pronoun, *she-she* (effeminate).

3. There are also many other compound words: *wall-house* (house made of cement), *night-dew* (dew), *just-now* (a moment ago), *beach-front* (coast), *knock-off* (finish work), *motto-car* (car).
4. The auxiliary verb is sometimes omitted, e.g.*I name, I telling.*
5. The passage is in the present tense, but the incident probably took place months ago. Other devices are employed, however, such as time words, to show the action was in the past, e.g. after, *did-just, previous, I just get, race-she-way, lick-down*
6. *She stannup so, look!*: Winken has omitted the words and used action to convey his meaning.
7. The lexis varies from Raw Bajan through to Standard English. Many words are familiar Bajan words still used by the older generation, e.g. Bajan: *having a thing* (carrying on an affair), *humbugging* (pestering); Raw Bajan: *benn-me-up* (hurt me badly), *lick-me-down* (knock me over), *race-she-way* (send her away), *skin- round* (turn round).

    With regard to the words *muh-guffy* and *gorilliphant*, the speaker in an oral culture is never at a loss for making up words to describe a visual event. It shows the creativeness of language. *Gorilliphant* emphasises Winken's attitude, his assumed power and physique. It is a nonsense word, as is *muh-guffy*. Bajan abounds in these; many are individual creations, used extensively in children's songs. These two words show the creativity and structure-dependency of language, and that variation can spring from the creative impulse of the individual or group. Thus they become part of Winken's idioloect.

8. The Creole vocabulary retains archaic and biblical phrases no longer in use in standard English, like *aforemention, tender mercies,* and *affronts.* These words are mainly in the vocabulary of the over-forty generation; many are redundant. Cruikshank (1916) has a chapter on 'Negro dialects in Barbados', which includes the variant *aforesaid*, and shows the influence of 18th century English on Barbadian Creole. Cruikshank obtained most of his material by talking to Afro-Caribbean people and visiting plantations in the Caribbean. He claims, for example, that *jouk*, as in *jouk out your eye*, is a corruption of a heraldry term, originally *jupe* (to pierce), probably from Scotland, where French terms of heraldry were frequently used. (Modern linguists, however, may suspect a convergent influence from Pula (Fulani) *jukka* (to stab, pierce).) He adduces a number of other Irish, Scottish and English archaisms, including some used in *The Canterbury Tales*, which were present in Bajan at the beginning of the century; some are still in use.
9. Finally, most of the words seem English in origin, but a close inspection of the morphological syntactic structure shows words to be influenced by African languages, as for example in the compound formations noted

above, and in the use of *hand* and *foot* to include the whole arm and the whole leg. There is also no lexical distinction between these parts of the body in many West African languages.

EXAMPLE V: A private letter.
A paragraph from a private letter to the writer.

> Good day/night to you. This has been a few months since I received your letter. I guess you probably saying to yourself 'Paul like he ain't bothering bout replying!' Now you know those are wrong thoughts.

Private letters rarely use Bajan. This is an exception. The writer is aged about 25 and of middle-class background.

In his third sentence *like* is used elliptically; there is no noun/verb concord between *Paul* and *like* because like is a 'manner preposition' (cf. Bailey, 1966, pp.70-71). It does not have the same meaning as 'Paul likes'. Another noticeable omission is that of the prefix a in the 'place preposition' *about*. The word is pronounced *bo't*; the a and the u are omitted and the t is silent.

The author of this letter was quite conscious of the change in language; the mixing of standard and Creole has a particular place in the letter. This one sentence is used primarily for effect; the oral and written are seen as overlapping.

In conclusion one may say that a word may belong to Raw Bajan alone, or to educated middle-class speech alone, or it may be used anywhere in the spectrum. Thus no single phonemic system will suffice for all words. Also, dialect words used by middle-class or educated speakers may be normalised and used unselfconsciously or they may retain their dialect pronunciation, showing that the speaker wants you to know that they are part of his ideolect and not his educated vocabulary. Finally, whatever phonological system is utilised, there is still a choice between an orthography conventionalised on the standard English pattern or an attempt at a phonetic or Bajan orthography (cf. Le Page and Cassidy, 1967).

BAJAN POETRY AND PROSE

The work of Bruce St. John is outstanding above all others in this field. One may examine the influence of standard English in his writing; but the voice is a unique Barbadian one, distinctly African in semantics and character. It is invested with an indispensable orality; its metres, tones, runs and switches if rhythm are an intrinsic part of its coherence. It carries most of the time a built-in implication of audience response. He exploits this to the full in the poem *Bajan Litany* when the audience actively participates. In his poem *Bajan Language* (St. John, 1974), he gives his opinion on the question of Bajan Creole being 'limited': here are two brief extracts:

> We language limit!
> De Yankee does read we short story
> All nation does read we short story
> An like um too.
> Dem doan onnerstan' a single word,
> An dem does laugh de right time
> An cry de right time
> An ask fuh mo'
> And ask fuh book widit...
>
> ...English Bajanise a delightful ravage
> An a lemonade language in de town.
> Each language got a rhythm but Bajan
> Lick guitar drum an banjo stiff wid blows...

Finally there are examples of Barbadian Creole in the novels of George Lamming (1979), Paula Marshall (1982), and a variety of writers whose work appeared in Gray (1969). The literary magazine *Bim* has also given authors like Austin Clarke, Timothy Callender, and the ex-teacher Bernard C. Graham a medium through which they can reach a sensitive reading public despite its negative preconceived ideas about Creole. The works of these authors have brought Creole into the classroom and given it a new status.

THE PRESENT AND THE FUTURE

The present-day linguistic continua within Barbados originate in the plantation hierarchy system, with house-maids at the top speaking a variety closer to the dominant language, those working in the 'yard' around the house speaking a mesolectal form and those in the field speaking a basilectal form. Except at the two extremes, it is difficult to say of anyone that they are or are not a Bajan speaker. It is, moreover, difficult to define the ideolect of some speakers in the sense that one cannot predict 's/he will say that, but not this'. All Barbadians are liable to vary their speech according to the social context, so we can say a language is not a uniform object. Variation of code is a basic principle of sociolinguistics.

In Barbados, then, the choice of language is determined by the subject of conversation, the situation and the degree of intimacy between speakers. There are rules speakers follow in choosing their speech patterns and the speakers' social status is of little or no importance in determining the variety used.

In informal situations - telling a joke, at the rum shop, slamming dominoes - where participants are friends, Bajan is usually chosen. In formal situations - a job interview, a lecture - the choice is more likely to be some approximation to standard Caribbean English, but many of the older rural people, labourers and poor Whites operate between the basilect and mesolect span. Many do not have a command of the acrolect span.

With social, economic, political and educational advancement, the language is moving closer and closer to the dominant language, and what variation is left is being systematically eradicated by mass communication. African cultural heritage is, however, gaining an increasing status and popularity in Barbados, and it is likely that although there may be decreasing variation within Bajan, the boundaries between it and standard English may become more formally marked, even if the distance between them has narrowed.

ACKNOWLEDGMENTS

My thanks go first to Yvonne Collymore of the Caribbean Communications Project who gave me a list of individuals and resources in Barbados to help start my research. Also to Dr. Richard Allsopp of the University of the West Indies and Glynn Waldron. I would also like to express my deep appreciation to those whom I interviewed, especially the headmistress and staff of St Michael's Girls' School, and Claimont Tate at CBC. Also Eltone (Elombe) Motley, Director of News and Current Affairs at CBC and his staff, especially Trevor Scott, who did the recording of the 'Rasta' extract. Finally, my thanks to Cathy Wallace at Ealing College of Higher Education, who suggested areas of research that led to this paper.

REFERENCES

Alleyne M. (1981) 'Linguistic Aspects of Communication in the West Indies' in Cuthbert M. and Pidgeon M. (eds.) *Languages and Communication in the Caribbean*, Third Edition. Cedar Press, Bridgetown, Barbados

Allsopp R. (1972) 'The Question of Barbadian Culture', *Bajan Magazine*, Barbados

Allsopp R. (1980) 'The Current State of Studies of the African Cultural Heritage' in *Barbados*. UNESCO, Paris and Bridgetown, Barbados

Bailey B.L. (1966) *Jamaican Creole Syntax*. Cambridge University Press, Cambridge

Blackman M. (1982) *Bajan Proverbs*. Cedar Press, Barbados

Carrington L.D. (1974) 'Some Applications of Linguistic Research to Educational Problems', *Language and Society*, 3

Cassidy F. and Le Page R.B. (1967) *Dictionary of Jamaican English*. Cambridge University Press, Cambridge

Colleymore F. (1970) *Barbados Dialect*, Fourth Edition. The Barbadian National Trust, Barbados

Craig D.R. (1971) 'Education and Creole English in the West Indies' in Hymes D. (ed.) *Pidginization and Creolization of Languages*. Cambridge University Press, Cambridge, p.371

Cruikshank J.G. (1916) *Black Talk*. Argosy, Demerara

Cuthbert M. and Pidgeon M. (eds.) (1981) *Languages and Communication in the Caribbean*, Third Edition. Cedar Press, Bridgetown, Barbados

Gray C. (ed.) (1969) *Response - A Course in Narrative Comprehension and Composition for Caribbean Secondary Schools*. Nelson, London

Hughes M. (1981) 'Some Contributions of Linguistics to the Use of English Studies' in Cuthbert M. and Pidgeon M. (eds.) *Languages and Communication in the Caribbean*, Third Edition. Cedar Press, Bridgetown, Barbados

Hymes D. (ed.) (1971) *Pidginization and Creolization of Languages*. Cambridge University Press, Cambridge

Lamming G. (1979) *In The Castle of My Skin*. Longman, London

Leitch J. (1980) 'A Perspective on Caribbean Language and Dialect', *Caribbean Communications Project Occasional Papers on Caribbean Language and Dialect*, 1

Marshall P. (1982) *Brown Girl, Brown Stones*. Virago, London

Rice F.A. (1962) *Study of the Role of Second Language in Asia, Africa and Latin America*. Centre for Applied Linguistics of the Modern Association of America, Washington DC

Stewart W.A. (1962) 'Creole Languages in the Caribbean' in Rice F.A. (ed.) *Study of the Role of Second Language in Asia, Africa and Latin America*. Centre for Applied Linguistics of the Modern Association of America, Washington DC, p.34

St. John B. (1974) *Bruce St. John at Kairi House*. Laird, Barbados

Walrond O. (1981) *The Children's Voice*. Stockwell, Ilfracombe, Devon

Willesford M. (1967) 'Bajan Dialect - English or Sudanic?', *Bim*, 12(44), p.258

Willesford M. (1968) 'Africanisms in the Bajan dialect' *Bim*, 12(46), p.90

Winford D. (1974) 'Aspects of the Social Differentiation of Language in Trinidad', *Caribbean Issues*, 3

Phonological Relationships within Caribbean English

J.C. Wells

SOUND CHANGES

Where two language varieties share a common origin but are now phonetically different from one another, each point of phonetic difference must have arisen because of sound changes which have affected one variety (or both) since the date the two varieties became distinct (Wells 1973, 1982). For example, the vowel of *short, fork* used to be distinguished from that of *sport, pork* in all kinds of English; this distinction is preserved in Jamaica and Barbados, as well as in Scotland and Ireland, although in England it has mostly disappeared through a sound change. On the other hand the vowel of *beer, fear* is still distinct form that of *bare, fair* in England, but this distinction is no longer usual in the West Indies.

COMMON CHARACTERISTICS

There are some phonetical characteristics which seem to be common to all parts of the English-speaking Caribbean (or to all Caribbean English-based Creoles, and in some cases to their related mesolects and acrolects). One example is the sound [ɥ] (labial-palatal approximant), the special variety of /w/ used before front vowels, as in *wet* [ɥet], *wheel* [ɥiil]. This seems to be traceable to an African origin, since the same relationship between [ɥ] and [w] applies in Akan (Twi, Fante) but not (as far as I am aware) in any non-Caribbean variety of English. The use of plosives [t, d] where standard accents (including acrolectal Caribbean English) have fricatives [θ, ð] as in *thick, father* may also reflect African influence, as may the cluster reduction exemplified in *next* [neks], *hand* [han] (which is again something sociolinguistically variable in the West Indies). On the other hand the use of clear (l) as in *milk, feel*, (shared with Irish and south Welsh English, for example) is merely a conservative feature, probably a characteristic of all 17th century English. Likewise the typical Caribbean quality of the diphthong in words like mouth, namely (ou), is perhaps just old-fashioned as compared with the [au]-type diphthongs which prevail elsewhere.

REGIONAL VARIATION IN THE CARIBBEAN

It is striking that the speech of Jamaica is phonetically quite similar to that of Guyana, even though they belong geographically at opposite ends of the Caribbean crescent, while that of Barbados is very different from that of, say, Antigua, which are closer neighbours. This can be seen, for instance, in the fate of historical [r]. In Barbados it is preserved in all positions, so that Bajans still generally pronounce [r] wherever r appears in the spelling, just as most Americans do. In the Leewards and Trinidad, however, [r] has been lost wherever it was preconsonantal (*start, beard, force*) or word-final (*star, beer, four*) just as it has been in RP (the standard accent of England). Jamaica and Guyana show an intermediate situation, since they have lost [r] preconsonantally but preserve it word-finally (with some variability in both sets of environments). This is tabulated at the top of Table 1 (1, 2).

	Jamaica	Leewards	Windwards/ Trinidad	Barbados	Guyana
1. [r] lost before C	(yes)	yes	yes	no	(yes)
2. [r] lost finally	(no)	yes	yes	no	(no)
3. merged [a]	(yes)	(yes)	no	no	(yes)
4. [ie, uo]	(yes)	(yes)	no	no?	no
5. Special Stress	no	no	no?	yes	yes
6. [oŋ] for [oun]	(yes)	no	no?	yes	yes
7. glottal stop [t]	no	no	no	yes	no
8. [ai]	no	no	no	yes	no

Table 1: Selected phonetic characteristics that are regionally variable in Caribbean English (parentheses = entry applies to basilectal speech, but not necessarily in the mesolect/acrolect). 1-4 seem to be centred on the Leewards, 5-8 on Barbados

The vowels of *trap* and *lot* (3) are merged in basilectal Jamaican, Leewards, and Guyanese speech, so that *black* is pronounced identically with *block, rat* with *rot*; but in Barbados and Trinidad they remain distinct. I am not certain whether they are ever merged in the Windwards. The vowels of words such as *face* and *goat* (4) were monophthongal [ee, oo] in seventeenth-century English, although in most parts of England they have now become closing dipthongs. They remain monophthongal in Barbados, Guyana and Trinidad, as well as acrolectal Caribbean English elsewhere; but in basilectal Jamaican and Leewards speech they have developed into opening diphthongs [ie, uo], thus [fies, guot].

In points (1-4) we thus see an innovation adopted in the Leewards and to some extent in Jamaican and Guyana, but not in Barbados. Points (5-8), on the other hand, constitute innovations adopted in Barbados but not in the Leewards. This may reflect the position in Antigua and Barbados as the earliest focuses of English (-Creole) -speaking settlement in the Caribbean, with Jamaica and Guyana being settled later and receiving their population largely from these two focal points. The Windwards and Trinidad occupy a special position, in that they have adopted English (an English-based Creole) only relatively recently.

From Barbados and Guyana there are reported special uses of stress (or tone?) (5) which give minimal pairs such as *tailor* vs. *Taylor*, *father* 'parent' vs. *father* 'priest'. The exact nature of this contrast still remains to be worked out, as does its geographical extent. It is again Bajans and Guyanese in whose speech we most typically find the use of the sequence [ong] (6) where other accents have [oun] or its equivalent: thus [kongt] *count*, [tong] *town* (homophonous with *tongue*). To some extent this is also found in basilectal Jamaican [dong] *down*, but not, apparently, in the Leewards. It may well be a Bajan innovation.

The use of the glottal stop for word-final [t] (7) is a striking Bajanism, thus (plee?) *plate*, (staar?) *start*. This phenomenon is of course widespread in Britain (though apparently quite recent), but is otherwise unknown in the Caribbean. In Barbados it probably arose independently.

Another very typical Barbadian feature is the use of a diphthong of the [ai] type (8) in words such as [prais, taim] *price, time*. From a historical point of view, this could well be an archaism rather than an innovation: the Leewards, Jamaica, Guyana, and Trinidad have the newer [ai] type.

A QUERY

In this connection Kephart's paper in this book raises interesting questions. If the phonemic analysis of Carriacou Creole which he gives is correct, Carriacou stands out as not distinguishing the vowels which others distinguish as /ii/vs. /i/ (sheep vs. ship), /uu/ vs. /u/ (*Luke* vs. *look*), and /aa/ vs. /a/ (pat/pot vs. path/ (part)). The last of these is not implausible, given their merger in basilectal Trinidadian (although Trinidadians do distinguish *pat* from *pot*); but the first seems to be unparalleled in the other Caribbean varieties I have been considering. Now it is true that the *sheep-ship* distinction is not made in Krio, and Alleyne regards it as having been historically lost in the early stages of Creole and then reintroduced into Jamaican and Guyanese (and implicitly into other Caribbean and American varieties) 'as a result of English influence' (1980, p.41). I confess I have my doubts about this claim. The absence of the opposition certainly seems to lead to some intolerable homophonic clashes, which I would expect to have given rise (as in Krio) to lexical replacement. In Kephart's goat story, when the goat asks *Du yu si big tit layk dis* (incidentally using a surely non-Creole syntactic inversion!) how do Padli and Mona know he is asking about his *teeth* rather than his *tit(s)*? Is Carriacou /mi tit-dem big/ not intolerably ambiguous? Kephart says he first assumed, but then threw out, the long vowels */ii/ and */aa/

REFERENCES

Alleyne M.C. (1980) *Comparative Afro-American*. Karoma, Ann Arbor
Kephart R. (1984) *An Orthography ans Sample Materials for Teaching Reading in a Creole-Speaking Community*. Conference Paper.
Wells J.C. (1973) *Jamaica Pronunciation in London*. Blackwells, Oxford
Wells J.C. (1982) *Accents of English*. Cambridge University Press, Cambridge

What Is 'Mother Tongue'? Some Problems Posed by London Jamaican

Mark Sebba

WHAT IS MOTHER TONGUE?

What exactly is a 'mother tongue'? In some cases, this question is easy to answer. If my parents, carers and peers for the first five or six years of my life are all monolingual speakers of, say, English, then it is clear that English is my mother tongue. But what if my mother is a Panjabi-speaking monolingual, my father speaks Panjabi and writes Urdu but always speaks to me in English, and the language of most of my playmates is either English or Urdu? My 'mother's tongue' is Panjabi but under these circumstances, could my 'mother tongue' be English? Or Urdu? Or two of those, or all three? The question is important not only because we should have a clear idea what terms like this mean, but because, educational, social and economic decisions sometimes depend on it. For example, in 1951 a UNESCO panel of linguistic experts made the following influential statement:

> On educational grounds we recommend that the use of the mother tongue be extended to as late a stage in education as possible. In particular, pupils should begin their schooling through the medium of the mother tongue, because they understand it best and because to begin their school life in the mother tongue will make the break between home and school as small as possible (UNESCO 1951, p.691).

In some countries, including England, there are special educational provisions for children whose 'mother tongue' is not the main language of education. In others, like Singapore, children are required to learn through the medium of their 'mother tongue'.[1] In either case, a child's 'mother tongue' is determined for administrative purposes, and will have an impact on the nature of the child's schooling, and where education is entirely in a 'mainstream' language, having a different 'mother tongue' from the majority may release financial resources and entitle one to certain kinds of educational support. This was the issue behind the famous Ann Arbor case (Labov 1982) where the court had to decide whether the language of black primary school children was sufficiently different from English to be a barrier to their learning through the medium of English. If so, the school system would be required to take account of that fact.

Given the importance attached to the notion of 'mother tongue speaker', it has had less discussion in the linguistic literature than one might expect.[2] An early reference is Jespersen (1922, pp.146-47). He does not explain exactly what he means by 'mother tongue speaker' though he does indicate that it is not necessarily to do with the language of the mother:

> The expression 'mother tongue' should not be understood too literally; the language which the child acquires naturally is not, or not always, his mother's language [... but] of those with whom the child comes into closest contact from the age of 3 or so, thus frequently servants [sic] but even more effectually playfellows of his own age or rather slightly older than himself...

Jespersen's remarks show some awareness of the complexities which may arise in a multilingual or multidialectal setting. More recently, Le Page and Tabouret-Keller (1985, p.189) show a much clearer perception of the problems which arise in trying to define 'native language' or 'mother tongue' whether in a supposedly monolingual or a multilingual setting:

> For some people in the world it is true that one particular variety of linguistic behaviour has a peculiar force and intimacy from being powerfully associated with early childhood: for others it is not true. But whether true or untrue, such a variety is likely to be only one of several learned in childhood, since no society is totally homogeneous. Moreover, the concept of 'native language' or 'mother tongue' is like all concepts culturally conditioned... In multilingual settings the term 'native language' or 'mother tongue' may have little meaning because children are exposed to many linguistic systems from birth.

However, such a view, though informed by notions of multilingualism and cultural conditioning, is challenged by other writers who also take these factors into account. Skutnabb-Kangas (1981, ch.2) considers possible definitions of 'mother tongue' in terms of (parental) origin, competence, function and attitudes. By each of her possible definitions it is possible to have more than one mother tongue, and by each except 'origin' it is also possible for a speaker's mother tongue to change in the course of his/her life. For Skutnabb-Kangas, 'one cannot decide whether complete bilingualism is possible [...] both monolingualism and bilingualism demonstrate great variation, which we have to accept' (p.38). She cites anecdotal evidence to show that for many bilingual individuals 'their second language which they learnt later in life, feels colder, more alien, less rich in words, less subtle, and on the whole poorer. It does not affect them as strongly as the first' (pp.49-50). On the other hand: '[...] it has emerged from a number of investigations in different parts of the world that there are a good number of individuals who identify with both their languages (and cultures) and who prefer alternatives which confirm their double identities whenever such alternatives are given [...] according to both of the definitions by attitude, it is thus possible to have two 'mother tongues' (p.34).

According to Skutnabb-Kangas, bi- or multilingual speakers have at least one variety which has for them (to use Le Page and Tabouret-Keller's phrase) 'a peculiar force and intimacy'. For some of these, two, perhaps more, languages possess this quality by the speakers' own assessments: thus a 'mother tongue' need not be unique, but everyone has at least one.

In contrast to the foregoing more individual-centred views of determining 'mother tongue,' Pattanayak (1981, p.54) draws attention to a more cultural and societal aspect, when he says:

> ... mother tongue is both a sociolinguistic reality and a product of the mythic consciousness of a people. It provides social and emotional identity to an individual with a speech community... One may also be such a perfect co-ordinate bilingual or trilingual that one may be said to have two or three mother tongues. Any primacy among these can be established on the basis of parental preference, culture, language identity, personal emotional associations, attachments and involvements.

Within a societal rather than an individual context, what is perceived to be 'mother tongue' relates not just to primacy or fluency but to issues of ethnicity and status. Language pride and ethnic differentiation may be issues affecting not only what languages are used, but also what languages are claimed as 'mother tongue', with the possibility of prescriptive and puristic attitudes playing a role. Speakers from a particular group may prefer to claim as their 'mother tongue' a language which has greater prestige or which is associated with more prestigious functions than their 'actual' mother tongue. For example, Romaine (1995, p.21) reports, based on Saifullah-Khan (1980), that Pakistani speakers of Panjabi in Britain 'will claim Urdu, the national language of Pakistan, as their mother tongue, and not Panjabi, which is a spoken language used in the home.'

Particular groups may feel the need for a 'mother tongue' as part of their ethnic or group identity. Barros, Borges and Meira report the unusual case of the Bare of Brazil, whose original ethnic language has almost died out, superseded in everyday life by Portuguese. The Bare have adopted Lingua Geral (a contact language originally introduced to the region by European colonisers) 'as their 'traditional language' vis-a-vis the white society, with a clear objective of ethnic differentiation and affirmation. [...] the language has a fundamental role in marking a differentiation which simultaneously transforms them and keeps them Bare, or rather, a group distinct from the 'others'' (1994, p.67). Among the Bare, it seems, the need for an ethnic language which keeps them distinct has allowed their 'mythic consciousness' (Pattanayak's words) to reinterpret the origins of Lingua Geral and assign it a role which traditionally it never had.

While not all groups go to the extent of the Bare in order to have an ethnic language, it is clear that for many, maintenance of the 'mother tongue' is an important part of ethnic identity and distinctiveness, and its loss - or even the prospect of its loss - is perceived as threatening[3].

'LONDON JAMAICAN' AND THE MOTHER TONGUE QUESTION

With respect to issues of 'mother tongue,' Britain's Caribbean community occupies an unusual position. Linguists have been arguing for some decades that the vernacular and majority language of most of the so-called 'Anglophone' Caribbean is not English, but one of a range of Creole languages which are similar to English in their vocabulary. However, this view is not universally accepted or understood in Caribbean society, where the idea that Creole (also called 'Patois'[4] or Patwa) is just 'bad English' is still prevalent, though less so than it was. Nevertheless, there is a part of the Caribbean community, both in Britain and the Caribbean, which values Creole and would like to raise its status.[5] For those of this persuasion in Britain, claiming Creole as a mother tongue for the generations of Caribbeans born here is a necessary part of laying claim to resources for maintaining and developing the language.[6] The issue of what the 'mother tongue' of British-born Caribbeans actually is, is therefore a live one.

Migration to Britain from the Caribbean was not from one or two places only, but from all the formerly British territories of the region. In London - the British city with the largest Caribbean population, and the focus of my research - we can find second or third generation Caribbeans who can trace their connections to each of those places, and many individuals have associations through family with more than one Caribbean country. Although culturally and linguistically distinct in the Caribbean itself, the people of the different Caribbean countries have not maintained that separateness in Britain, and the traditional island identities have been supplanted to a large extent by the notion of 'Black British' (see Gilroy 1987).

As we might expect, most if not all the individuals in the second and third generation of London Caribbeans are fluent speakers of London English. This is no surprise, given its prevalence in the London environment (in school in particular), and given also the belief, widespread among the first generation of migrants, that they were English-speaking to start off with anyway. In fact, my research indicates that London English is the language variety which Caribbeans in London use most of the time, both at home and outside it (see Sebba 1993).

Most second generation[7] Caribbeans are also speakers of Creole. But which Creole exactly? If we take literally implications of the concept 'mother tongue', then we would expect the Caribbeans of London to speak a range of different 'mother tongues', varying from individual to individual depending on the variety of Creole spoken by their parents in their home country: Guyanese Creole where the parents are from Guyana, Trinidadian where the parents are from Trinidad, etc. However, though a child of, say, Trinidadian parents is likely to have a passive knowledge of the Creole of Trinidad, this is not the Creole they are most likely to use *actively*. Instead, the widely used Creole of London youth is specifically a variety of *Jamaican* Creole. The term 'London Jamaican' (Sebba 1993) for this variety was first brought into use by Rosen and Burgess (1980)), though its users are most likely to call it *Patwa* or *'Black Talk'*.[8]

London Jamaican is first and foremost a language of adolescence and youth, and its speakers tend to be young and Caribbean or African, though some are white. It is closely associated with the Black youth culture of London, and its music, in particular with the Reggae music of the 1970s and 1980s and its successors, and with Rastafarian culture. Pre-adolescents are usually excluded from this culture and anecdotal evidence suggests that they do not have much interest in speaking London Jamaican and have restricted competence in it. It is in adolescence that London Jamaican comes into its own, both as an in-group language and a non-legitimated language variety. This leads to a number of anomalies if we want to see London Jamaican as the mother tongue of its speakers:

1. London Jamaican is not identical to the Creole spoken by the parents of its speakers. This is true even when the parents are from Jamaica, as London Jamaican is distinctively 'London'. It is all the more true when the parents are from other places in the Caribbean, or are African, or White British. Speakers from non-Jamaican backgrounds are often highly fluent in London Jamaican.[9] Clearly for those Caribbeans without Jamaican ancestry, this Creole is not 'mother tongue' in any strict sense.
2. London Jamaican is not necessarily the first language variety learned, and is not always used in early childhood. It is most likely to be used in adolescence, when peer group influences are strongest.
3. London Jamaican is mainly transmitted through the peer group, not the parents; indeed, as Creole is stigmatised both in the Caribbean and in Britain, many parents go out of their way to avoid using it at home, and discourage their younger children from speaking it. In the case of white adolescents who use London Jamaican, it is clear that the language has been acquired from peers and not parents.

Thus while London Jamaican is the main candidate for 'mother tongue' for Caribbeans in London, it is in some ways a rather unlikely one. It has a currency among London youth which extends beyond the community which might identify it as its ethnic language; it is not necessarily acquired in early childhood; it is a peer, rather than a parental, language.

'CHATTIN' PATWA': CONSTRUCTING A LANGUAGE THROUGH TALK

In Sebba (1993), I argued that for many speakers, 'Patwa' is a 'second dialect,' a language learnt after London English, and constructed by means of verbal gestures in the direction of the intended target, Jamaican Creole. This means that for many adolescents, to 'talk Patwa' means simply to sound Jamaican. This can be achieved by using appropriate quantities of the tokens of Jamaicanness which have stereotypical value. These include features of grammar, phonology and discourse. Certain lexical items are of particular importance: taboo words (for males such as *blodclaht*[10] *bomboclaht, rassclaht,* and *rass*); forms of address like *man, guy, bwoy, star, spar* and *massa,* and tags such as *you know, you know what I mean, seen?* and *you (no) see (it)?* Just inserting one of these may be enough to mark an utterance as Patwa.

For speakers who have begun using Creole in adolescence, 'Chattin' Patwa' (as this activity is often called) consists of a making a larger or smaller number of adaptations of London English in the direction of Jamaican Creole. Inevitably, the resulting talk has features of both varieties, as speakers for whom it is not a first language cannot - *but also do not need to* - hit the target exactly. In the cooperative activity of conversation, a mastery of Jamaican Creole is not necessary. Provided that a speaker does the right things to produce 'Patwa' some of the time, other speakers will (and must) play the game by allowing these as instances of 'Patwa' and responding to them as if they were indeed that.[11]

But if 'Patwa' is constructed jointly in conversation by the participants together, what happens in narrative, where one party alone is mainly responsible for the talk? In my data, there are relatively few examples of extended narrative. Stories occur frequently, but they tend either to be very short, or to be in a question-and-answer format where the story is told in the course of conversation rather a monologue. The story below (Appendix 1) is unusual firstly in being a complete story recounted in a monologue, and also because it was elicited, both as a 'story' and as 'Jamaican', by the researcher who made the recording, R. B. Le Page.

V, a 16 year old boy of Jamaican background from South London, was recorded in a private house in 1984. With him at the time was a schoolfriend of the same age, also of Jamaican descent. The researcher asked V to tell a story 'in Jamaican', and he chose to relate an incident which his aunt had written about in a recent letter. While telling the story V and his friend were left alone in the room, although the researcher was not far away. V had previously been asked about his knowledge of Creole and had said that he had no problems understanding it, while speaking Jamaican simply involved 'talking faster' than when using London English; for example, saying *wha' appen?* /wa apm/ instead of *what happened*.

Two things are particularly striking about the story. Firstly, the first half of the story is as much in London English as in Creole, so that Creole is pretty well interspersed with London English throughout. The second half is much more consistently in Creole. Secondly, the whole story (but particularly the first half) is characterised by variation in syntax and pronunciation, so that both the London Jamaican and London English versions of various constructions and lexical items occur close together and sometimes even in the same sentence. The story illustrates nicely the choices between varieties which the speaker has to make at each point in his talk, and thus the nature of the variation which is characteristic of London Jamaican speakers.

The transcription in Appendix I is in a modified Standard English orthography with the parts which show distinctively Jamaican phonological or grammatical features in bold. Words which contain distinctively London phonological features (such as use of the glottal stop, written here as %) are in italics.

A line-by-line analysis shows the points of variation.

Some Problems Posed by London Jamaican

Lines 1-4: This section is V's preface to the story he is about to tell, and is done in London English. Although he intends to tell the story in Jamaican as he was asked to do, the prefatory remarks are presumably 'exempt' and need to be done in London English as they provide a commentary on the forthcoming Jamaican narrative. After *it goes* (1.4) there is a long pause (5.0 seconds) and then V begins with *de gal* ('the girl'), breaks into laughter and then stops. While *de gal* is clearly marked as Jamaican by its phonology and can thus be taken as the Jamaican 'lead-in' to the story, it is not clear how this phrase 'the girl(s)' is linked to the rest of the story, which has nothing to do with 'girls'. At any rate, this line is aborted and after a two second pause V continues with a further introductory remark in London English (1.7-8) about his mother's name (again this is not relevant to the story he tells in the end). At this point there is a long pause (5.0 seconds) and, apparently to avoid the embarrassment of an even longer one, V stops the tape. When the tape starts again, V begins (1.7) with the phrase *check dis, right*, which is not specifically London English or Jamaican Creole on the basis of its syntax, and which phonetically sounds closer to London English: nevertheless, the use of the 'slang' expression *check dis* suggests that V is marking the beginning of his 'Jamaican' story. After a three second pause V starts with the topic of his story, '*my mudder('s) sister*'. The possessive pronoun 'my' ([mɐɪ]) is more characteristic of London / Standard English speech than of Jamaican Creole, but even in Jamaica it is found in variation with the more 'Creole' form /mi/. Thus it does not mark the phrase strictly as belonging to one code or the other. The same is true of the noun it modifies, 'mother's', since the final [s] is appreciably lengthened, representing the possessive ending -s of mother's: but the [d] (for orthographic th of mother) belongs to the Jamaican and not the London English system, which has [ð] or [v] in this word. *Mudder's* is thus a hybrid of the Jamaican and Standard / London English systems. The uncompleted *sist* again is neutral. At this point V interrupts himself, starts again, aborts his utterance, clicks his tongue and then re-starts; '*yes, mi mwoda sister*'. This time the possessive pronoun has its Jamaican form; the /m/ of mwoda is strongly lip rounded: the vowel is Jamaican [ɔ] rather than London [ʌ]; and the possessive inflection is not present. The second version of '*my mother's sister*' is thus substantially more 'Jamaican' than the first. This is the first instance in the narrative of a pattern which V shows several times: repeating something just said in a more 'Jamaican' way, though the opposite may also happen, as we shall see.

The glottal stops (% in this transcription) in line 8 and the phonetics of the stretch put in the letter generally mark it as London English; *she 'ave a son* (lines 8-9) is more complicated since *she 'ave* is definitely not Standard or London English (for which it would have to be *she has* or *she had*), and is probably meant to be Jamaican, but the vowel of *'ave* is [æ], not the Jamaican [ɐ]. On the other hand, the vowel of *son* is [ɔ], the Jamaican vowel corresponding to [ʌ] in *son* and *sun*. As *son* is not a typically

115

Jamaican word, V paraphrases in line 9: a *pickney*, where *pickney* is strongly marked as a Jamaican form meaning 'child'.

Now (line 9) is clearly pronounced as London English, with the London low front to central glide [æə] as opposed to [αω] in the same word in Jamaican; however, the next sentence, *de fader live nex' door* (line 9) is Jamaican in its grammar (*live* lacks any inflexion) and phonetics. Apart from the phrases *de pickney* and *de godparents we call dem* the next 4 lines are virtually all characteristically London English, down to *well anyway* (1.21) which has perceptibly higher pitch and a Jamaican clear /l/ in [wel], contrasting with the British English dark /l/ which in London is vocalised in this context, becoming a vowel similar to [ʊ] (Wells 1982, p.313), as well as the typically Jamaican pronunciation [ɩə] for *ay* in *anyway*. The change to Jamaican is short-lived, however, for after a 1.2 second pause, V continues in London English (line 14): *'they 'ad a argument'* but then interrupts himself to give a more Jamaican version of the same statement: *a argument brok out*. While this may be more Jamaican in idiom, and the lexical item *brok* (for present as well as past tense) is identifiably Jamaican (the vowel is [ɒ] rather than [əω] as in *broke*) the rest of this restatement is London English: the vowel of *out*, for example, is London [æə] not Jamaican [oʊ].

After this sentence V pauses for 30 seconds and then stops the tape. After restarting the tape, V utters something unintelligible, says *'and'* then pauses another 3.0 seconds before taking up his last theme with *them brok out* (line 16). This is 'pure' Jamaican, with the subject form *them*, the Jamaican vowel in *brok*, and the Jamaican diphthong in *out*. The only hint of Standard / London English here is the pronunciation of *th* in *them* as [ð]: in 'classical' Jamaican, it would be [d], though [ð] is in variation with [d] in this context even in Jamaica.

From this point onwards the Jamaican becomes much more constant: it is no longer interspersed with London English stretches, and the lexical and syntactic content conforms more closely to Jamaican stereotypes (e.g. the past and present tenses are the same as the English present, pronouns belong to the Jamaican system, etc). There are few instances of London English nevertheless. In line 18, *'so, next minute my aunt'*, has a characteristically London English pronunciation, shown by the diphthong [ɐʊ] in *so*, the glottal stop in *minute* ['mɪnt?] and the possessive pronoun *my* (though the last is also possible in Jamaican, see above). Interestingly, the vowel of *month*, which in London English is [ʌ] and in Jamaican Creole [ɒ], is not consistently realised by either in V's Jamaican; compare [mɒnt] (line 24) with [mʌnt] 'month' (line 25) and [mʌs] 'must' (line 23). This has been observed in other London Jamaican speakers of this age group.

There are, however, several things which distinguish V's 'Jamaican' (as exemplified by lines 16-27) from 'classical' Jamaican Creole as described by B.L. Bailey (1966), for example: the use of *to* (/tu/) instead of *fi* as in *tell di obiah man to take to take it off her* (line 22); the use of inflections like the -s plural marker in *fedders* (line 23) and the suffix *-in* in *'start feelin'* (line 25), where Jamaican Creole would have *start feel*, the form actually found

Some Problems Posed by London Jamaican

in line 18; the use of *a* rather than *wan* as indefinite article; and the use of a feminine singular pronoun, *she*, where 'classical' Jamaican Creole has invariant *im* for all genders, as in *she ave a son* (line 9). All these could be due to influence from London English on V's 'Jamaican': but all are also found in Jamaica, where they are characteristic of more educated, urban styles of Creole which are closer to Standard English. This suggests that London Jamaican should not be thought of as a variety of 'deepest' Jamaican Creole, but as having more affinity (at least syntactically) with the varieties higher up the post-Creole continuum (De Camp 1971).

The detailed linguistic analysis of V's story above shows that it contains frequent hesitations, sudden code-switches, self-corrections and inconsistencies of usage, especially near the beginning. Yet it is clear that V has no trouble telling the story as such; it comes across clearly enough, as an instance of a 'recountable event'. The problem seems to be with the language which the researcher has prescribed for this narration: V was asked to tell the story 'in Jamaican,' with the result that V on several occasions tries to find a more 'Jamaican' way of saying something which he has already said. The impression is one of a person struggling to narrate a story in a language which he does not feel completely comfortable with.

This view is confirmed by two native speakers of Jamaican Creole who heard the tape of V's story. One said that V's Jamaican sounded 'put on'. The second, E, said that V's way of telling the story was completely unlike the way it would be done in Jamaica. E, who was brought up in Jamaica, immediately noticed the stylistic differences which make V's story seem very poorly told from the point of view of someone acculturated to Jamaica. E was able to re-tell V's story in his own words, as 'they would tell it in Jamaica'.

CONCLUSION

What is V's 'mother tongue?' His parents are Jamaican Creole speakers; it is clear that he understands Jamaican Creole; he says he can speak it - in fact, he says, it just involves 'talking faster'. Clearly, V has a good idea of what Jamaican Creole is like and in speaking it, he goes way beyond simply 'talking faster.' But it is also clear that V's story was not told as it would be told by a Jamaican Creole speaker from Jamaica. Part of the story was in London English; even the part which was not, had some features of London English in it; and native Jamaicans judged his Creole to lack 'genuineness' and his narrative style to be un-Jamaican.

What does this mean? One thing it certainly does not mean is that V is somehow incompetent as a speaker. The fact that he code-switches between London English and Creole, for example, does not mean that he lacks competence in either; code-switching is a common strategy found among fully fluent bilinguals in many language communities. What is apparent is that V is not good at telling a story *consistently* in Creole. It is the demand that the story should be 'in Jamaican' that poses a problem. Could V's 'mother tongue' be not Creole, but London English *mixed* with Creole?

Given the range of V's linguistic competence, there seems to be little point in arguing about what his 'mother tongue' is. The difficulty is with the term itself, which has built-in assumptions about the nature of linguistic communities and how language is acquired and transmitted. V's linguistic competence is different from that of his parents - something that in fact, is true of all of us, as all languages change from generation to generation. More significantly, only part of it seems to have been acquired from his parents: some of it can be attributed to his peer group.

By examining the case of one particular speaker, and one narrative produced by him, I have tried to show that the term 'mother tongue' is a particularly problematic one in the context of Caribbeans in Britain. I would suggest that the most appropriate thing to do is to abandon it, in favour of more accurate and research-based descriptions of the actual language competences and practices of speakers.

APPENDIX 1: V'S STORY TRANSCRIPTION CONVENTIONS

#	Pause of <1.0 second
##	Pause of <2.0 seconds
###	Pause > 2.0 seconds
*	Unintelligible syllable
%	glottal stop (feature of London pronunciation)
↑	raised pitch
italics	stretch containing London English grammatical/phonological/lexical feature
bold	stretch containing Jamaican Creole grammatical/phonological/lexical feature

1   de story goes as follows ### my muv # mum # my murver was reading me
2   de um ## the le%%er that'd come the uvver day # come dis week or:: ##
3   weekend or sumpn like that ## and er # she was jus' reading me parts of it
4   ### well um er first of all # it goes ### **de gal** hhhh ### * * **sister** ###
5   **sister Etta** da's me **mudder**'s name / ## **sister Etta** ###
6   ((TAPE PAUSED))
7   check dis right ### my **mudder**'s sist # ma ((CLICK)) yes **me mwadder**
8   **sister**, right (.) pu% in the le%%er (0.8) that (0.6) she 'ave a:: # she 'ave a
9   son right ## a **pickney** right # now # **de fader live nex'** door ## an dey
10 use to share de pickney come weekends right # but ## di # **de godparents**
11 **we call dem right** # used to um ((CLICK)) ↑~ *live next door* inni% # to
12 my aun% ## an come weekends and she used to # take the **pickney** right
13 so they used to 'ave it all weekend and tha% ### ↑~ *well anyway* ## they
14 'ad a argument the- # **argument brok** out an um ### the **pickney** got
15 shared (TAPE PAUSED)

16 and ### and **them brok out** # so ### the people next door **dem go to the**
17 **obiah man** ## tell him seh ### me auntie do sinting wicked to them to
18 do wid de pickney # so ## next minute # my aunt start feel sick she she
19 say she get skinny ## she lose she lose about five stone, a:h? # so ###
20 she just ## she hafi get up one day and go see obiah man 'im- herself
21 and it true seh she find out # dem ## put put s- curse 'pon her #
22 anyway # she she tell di obiah man to take # to take it off her and he
23 give her some fedders # some chicken fedders ## and she say he mus'
24 keep dis by her for a mont' # and she do dat # and she feel de eh #
25 after dat mont' she feel she start feelin' better ## and she put on back
26 her weight and sinting like dat ### but up till now she naah talk # to
27 di godfader again
28 (TAPE PAUSED)

FOOTNOTES

1. In Singapore, "mother tongue" is defined by law according to ethnic group membership, and on the basis of the father's ethnicity. Thus the child of a Cantonese-speaking father is deemed to be a speaker of Mandarin (Chinese ethnicity) and will learn Mandarin at school (See Gupta 1994). All children also learn English.
2. Though Romaine (1995) provides a recent detailed discussion. See also Singh (1998) for a selection of papers on the related concept, 'Native Speaker'.
3. As evidenced by, for example, audience reaction to the original Conference version of this paper. Some members of the audience, themselves Caribbeans, objected strongly to what they (incorrectly) thought to be the message of the paper, namely, that Caribbean children born in London "could not speak their own language".
4. This term, although apparently of French origin, is in general use for English-lexicon Creole.
5. It is not possible to deal here with the many issues which are raised by this. See Devonish (1986a, b) for discussion.
6. At one time, language issues concerning Caribbeans were hotly contested in British schools (see Edwards 1979). This is no longer the case, and in practice, there is no longer any possibility of releasing educational resources aimed specifically at helping mother-tongue Creole speakers in the education system. Other types of national and local government resources (e.g. library resources, adult education) are still theoretically available.
7. Research remains to be done on the third generation, who are themselves by now young adults.
8. The terms 'London Jamaican' (a linguist's / educationist's term), 'Patwa' (a term in everyday use among the Caribbean community) are used interchangeably in the remainder of this paper. 'Creole' (used by professionals and informed members of the public) is used in a more general sense, to mean an English-lexicon creole language.

9. Even some white adolescents are credible speakers, though they have no family connections with the Caribbean at all (Hewitt 1982, 1986). See also Footnote 11 (below)
10. Recent evidence suggests that this term has become an insult within the young White community as well, but is interpreted as being derived from Standard English *bloodclot* rather than Jamaican *bloodcloth*, i.e. sanitary towel.
11. Recently, a kind of constructed Patwa has become widely known as a result of the popularity of the controversial British comedian, Sacha Baron Cohen. In the persona of 'Ali G.', a streetwise youth/gang leader of ambiguous ethnicity, he conducts interviews with unsuspecting politicians and celebrities, trapping them into embarrassing self-revelations. There are various contested interpretations of 'Ali G.'; the predominant one is that the act is a satire on comfortably off British young people not of African or Caribbean ancestry, who try to associate themselves with street culture by affecting the language, styles and attitudes stereotypically identified with black gangs in Britain and America. Language is an important part of Ali G.'s persona, and his version of 'street talk' is propagated and mimicked in numerous e-mail bulletin boards and web sites which have been set up by himself and his fans.

    Though part of the joke is that 'Ali G.' is from the humdrum English town of Staines, divorced from any kind of 'ghetto culture', and can't understand real Creole when it is spoken to him, Ali G.'s language in fact shows many of the stereotypical 'Creole' tokens which are used to construct Patwa by Caribbean adolescents. These include: Creole pronoun forms and the verb form *is* with first person pronouns, e.g. *'me is using me Walkman right now'*, *'him has got a GCSE - a real one'*; /d/ in place of initial /ð/, e.g. *dis, da* for *this, the*; and frequent taboo lexical items such as *punani*, 'vagina'. We also find stigmatised forms from Southern British English such as 'double negatives' and /f/ and /v/ for RP /θ/ and /ð/, and the frequent tag *innit?* which even features in the title of the first Ali G. video, *Ali G. Innit*. Ali G.'s Patwa is thus constructed to some extent in the same way as the actual 'Patwa' used by some adolescents of genuinely Caribbean heritage, namely by grafting salient features which have stereotypical or symbolic value as Creole on to a base which is essentially local British English. (Examples from an interview with Ali G. by Danny Plunkett in LOADED magazine, Issue 61, May 1999, available at http://meltingpot.fortunecity.com/morocco/518/).

ACKNOWLEDGEMENTS

The research on which this paper is based was part of the project 'Sociolinguistics of London Jamaican English' funded by the Economic and Social Research Council, whose assistance is gratefully acknowledged. I am grateful to Prof R.B. Le Page for the use of his tape-recorded data, and to him, Mr. M. K. Verma and Dr. R. Hewitt for comments on an earlier version of this paper. Any shortcomings in it, are of course, entirely my own responsibility.

REFERENCES

Bailey B.L. (1966) *Jamaican Creole Syntax: A Transformational Approach*. Cambridge University Press, Cambridge.

Barros M.C.D., Borges L.C. AND Meira M. (1994) 'A Lingua geral como identidade construida', *Papia (Revista de Crioulos de Base Ibe'rica)*, 3(2), 62-69.

Bloomfield L. (1935) *Language*. George Allen and Unwin, London.

De Camp D. (1971) *Towards a Generative Analysis of a Post-Creole Speech Continuum*.

Devonish H. (1986a) *Language and Liberation: Creole Language Politics in the Caribbean*. Karia Press, London.

Devonish H. (1986b) 'The Decay of Neo-Colonial Official Language Policies. The Case of the English Lexicon Creoles of the Commonwealth Caribbean' in Gorlach M. and Holm J. (eds.) *Focus on the Caribbean*. John Benjamins, Amsterdam.

Edwards V.K. (1979) *The West Indian Language Issue in British Schools: Challenges and Responses*. Routledge and Kegan Paul, London

Hymes (ed.) (1968) 'Pidginization and Creolization of Languages', *Proceedings of a Conference held at the University of the West Indies*, Mona, Jamaica, April, pp.349-370. Cambridge University Press, Cambridge.

Gilroy P. (1987) *There Ain't No Black in the Union Jack*. Hutchinson, London.

Gupta, A.F. (1994) *The Step-Tongue: Children's English in Singapore*. Multilingual Matters, Clevedon, Avon.

Hewitt R. (1982) 'White Adolescent Creole Users and the Politics of Friendship', *Journal of Multilingual and Multicultural Development*, 3(3), pp.217-32.

Hewitt R. (1986) *White Talk, Black Talk*. Cambridge University Press, Cambridge.

Jespersen O. (1922) *Language, Its Nature, Development and Origin*. George Allen and Unwin, london.

Labov W. (1982): 'Objectivity and Commitment in Linguistic Science: The Case of the Black English Trial in Ann Arbor', *Language in Society*, 11, pp.165-202.

Le Page R.B. and Tabouret-Keller A. (1989) *Acts of Identity: Creole-Based Approaches to Language and Ethnicity*. Cambridge University Press, Cambridge.

Pattanayak D.P. (1981) *Multilingualism and Mother Tongue Education*. Oxford University Press, Delhi.

Romaine Suzanne (1995) *Bilingualism*. Second edition. Blackwell., Oxford

Rosen H. and Burgess T. (1980) *Languages and Dialects of London School Children*. Ward Lock Educational, London.

Saifullah-Khan V. (1980) 'The 'Mother Tongue' of Linguistic Minorities in England', *Journal of Multilingual and Multicultural Development*, 1, pp.71-89.

Sebba M. (1993) *London Jamaican: Language Systems in Interaction*. Longman, London.

Sebba M. and Wootton A.J. (1998): 'We, They and Identity: Sequential vs. Identity-Related Explanation in Code-switching' in P. Auer (ed.) *Code-Switching in Conversation*. Routledge, London, pp.262-289.

Singh Rajendra (ed.) (1998) *The Native Speaker: Multilingual Perspectives*. Sage, New Delhi.

Skutnabb-Kangas T. (1981) *Bilingualism or Not: The Education of Minorities*. Multilingual Matters, Clevedon (Avon).

Jamaica Speech: A Language or a Variety of Language (Dialect)?

Dimela Yekwai

The idea of Jamaican speech being a language or variety of a language (dialect) is a controversial one. What constitutes a language and on the other hand a language variety? Taking a dictionary definition (Barnhart 1979), language is 'human speech, written or spoken: without language men would be like animals; language is the basis of man's uniqueness and the essence of his culture...' On the other hand, a variety is defined as a 'form of speech peculiar to one locality or district of the geographical territory of a language; one group of closely related languages. Some of the dialects descended from the Latin language are French, Italian, Spanish and Portuguese'. This paper illustrates fundamental differences between Jamaican speech and standard English thereby discrediting the argument that it is a variety of the English language.

To understand the development of Jamaican speech we need to examine the socio-historical background of its speakers. Many of the Jamaican people were forcibly removed from an area in Ghana where Twi was spoken. In the new environment these 'subdued' Afrikans were forced by the plantocracy to use English. By this it was hoped that any conspiracy on the part of the Afrikan enslaved population would be detected by the slavemasters or Europeans. These Afrikans, however, in order to keep their traditional identity intact, continued to use the syntax or structure of their parent languages onto which they grafted English words. Taking this process further some English words were changed to fit into the Afrikan intonation and actual Afrikan words that have similarities with the English language were incorporated. What came out of this was a speech form sufficiently removed from the English language to prevent the easy understanding of the new language by the plantocracy as was originally intended (Barratt 1979).

To illustrate this difference, I will use the following sentence - *Me kaan tap now atalll* (I can't stop now). The use of the pronoun *me* rather than 'I' is significant. With 'I' the egoistic individual becomes the important concept whereas 'me' becomes objective - external to the speaker. It follows, therefore, that the speaker does not demand attention for him/herself in the case of the Jamaican speech but sees him/herself as part of the wider community. In fact the listener is considered no less important than the speaker, hence the Jamaican saying '*half empty gourdy make the most noice*'. Metaphorically speaking this is saying that a person who talks too much has no time to listen and therefore, does not learn anything new. Jamaican speech is more egalitarian as a result of its emphasis on community rather than individuals. This egalitarianism can also be seen in the use of the pronoun 'him' across sexual boundaries, whereas, in the case of standard English, there are marked differentiations. Hence 'she is walking down the road' would become *im a walk dung de road*. This is also a feature of the Afrikan language, for example Twi *i* = s/he.

Verb forms can also be seen as clearly different from standard English, as shown in the case of *im a walk*. 'A', in this case, is used to make the following verb a present participle rather than walking as would be the case in standard English. In the case of past tense, however, as in *Me see im yessedae a walk dung de road* and for the future as illustrated here, *Tommara me a go walk dung de hill fe see Miss Matty*, time words are used to show tense. These differences draw on the Afrikan syntax.

Grafting, in which Afrikan words with intonation similar to English are used, was a further strategy used to disguise the language. This is shown clearly in this sentence *Yu bancra look heaby, wha yu hab in de - dutty? (Your basket looks heavy what is in it - dirt?)*. The similarities in the italic words are very striking and people tend to believe that for example *bancra* is from an English language variety for 'basket', but this is a Twi word meaning the same thing. The same is also true for the Twi word *dutty*, also meaning 'dirt'.

The implication here is that Jamaican speech is definitely not a variety of standard English but a language in its own right, having its own syntax. If, however, we insist on it being a language variety, then it is a variety of Twi, the Ghanaian language.

Should this, however, be recognised and accepted, then even more volatile political and economical implications arise. The arguments so far, have tried to show that this language is very egalitarian. Language reflects culture; but the Jamaican culture as reflected in politics is not egalitarian; hence the degradation and rejection of the Jamaican speech by the ruling elite. The dominance of standard English is functional for this dominant group, as the 'yard-stick' by which excellence is measured, emanates from foreign influences, outside the Jamaican community, to which they do not have easy access. This situation socialises the Creole speakers, who comprise the majority of the Jamaican population, to develop a feeling of inadequacy.

Should this Creole, then, become accepted as a language, it would have tremendous repercussions for the capitalist elite and the structure of the Jamaican political and economic environment. I argue that the traditional Afrikan culture, language and values from which Jamaican speech is derived, are in direct opposition to this capitalist ethos, and emphasise community rather than individualism - as in the Afrikan saying, *I am because we are and we are because I am*.

The implication this has for teachers in multi-racial/cultural Britain, is that Jamaican speech is not given its full credibility. Regardless of good intentions on the teacher's part, it is often utilised in a very patronising way, namely in an entertainment capacity. Its full value in the wider sense of language usage is ignored and undervalued. The teacher is placed in a dilemma. If s/he ignores this language form, then s/he runs the risk of alienating his/her pupils by implying that their cultural experiences as reflected through language are not valid.

The resourceful teacher with a flair for language must use standard pedagogic literature procedures to help students develop the art of appreciating the natural beauty of this language form. In this sentence taken from a poem by Dr Louise Bennett: *An hab a boonoonoonus time* ('And have a good time'), *boonoonoonus* is an adjective denoting enjoyable, nice, pleasant time. Drawing on the culture from which this word derives implies to have a good time demands dancing and merriment in that fashion. Drumming would, therefore, be an essential part of this merriment and *boonoonoonus* carries in its sound the rhythm of drumming and dancing. This makes it onomatopoeic. The language of the poem uses proverbs which can be discussed in classes. Students looking at poems written by the dub poet Mutubaruka or Anum Iyapo would not be less knowledgeable about literature than a student studying Robert Louis Stevenson. The difference is that the student would become aware that these poets have drawn on different cultural experiences for the basis of their poetry.

Regardless of the status given to this speech form, it is rich and living and, therefore, deserves serious attention. To determine whether or not it constitutes a language or a language variety depends on the individual's conception of what is a language or a variety. This dichotomy arises because, even in Jamaica, the source of its development, it is not given any credibility and, therefore, has no accepted criteria for assessing its worth. Until such time as recognition is given by the Jamaican government, then it will continue to be an area of controversy. This situation means that for the teacher in the Jamaican classroom, it depends entirely on him/her, whether this speech form is utilised in a positive way: a situation that is clearly dependent on the teacher's attitude to the language and its speakers.

REFERENCES

Barnhart C.L. and Barnhart R.K. (1979) *The World Books Dictionary*. Thorndyke-Barnhart, New York

Barratt, L. (1976) *Sun and the Drum*. Heinemann/Sangsters, London

Bennett, L. (1981) *Yes My Dear*. Island Records, London

IYAPO A. (1985) *Song of the Motherland*. Ankh Arts, Kingston

The Status and Prospects for Romanes in Germany

Marion Papenbrok and Herbert Heuss

Romanes, the language of the German Sinti, has been for centuries a 'private' language, strictly limited to the inner-familiar use. As its speakers never claimed any political power, the authorities in general did not try to forbid Romanes, as has happened to the languages of other minorities all over the world.

When, from the 18th century on, Romanes aroused the curiosity of linguists (Rüdiger, Grellmann, Pott) and criminologists (Liebich, Bischoff), the former studied that language because of its Sanskrit heritage, the latter as a means of a more effective control over the Sinti. They were not particularly interested in the emancipation of its speakers or the recognition of their culture. They did not yet, however, participate in their persecution and extermination.

A dramatic change took place in the 19th century. The persecution of the Sinti sharpened; as part of that, they were systematically excluded from education.

From 1939 some, and from 1941, all, Sinti children were denied the right to attend school. This is the reason for the absurd situation that nowadays, there is a smaller percentage of illiterates amongst the old than amongst younger generations. During the Nazi period, linguistic knowledge was used to prepare the Sinti genocide. The racial anthropologists Dr Robert Ritter and Eva Justin, both speaking Romanes, managed to win the confidence of many Sinti families and to establish the genealogies of practically the whole Sinti population in Germany - including families who were completely integrated, for example some peasants in Northern and Eastern Germany.

The direct consequence of this type of 'research' was the registration, deportation and murder of about 20,000 German Sinti. It is easily comprehensible how, up to now, the immense majority of the German Sinti are strictly opposed to non-Sinti learning their language or doing research without giving clear evidence about the purpose and the practical use of its results.

The horrible events of the Nazi period resulted in a profound shock among those who survived, and a lack of both cultural and economic continuity in the families. The death of a great number of old people, who used to keep and transmit old customs, laws and traditional crafts, weakened the family structure, the cultural security and the economic basis.

Concerning the attitude of the families towards their language, one can roughly distinguish four tendencies:

1. Families who after the war stopped speaking Romanes. These are mostly isolated middle-class families, who had few contacts with other Sinti, and those who after the traumatic experiences of the past decided to 'pass', to escape discrimination and acquire a higher social status by disguising their cultural identity;
2. Families who bring up their children with Romanes as a first language and who are very distrustful towards schooling and 'kindergarten', which they consider a threat to their culture;
3. Families who consciously continue to speak Romanes at home, wanting, at the same time, a good 'German' schooling for their children;
4. Families who speak a poor Romanes and a poor German, restricted in both languages, being excluded from both, the major society, and the traditional Sinti groups.

What all four groups refuse, is:

1. Special schools for Sinti children, which they consider 'ghettos'
2. A written codification of Romanes

In these aspects the Sinti agree with their organised Civil Rights Movement which, in the cultural and educational sector, has three main demands:

1. Adult literacy work
2. Improved schooling for Sinti children
3. A cultural centre, dealing with documentation, vocational training and community work, in order to preserve and develop the culture of the Sinti and to help to improve, in the long run, the social and economic situation of this minority in Germany.

These demands do not include, for the reasons mentioned above, the use of Romanes in education. Sinti continue to consider their language as a 'secret' one, although one has to say that it is not secret, as the language is known, due to the work of the linguists like Wolf, Reinhard, and Knobloch, if we only mention the most important names of present-day German scholars.

There are few publication in Romanes: one bible translation and several songs; their number, however, is growing.

When Häns'che Weiss and his group recorded, some years ago, the first song in Romanes 'Lass maro tschatschepen' (Let's demand our rights), this was considered sensational and caused a great deal of ambiguous reactions. Since then, every Sinti orchestra has included some songs in Romanes in their programme. Thus, a certain public awareness of the language has been developed, as a vehicle of demonstrating the viability of a culture and of using an old language to demand the rights of a minority in the society of today.

REFERENCES

Grellmann H.M.G. (1783) *Die Zigeuner*. Dessau, Leipzig

Knobloch J. (1953) *Romani-texte aus dem Burgenland*. (Burgenländische Forschungen No. 24), Burgenländisches Landesarchiv, Eisenstadt

Liebich R. (1863) *Die Zigeuner in ihrem Wesen und in Ihrer Sprache*. F.A Brockhaus, Leipzig

Pott A.F. (1844-5) *Die Zigeuner in Europa und Asien*. Heynemann, Leipzig.

Reinhard M.D. (1976) 'Die Sprache der deutschen Zigeuner', *Mitteilungen zur Zigeunerkunde*, 1

Rüdiger J.C.C. (1782) *Neuster Zuwachs der deutschen, fremden und allgemeinen Sprachkunde in eigenen aufsätzen, Bücheranzeigen und Nachrichten*, Leipzig u. Halle, 1, pp.37-84

Wolf S.A. (1960) *Grosses Wörterbuch der Zigeunersprache*. Bibliographisches Institut, Mannheim

Shelta/Gammon in Dublin

Alice Binchy

Irish Travellers occupy a position in Irish society similar to that of Gypsies in other countries, and they share many aspects of the same lifestyle. The fact that Travellers had a secret language first came to academic attention the 1880s, with the work of Charles Leland. Leland's primary interest was Gypsies, but he discovered some Irish Travellers who spoke a language that bore little resemblance to Romanes, and that seemed to be based on Gaelic. All the contributors to subsequent work on the language agreed that Shelta/Gammon was exclusive to Irish Travellers, as opposed to Gypsies. (Shelta, incidentally is the name used by academics; Travellers call their language Gammon or Cant). The language seemed to be formed by the application of certain rules to Gaelic or English words: thus, Gaelic *doras* 'a door' becomes *rodas* in Shelta; English 'waistcoat' becomes Shelta *graskot*. Even at the time of its discovery, Shelta/Gammon had no grammatical structure of its own: it functioned as a lexicon inserted into a predominantly English syntax.

As academic interest in Shelta/Gammon grew, so too did speculation about its origin. Kuno Meyer, the German folklorist and scholar who worked in Ireland around the turn of the century found what he considered to be evidence of great age in Shelta/Gammon. Certain words were preserved in disguise which had been obsolete in Gaelic for centuries. Moreover, some Shelta/Gammon words seem to have been produced from Old Irish forms. For example, *tobar* 'road' appears to have been formed before modern Gaelic developed the phonological rule of lenition. By this rule, the Gaelic word *bothar* is pronounced 'bo'her' instead of as it is written. *Tobar*, formed from *bothar*, shows no sign of lenition, which led Meyer to conclude that the word, at least, had been formed before the eleventh century.

Although more recent work has been done by Harper, Acton, Kenrick and Hancock, the definitive work on Shelta is still Macalister (1937). Macalister's theory of the origin of the language rested on the proposition that the ancestors of today's Travellers were the 'untouchables' of ancient Ireland, who roamed the country with assorted rogues and vagabonds. Macalister supposed that, like underworld groups everywhere, these ancient Travellers had an exclusive jargon or cant of their own. When Christianity came to Ireland, druids and supporters of the old religions became outcasts and, Macalister surmised, since they had a tradition of language disguise for magical/sacred purposes, they superimposed their cryptic devices onto the underworld cant. At various times during history, other groups were forced onto the roads and, according to Macalister, joined the band of Travellers and perpetuated the use of Shelta/

Gammon. Macalister's conclusion was that the language was predominantly modern, that is, between two and three hundred years old, though containing some unspecified ancient material. MacAlister's work can be criticised on many fronts. His explanations of word derivations are sometimes stretched to extreme lengths, e.g. the English detective fiction term 'to shadow' is proposed as a possible source of the Shelta/Gammon word for policeman, *shaydogue*. The rules he constructs for word formation in Shelta/Gammon are arbitrary and over-elaborate. For example, he claims that Shelta/Gammon *skurlum* is formed from Gaelic *loisg* by a process of metathesis + insertion of r + addition of a suffix. He dismisses Meyer's theory of the origins of the language on the basis that lenition in Old Irish was 'far older' than the oldest manuscript in which it was indicated. Thus, if Shelta/Gammon words had been formed in pre-lenition times, Shelta/Gammon 'would not be a mere relic of the eighth or tenth century AD: it would be prehistoric'. However, Macalister's own explanation of the formation of the language is far from convincing, He argues that words like *tobar* must have been formed by literate people who invented the language by 'work[ing] out from written forms of Irish' (1937:166). This curious explanation would effectively rule out Travellers as originators of the language.

MacAlister's work was reviewed in 1979, in an unpublished manuscript by Sineád ní Shúinear. She hypothesises that, when the Celtic invaders arrived in Ireland, those of the natives who did not cooperate with them were made outcasts. Later, when displaced druids were forced onto the roads, these two groups came together Shelta/Gammon was jointly formed by them. If her theory is correct, the native outcasts would have preserved their non-Celtic language, and the druids would have grafted onto the language their techniques for disguise. The difference between MacAlister and ní Shuinear, therefore, is that, while MacAlister took the position that Shelta/Gammon is essentially an artificially constructed language, ní Shúinear considers it to be the remains of a 'natural' language.

My own position is closer to ní Shúinear than Macalister's. I believe that the core of Shelta/Gammon is neither Gaelic nor English, but a third language. All the social evidence suggests that Travellers are the descendants of an indigenous people; moreover, Travellers' own legends exclude a foreign historical source and aspire to an Irish tradition which extends back at least as far as the time of St Patrick, over 1500 years ago. Many of the commonest words in Shelta/Gammon are accepted by Macalister and others to have no satisfactory etymological origin in Gaelic or English, e.g. *beor* 'a woman', *cena* 'a house', *inoch* 'a thing', *galyune*, an exclamation which many Travellers translate as God. (Michael McDonagh of Navan, Co Meath, a Traveller with a deep interest in the language, points out the similarity between *galyune* and the name of the pre-Christian god *Dhalon*, who is credited with the invention of the cryptic language Ogham). It seems reasonable to posit that the pre-Celtic language, insulated from change to some extent by the fact that its speakers were outcasts, was supplemented at various times by words from the majority language, disguised by traditional cryptic devices. There is some evidence that Shelta/Gammon was a first language at some stage, spoken all the time rather than only in cases of cautious contact with non-Travellers, and Travellers have told me that they remember their grand-parents speaking it habitually. Anthony Cash (1977), himself of Traveller descent, quotes some Shelta/Gammon words which he considers belong only to intimate contexts. He is doubtful of the proposition that Shelta/Gammon was invented and used only for the purpose of secrecy in the presence of outsiders. To the words he isolated can be added the common Shelta/Gammon phrases, given to me in varying forms by several Travellers, which translate as 'get some sticks for the fire' and 'get up out of bed', which seem more likely to be used in private familial contexts than in situations of confrontation. The fact that Shelta/Gammon is acquired in infancy by Traveller children, jointly with English, may perhaps indicate a wider range of contexts than merely cryptic communication.

Perhaps the perception of Shelta/Gammon has been put out of focus by its designation as a 'secret' language. Rather than concentrating on the disguise function of the language, researchers might more usefully have examined the secrecy of the language in the primary sense of sacred, special, apart, with secrecy of communication in front of outsiders very much secondary. I would argue that the dwindling vocabulary of a 'natural' language was expanded by disguising (i.e. making secret) words from its speakers' other lingua franca vocabulary, not primarily to exclude outsiders, but to preserve the ancient heirloom, the secret language. Gypsies have a secret language too, and nobody now suggests that it was constructed to confound non-Gypsies, because the history of their language is known. Writings by Kenrick (1971) and Acton (1974) among others have shown that the secrecy of Romanes has a deep symbolic meaning for English Gypsies. Because Shelta/Gammon is primarily used for secrecy today does not mean it always was. In fact, I would argue that the secrecy function is comparatively recent. Documentary sources, as well as folklore, indicate that, in the past, relations between Travellers and settled people were based on respect for mutual differences. In these circumstances, the need for construction of a complicated code, with a wide-ranging vocabulary seems unlikely.

Shelta/Gammon today consists of lexical items used almost exclusively in an English syntactic structure, e.g. *the gallya is lush-ing alamach*, 'the child is drinking milk'. Since the language is unwritten, there is a great deal of variation in renderings of the same word. Macalister gives the word for shawl (an essential item of clothing for older Traveller women) as *mirsrun*: today some Travellers say *meersoon* and others say *meersoom*. There is evidence of a certain amount of interference from English, e.g. the word *talop* 'belly' is more often given as *trollop*, and *shuri* 'to run has become *scurry*. The word for an eye, *lurc* had been extended in Macalister's time to mean a watch. But most Travellers now say *geig the lurc*, for 'ask (someone) the time': the original word for time, *turc*, has been eclipsed. Folk-etymology also plays a part. Macalister gives the word for sleep as *kuldrum*; I was given the word as *kudlum* by a young

Traveller who explained it in this way: 'if you have a child, and you're trying to get him to sleep, you cuddle 'im'.

There is no evidence of the elaborate word coining by compounds which has been commented on by many writers on Gypsies. When words are needed in Gammon, they are generally formed in the traditional ways, for example by the prefix gr- or sl-. Thomas Acton has mentioned that Irish Travellers he knows in London say *groilet* for 'toilet'; I was given *slag* for cigarette which comes via the slang 'fag'. A teenage boy gave me the word *graydogue* for policeman, or guard as this is called in Ireland. This seems to be a further disguising of the Shelta/Gammon word *shaydogue* for policeman, perhaps reflecting the fact that its abbreviation *shade* is known to the police. An older Traveller who had never heard this reworking of the old word, suggested that it sounded like the Shelta/Gammon for goat, *grayvogue* in which case it would seem to be analogous to the term 'pig' for the police in some circles. Quite young children are aware of the basic rules for disguising language in Gammon; one seven-year-old girl, when asked the word for apple, at first said she didn't know, then laughed and said *grapple*. In Macalister's time the word for apple was *grula*, formed by a similar process from Gaelic 'ul'. Ad hoc words like this are very common, but it must be said that, as a code, this is easily broken, which in my view casts additional doubt on Shelta/Gammon's classification as a secret code.

The secrecy of Shelta/Gammon is, however, very jealously guarded. Children who were asked if they knew any words looked blankly for a moment, and only started giving words in response to my offering some. In recordings done in a Dublin school for Travellers, the contrast between the early part of the tapes and the later is very marked. In the first part, when I asked the children to tell stories or sing songs (in English: this was designed to get them used to the tape recorder) the atmosphere was decorous. The children tried not to interrupt each other, and accepted the principle of taking turns to perform. In the second part, from the moment Gammon was mentioned, the atmosphere was completely different. After the first couple of words, which emerged haltingly, the room erupted. All the children started shouting words, and a lot of expressions that were not Gammon, but belong to the same range of contexts (for instance, 'I'm going to rob Alice's purse') could be heard. It appears the children considered that they had been encouraged by an adult to do something naughty, i.e. to give Gammon words to a stranger.

Adult Travellers too are very wary of interest in the language. The first issue of the Travellers' newspaper, The Pavey, contained a warning that some policemen in Dublin were trying to pick it up, for the purpose of trapping Travellers who used it at the police station. Whenever I said that I was doing a study of Shelta/Gammon, I met a stone wall response. On the other hand, if I said that I was doing a study of Travellers, and enquired about the language in the wider context of Travellers' lifestyle and culture, my interest was accepted and seemed not to be threatening.

The future of Shelta/Gammon is an interesting question. In the past,

Travellers' social situation as an excluded minority may have played a part in the survival of their language: when they lived on the edges of Irish society making their livelihood from the settled majority but intent on revealing nothing of their internal community life to them, an ability to communicate exclusively with their own group in the presence of outsiders may have had an inherent value. While Travellers are still marginalised in Irish Society, there is no doubt that they have moved from the edges somewhat. Travellers over the past twenty years have been increasingly colonised by State agencies. They have been drawn into the net of social welfare, public health and education, and public-provided accommodation. In consequence, many Travellers are now living their lives in close proximity to settled neighbours. Their material circumstances have changed but their identity as Travellers has not. On the contrary, the last twenty years have seen a marked growth in the notion of Traveller pride and this, together with increasing political awareness, especially among young people, has focused attention on the language. It is notable that, in the younger age group, it is those with most education who are most adamant that they will pass on Shelta/Gammon to their children. While the State encroaches more and more on visible manifestations of the Traveller way of life, traveller identity as a distinct group continues to flourish and, as long as travellers want to remain distinct, they will have a need for Shelta/Gammon.

REFERENCES

Acton T. (1974) *Gypsy Politics and Social Change*. Routledge Kegan Paul, London

Binchy A. (1994) 'Travellers' Language: A Sociolinguistic Perspective' in McCann, O Siochain and Ruane (eds.) *Irish Travellers: Culture and Ethnicity*. Institute of Irish Studies, Belfast

Cash A. (1977) 'The Language of the Maguires', *Journal of the Gypsy Lore Society*, 4th Series, I(3), pp.177-80

Kenrick D. (1971) 'Anglo-Romani Today' in Acton T. (ed.) *Proceedings of the Research and Policy Conference of the National Gypsy Education Council* . St Peter's College, Oxford, NGEC, Oxford

MacAlister R.S. (1937) *The Secret Languages of Ireland*. CUP, Cambridge

Meyer K. (1891) 'On the Irish Origin and the Age of Shelta', *Journal of the Gypsy Law Society*, 1st Series, II(6), pp.257-66

Ní Shúinear S. (1979) 'Commentary on MacAlister'. Privately Circulated Essay, Dublin

SECTION FOUR

Education and Language: Strategies

Introduction

Central to debates on the role of languages without a written tradition is the use of education as a legitimising or non-legitimising factor, especially vis-a-vis traditional standards. In the cases of Sylheti/Bengali, Cypriot/Demotic Greek, Kachchi/Gujrati and Creole/English, this legitimising factor is of crucial importance as traditional educational legitimacy has favoured the languages with a written tradition such as Bengali, Demotic Greek, Gujerati and English.

This role of education tends to be put into question, however, when the education is being run by the speakers of the non-written languages themselves, in their own community groups in Britain, as for example the Caribbean Communications Project.

Compromise solutions seem all to centre around the use of the mother-tongue, as non-written language, at the initial, primary and early secondary school stages, followed by the use of the written standard language in the acquisition of literacy from the late primary and early secondary school stages. The Mother Tongue Project seems to envisage outcomes like this for the Sylheti/Bengali and Cypriot/Demotic Greek divides. For the Kachchi/Gujrati divide in Britain, Alladina seeks a dual solution on the one hand through the struggle against monolingual racial bias in Britain, which favours first English and then other written languages, and on the other hand through the promotion of a genuine mutual respect for other people's languages in a multilingual society, seeking to use each other's differences for mutual development. In such an ideal situation, Kachchi culture would be valued as an invaluable source for Gujrati written literature, while Gujrati would be valued because it provided a written expression to Kachchi culture.

For the Creole/English divide the solutions proposed by our contributors are eclectic. On the one hand, there is the over-riding wish by Creole-speaking adults to master standard English. Within this context, the role of Creole is that of a contrasting language, whose differences with standard English should be pointed out to the Creole adult. On the other hand, Creole is the central core of Afro-Caribbean culture within which much of the predominantly oral literature of the Caribbean exists. Creole adults often want to explore these aspects of their culture and appreciate an analysis of both written and oral Creole as a means of bringing their cultural experience under conscious scrutiny.

Mace indicates similar concerns about the acquisition of standard English by working class adults whose oral language does not reflect the standard English norms.

The question of language is avoided in the analysis of the Beash Rom in Hungary by Varnagy and Pongracz. Instead, an art-based approach is made to communication and the assimilation of disadvantaged pupils into the Hungarian education system. Acton explains the historical background which differentiates the Beash linguistic situation from that of other Romani groups. As a non-written form of expression, however, painting also conforms to the compromise solution of oral/non-written forms of educational communication being used for pupils during earlier stages of schooling, followed by use of the written forms of a standard language in the later stages of schooling and for adults from these cultures and language groups without a written tradition.

As the debate has continued through the 1990s and into the 21st century, we have had to recognise that the class interests of the promoters of literacy in Creole, the 'super-literates', (who can read and write two or more languages), may vary from the interests of the lower class to whom they suggest Creole literacy would be an asset. The super-literates may fail to take account of the functions which underlie the development of literacy.

The written use of language has superseded the oral use of language in prestige partly because the written mode is a superior mode, (at least with respect to quantities of information stored) for the purposes of record-keeping and political/military power. The written mode has often been used by some literate groups to confuse non-literates and as part of the apparatus for oppressing them. The cleavage between the powerful and the powerless, between the 'developed' and the 'underdeveloped' worlds, may also coincide with the cleavage between the literate and the non-literate. In their bid to close the literacy gap, the peoples of the underdeveloped world have embarked on literacy schemes with extreme zeal. In many respects, both 'underdeveloped' and 'developed' peoples have been quite happy with this educational aim. In a number of cases, however, educational activities suggest a questioning of cruder, more assimilationist, types of the drive towards standardised forms of literacy as the examples in this book show

REFERENCES

Dalphinis, M. (forthcoming) *Caribbean and African Languages: Social History, Language, Literature and Education*. Second Edition. Whiting & Birch Ltd, London

Languages Without a Written Tradition and the Mother Tongue Movement: The Bengali/Sylheti and Cypriot/Greek Debate

Hasina Nowaz and Maria Roussou

BACKGROUND TO THE MOTHER TONGUE PROJECT

In May 1981 when the Mother Tongue Project was set up, ethnic minority communities were struggling against tremendous odds to organise Mother Tongue classes all over Britain. They were concerned about their children losing their culture, language and identity, and about the widening communication gap between the older and younger generations.

There was also a growing dissatisfaction in the communities about the children's poor achievement in their school education. This deepened their consciousness of the heavy loss they were suffering for little positive gain, and made them question the whole attitude and policy of schools.

One part of the Mother Tongue Project (MTP) brief was to examine current theory and practice of curriculum development and produce exemplar teaching materials in the two sample languages, Bengali and Greek, which had been selected on the basis of their statistical importance in London (Tansley 1986).

In July 1981 the Team selected members from the two language communities and set up two teacher groups to help them in planning and producing the materials. The first task of the team and the two teacher-groups was to define their objectives. Various factors were considered in the selection of the objectives such as:

1. The content of the materials: ideas, facts and themes for learning.
2. The teaching methods to be used.
3. The needs, interests and experiences of children growing up in Britain.
4. The competence in their Mother Tongue of children of the communities.
5. Societal expectations both within the particular communities and outside.
6. The school ethos.

The main objectives adopted for materials to be produced were that they:

1. Would be suitable for children growing up in a multicultural society and in a mainly urban British environment.
2. Would help to develop the language through oral as well as written forms at all levels of learning in the primary stage and in a variety of situations.
3. Would acknowledge the communities' hopes and aspirations and create links with the culture of the home and the family.
4. Could be used both by the community schools and the mainstream schools.

In studying the background of two language communities in Britain and their children, we found strange similarities in their socio-political situation. Both countries of origin had been under British rule, divided on the basis of religion, had large scale population movements both within the country and to Britain, and the majority of the people coming to Britain from the rural areas speaking an important variety of the national language, that is Sylheti and Greek Cypriot.

It was also found that, in both communities, the children were at various stages of fluency in their Mother Tongue, but the significant difference was that there were more first and second generation speakers among the Bengali speaking communities, while there was a preponderance of second and third generation learners in the Greek-speaking community. Most of the first generation children are fluent speakers of their home language while the second and third generation children generally have receptive competency in their Mother Tongue. However, the stages of fluency could not be strictly divided according to the three generations mentioned, but should instead be regarded as a continuum with the bulk of category of speakers being placed under each generation.

Fluency of Ethnic Minority Children

First Generation	*Second Generation*	*Third Generation*
Fluency speech which may be standard or a local dialect spoken fluently with some competence in reading or writing.	Losing Fluency - struggling to master literacy. English may be the first language.	May understand but not speak the community language. English is first language.

The most important causal factors seemed to be:

1. How long the children had been in mainstream schools;
2. How long their families had been in Britain - whether the children were first, second or third generation born;
3. Whether the families lived near, or within the language communities;
4. Whether the parents had links with their country of origin;

5. What social class the parents belonged to, and what their attitude to Mother Tongue was.

The working definition of Mother Tongue on which the MTP based its initial discussions was that Mother Tongue is the first acquired language, i.e. the vernacular of the home which in most cases of the populations we were concerned with, i.e. Greek and Bengali pupils aged 5-11, was a non-standard oral variety. We were aware of other definitions of mother tongue which emphasise the acquisition of literacy, i.e. Mother Tongue is the language of the country of origin with its written literature. There is some conflict between the first and second definition.

The Mother Tongue Project terms did not come out with a definite answer to the question: 'When is a language variety a language?' and had not anticipated all the implications of accepting the validity of the vernacular in terms of the response from the community, the perceptions of the children, the responses from Mother Tongue teachers and other mainstream teachers.

We aimed to prepare exemplar materials for developing both oracy and literacy. For developing oracy materials, we worked with the first definition of Mother Tongue as the first acquired language, i.e. the vernacular of the home. In pedagogic, educational terms, it means that a child-centred method and approach is guiding the teaching situation from issues of class organisation, issues concerning the content of the curriculum and of course issues of material developed for that purpose. That is how we interpreted the guidelines of the Bullock report (1975):

> No child should be expected to cast off the language and culture of the home as he crosses the school threshold, nor to live and act as though school and home represent two totally separate and different cultures which have to be kept firmly apart.

Philosophical and theoretical discussions concerning the development of oracy in the organised teaching situation (that is, at school as opposed to the learning that informally takes place at home, in the neighbourhood, in community social and cultural gatherings) suggest that the teacher should first assess what the child brings with her/him in the classroom and then organise the content of the curriculum on the bases of his/her abilities and needs. The ongoing debate about child-centredness in education linked with the acceptance and the validity given to the child's vernacular has encouraged a number of mainstream teachers to put into practice the social and educational arguments supporting and elevating children's talk into a form of interaction in the classroom; this has been mainly practised during a child's first years in formal schooling (infant schools). These teachers with their successful results have shown the value of children's vernacular and given a basis for further research and application. The acceptance on non-standard varieties of the English language in the mainstream classroom induced the Project to try out the same, or similar methods concerning non-standard varieties of Greek and Bengali.

SYLHETI AND BENGALI

We know that in the Bengali speaking community the majority of the children come from the rural areas of Sylhet in Bangladesh and speak the Sylheti variety. There is also a minority group from West Bengal who speak the standard Calcutta colloquial, which is very similar to the standard written form. The spoken and the written language of the two Bengali speaking communities from Bangladesh and West Bengal show some distinct differences where they reflect their different religion orientated culture, Muslim in one case, Hindu on the other. For differences between Bengali and Sylheti, however, we must look at the origin and development of Bengali language.

In the middle ages there were many Bengali varieties spoken in Eastern Indian. With the Muslim conquest in the twelfth the different tracts of Radha, Varendra, Vanga (with Srihatta or Sylhet) and West Kamrup were united under the common name Bangala or Bengal and a literary standard language was fixed which the Persian speaking Moslems called Zaban-Bangala. The people themselves called their language 'Vasha'. The speech of West, and North Central Bengal was regarded as the standard form of Bengali and called Gauda Vasha, and that of Vanga or East Bengal was regarded as a regional variety.

The literary language of Bengali developed from the dominant speech of the upper classes of Eastern Radha or West Bengal, and, during the British period, as Calcutta became the seat of learning, the colloquial speech of the educated class around Calcutta became standard Bengali. Vanga in the East came under many outside influences. The extreme Eastern forms of Vanga speech in Sylhet, Tippera, Chittagang have been influenced by the Tibeto-Burman speech, but they have retained some of common characteristics such as *ila iba* for past and future base, *ia* for conjunctive, *era, kera* for the genitive, *ke, re* for the dative etc. These pan-Bengali features make it possible for the Vanga varieties like Sylheti to be attached to the composite literary language. Bengali is now the national language of the Republic of Bangladesh and the state language of the state of West Bengal in India. It is also spoken in parts of the states of Bibar, Orissa and Assam.

Sylheti is regarded as a regional variety of Bengali in Bangladesh. It has not developed a separate script or written literature. Like all language varieties, Sylheti is rich in rhymes, folk songs and tales which have been incorporated in Bengali literature. Sylhet has always used literary Bengali for education, academic professions and for functioning nationally.

The Mother Tongue Project respects Sylheti as a variety of language through which the Sylheti child learns to understand and experience the world around him. The child's language needs to be acknowledged, recognised and supported. As the Bullock Report (1975) says:

> The aim is not to alienate the child from a form of language with which he has grown up and which serves him effectively in the speech

community of his neighbourhood. It is to enlarge his repertoire so that he can use language effectively in other speech situations and use standard forms when they are needed (p.143).

Parents and community members have all expressed their view that learning to read and write the standard must be the goal for all pupils. Accordingly, the Project has produced materials which aim to support the child's variety at the oral and early writing stage and use the standard form for introducing and extending literacy. Vocabulary from the speech of both the Bengali speaking communities has been used in the Primary Readers, the Workbooks and the Story Readers. During the trials of these materials in the various community and mainstream schools, teachers encouraged children to speak and write in their own varieties during the formative stages and led them gradually to the standard written forms. The children at one of the mainstream schools in Tower Hamlets had rewritten and dramatised the story of the Fox and the Mongoose in Sylheti. Most of the teachers had used a mixture of Sylheti and the standard form, or the standard form alone when telling a story but when retelling it the children almost always used Sylheti.

The trials for the Bengali materials in seven mainstream schools and 5 community schools had not shown that the use of regional varieties and the standard form had bewildered or confused the children. In fact, many teachers in both mainstream and community schools, said that the children had gained confidence and self-esteem through their achievement in Sylheti/Bengali.

CYPRIOT GREEK

The majority of the Greek speaking community in Britain consists of Greek Cypriots (180-200,000) who have migrated from Cyprus since the 1920s, firstly as young male soldiers, in the British army, or as labourers and students, and later, during and after the independence struggle 1955-1960, as whole families, searching for peace and work. The last influx of Greek Cypriots came as refugees after the invasion of Cyprus by Turkey in 1974. Most of these Greek Cypriots are of rural origin and are speakers of the Cypriot language variety as it was used in the 50s and 60s, in the various villages of the Nicosia, Famagusta, Limassol, Paphos and Kyrenia districts (Roussou and Ponteli 1990). They are mainly settled in North London and have well-organised networks of community organisations for social, educational and political purposes. Federations and central organising committees have brought the members of the Cypriot community in touch with each other.

What is the vernacular Cypriots in London use in their everyday interaction and how to they reproduce it in their children? Since most of the Greek Cypriots come from a rural background the few researchers who have involved themselves in issues of the Cypriot language variety have found phonological, lexical and syntactical differences when comparing it with Demotic Greek

(Standard Modern Greek). To these already existing differences (examined by Roussou in her other paper in this book) London Cypriots have added loan words from English with Greek endings, for example, the word 'market' became *marketta*, the 'a' sound being the ending of feminines in Greek, or the word 'bus' became *busso* - 'o' sound being the ending of the neuter. Besides these 'Greekified' words there are other loan words concerning everyday things, especially words that come from the new technology, e.g. *cooker, tractor, computer*, or words for the food, drink and customs of other cultures. The mainstream English includes, for example, words that have entered the Greek Cypriot vocabulary unchanged.

CONCLUSION

The Mother Tongue Project sought to support both Bengali and Greek children within the language contexts described.

A video compiled by the project shows how the Mother Tongue teachers of Bengali and Greek as well as their English mainstream colleagues accepted, both supported children's talk and guided them step by step towards acquiring the standard form of the language during the literacy stage.

In one particular extract when teacher and children are sitting on the carpet and talking about a visit to the Greek monastery of St Mary's on the Greek island of Chios, while being on an imaginary journey to Cyprus, one of the pupils starts describing in dialect what he saw on Chios. He is telling the group how he visited the monastery with his family and how he managed to drink holy water from a well. The boy, Yiannis, introduced English loan words alongside the use of the dialect. In some English words he actually adds a Greek plural feminine marker so the word 'cups' becomes κάππες. The teacher is aware that bilingual children may devise a rule based on the system of their other language when encountering new language items in one language, and she offers the equivalent standard form or rephrases his statements for the benefit of the other children as well as his, but without actually reproaching him for the use of dialect in its oral form. When it came to introducing literacy, both Bengali and Greek teachers of the Mother Tongue Project used the standard form of the languages in their most simple forms.

The project discussed with teachers involved in the trials various points concerning dialect and standard, that is:

1. Should the use of the dialect be encouraged or should the teacher insist on the standard form of the language both in oral and written form?
2. How can a teacher deal with parental pressure for the early introduction of the standard form of the language?
3. Parents may wish the school to give support to a language, or form of language which is not the natural mother tongue of the child, which may conflict with the teacher's educational objectives of building on the language that the child already knows. How should the teacher respond?

Having discussed all these points teachers opted for accepting the dialect form of the language taught in its oral form, and gradually introducing standard in formal teaching situations without any value judgements (cf. Roussou and Bell 1991). During the 'teacher training' period of the project we understood that the debate amongst the teachers involved sensitised them in a quite remarkable degree towards the principle of child-centred education, of acceptance of the form of language the child brings into the classroom.

REFERENCES

Department of Education and Science (1975) *A Language for Life*. The Bullock Report. HMSO, London

Tansley P. (1986) *Community Languages in Primary Education*. NFER, Nelson, London

Roussou M. and Ponteli S. (1990) *Greek Outside Greece II*. Diaspora Books, London

Roussou M. and Bell S (1991) *World Languages in Europe: Implications for Teacher Training*. Trentham Books, Stoke-on-Trent

The Status of Kachchi in Britain and India: Implications for Language Teaching

Safder Alladina

KACHCHI AND GUJRATI AS LANGUAGES

In the tradition of genetic description of languages, Gujrati is classified as Language of the Central Group (Inner Sub-Branch, Indo-Ayran Branch, Aryan Sub-family of the Indo-European Family). Kachchi is classified as a dialect of Sindhi (North-West Group, Indo-European Family). Sindhi is classified as a language of the North-West Group (Outer Sub Branch, Indo-Aryan Branch, Aryan Sub-family of the Indo-European Family). A diagrammatic representation of the relationship of these languages is given in Figure 1.

Figure 1
Genetic Relationship Between Kachchi, Gujrati and Sindhi

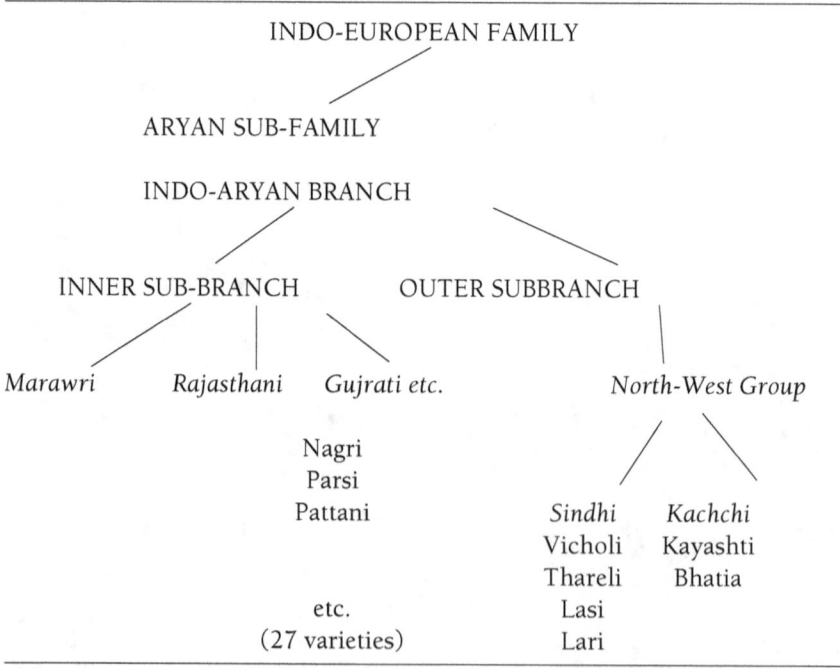

After Grierson (1926), Sarkar (1964) Census of India (1961a)

The Status of Kachchi in Britain and India

Thus linguistically Kachchi is not a dialect nor a variety of Gujrati. Genetically, it is closer to Sindhi. Languages can be defined genetically, culturally or politically but in the end it is the perceptions and loyalties of the speakers and users of a language that account for its life or death. The close relationship between Kachchi and Gujrati can be appreciated in light of the geo-political developments in the Gujarat peninsula. The more important commercial and maritime centres were located in the Gujrati speaking Saurashtra and parts of Kutch have always been the commercial and linguistic hinterland to it. After the creation of Pakistan, a large number of Muslim Kachchis moved to Kachchi. Kutch became part of the State of Gujarat in India where the official language of court, commerce and education is Gujrati. Thus the diglossic relationship between Kachchi and Gujrati got institutionalised. Developments in the use of Sindhi are pertinent to the status of Kachchi in South Asia today. In Pakistan, Sindhi is dominated by Urdu, the official language of the country. Political and linguistic assertion by the Sindhis is a recent phenomenon. As the use of Kachchi in Pakistan, although no data exist on this question, it can be assumed that Urdu, rather then Sindhi or Gujrati, is the language of literacy of Kachchi speakers in Pakistan. The pattern of language use among these Sindhis is that of language loss or attrition in favour of Hindi, English or the dominant language of the state they have settled in (Daswani and Parchani, 1978; Daswani, 1982). Thus, although Kachchi is a sister language to Sindhi, in Pakistan it is dominated by Urdu and India by Gujrati.

The Census of India gives separate figures for Kachchi and Gujrati speakers and the trend in the number of people who claim either of these languages as their mother tongue, between 1921 and 1971, shows some interesting features.

Table 1
Kachchi and Gujrati Speakers in India - 1921-1971

	1921	1931	1951	1961	1971
Gujrati (Millions)	8.8	10	15	19	20
% increase		1.7	50.0	26	0.5.
Kachchi ('000)	350	435	335	340	400
% increase/decrease		20	-23	1.5	17

From Census of India (1971) and Nigam (1972)

The changes in the number of people who respond to Gujrati or Kachchi as their languages do not follow trends in natural growth of population. The seemingly erratic trends may reveal some significant features to do with language loyalty, language shift and the pull of politics on language choice. Figures for 1951 were returned two years after the Independence of India and Pakistan. A rise of 50% for speakers of Gujrati and a fall of 23% for speakers of Kachchi may indicate the movement of language groups in and out of Gujarat.

However, an increase of 20% for Kachchi speakers in 1931 and 1.7% in 1971, compared to 14% and 5% for Gujrati speakers for those years, may be indicative of a rise, fall and resurgence of linguistic assertion on the part of Kachchi speakers in India.

KACHCHI AND GUJRATI IN BRITAIN

In the 1980s there was a paucity of information on linguistic resource of Britain. There was no comprehensive survey of languages in daily use in Britain. The Department of Education and Science estimated the number of pupils between the ages of 5 and 16 years whose first language is not English as somewhere between 375,000 and 500,000 - a difference of 33.3% between the highest and the lowest estimate. Information on languages in the repertoire of British school children does not exist. (Commission of the European Communities, 1984). The Linguistic Minorities Project, based at the University of London Institute of Education from 1979 to 1983 has produced valuable linguistic sketches of some of the major languages of Britain. Kachchi, however, gets subsumed under Gujrati in these reports (LMP, 1983). Similarly, the Inner London Education Authority, which has conducted language census in all its schools in 1979, 1981 and 1983, includes Kachchi speakers in the total number of Gujrati speakers (ILEA, 1983). The ILEA 1983 Language Census gives the figure of 2632 speakers of Gujrati out of a total of 50,353 school students who speak a language or languages other than or in addition to English.

From the point of view of developing teaching programmes and teaching strategies in Britain, information on Kachchi speakers and speakers of other languages with oral tradition is of great relevance. Quite often, this information is contained in the raw data in language censuses conducted in Britain and if such information can be extracted from that data, it would be of great value. Also, an in-depth analysis of the linguistic repertoire of school children in Britain would prove fruitful. The currently popular description of 'bilingual learners' in Britain disregards the multilingual nature of her school children and the 'bilingual initiatives' exclude speakers of languages that are not one of the twelve major languages of Britain. Table 2 sets out the possible range of languages that may exist in the linguistic repertoire of Kachchi and Gujrati speakers in Britain.

Table 2
Likely Responses from People of Gujrati Origin in Britain

1	2	3	4	5[1]	6[1]	7[2]
G-Hindu	G-Muslim	K-Hindu	K-Muslim	Other Hindu	Other Muslim	G-Regional
Gujrati	Gujrati	Gujrati	Gujrati	Gujrati	Gujrati	Gujrati
	Urdu	Kachchi	Kachchi	Kachchi	Kachchi	Memoni
			Urdu	Sindhi	Sindhi	Kookni
				Hindi	Urdu	Bhadala
				Marwari		Kharwa
				Marathi		Tribal
				Other	Other	Other
Shift	Shift	Shift	Shift	Shift	Shift	Shift

1. Other - Hindu or Muslim - people originating from Sindhi, Rajasthan, Maharashtra, Persia or elsewhere who have adopted a Gujrati political identity. For the sake of simplicity, Parsis may be included in one of these two groups and their declared language would tend to be Gujrati (Parsi variety).
2. G-Regional - those from other regions of Gujarat where the linguistic and cultural identity is marked enough for respondents to assert a separate description.
3. Identity Shift - Those who were brought up outside Gujarat and have abandoned their Gujrati or Kachchi identity. Declared language may be Swahili, English or any other language or culture they have identified themselves with (French, Flemish, Portuguese etc).

All these categories may have individuals who are bi- or multilingual

THE RELATIONSHIP OR DIGLOSSIA BETWEEN KACHCHI AND GUJRATI

In the late nineteenth century, the Gujrati vernacular Society published *Kachchi Kosha* - a Kachchi lexicon. Around the same time Khan Sahib nan Jianni published a book of poems called *Kachchi Kavita*. These developments are recorded by Khakhar (1876) whose Volume V on Collection of Gujrati Poetry includes Kachchi Kavya and Kachchi Dohana of the oral tradition. It should be noted, however, that the reservoir of Kachchi oral and literary tradition had already become included in Gujrati writings by this time. Gujrati has been used by Kachchi speakers as the language or education, wider commerce, business, letter-writing and formal occasions. The relationship is comparable to that between Sylheti and Standard Bengali, Sicilian and Standard Italian, a variety of Arabic and standard Arabic, Demotiki and Katharevousa in Greece. African-French Creole and standard French, and African-English Creole and standard English.

This relationship of diglossia brings about a situation where the speakers of the 'non-standard' language are under constant pressure to discard their language in favour of the standard variety. These societal pressures are compounded by the education system in the modern world where literacy can only be achieved through the school system. Pressures also operate at an individual level. For example, my mother who is Kachchi speaking, married into a Gujrati speaking family. Although my parents used Kachchi between themselves, the children grew up speaking Gujrati. Thus, my mother tongue is really my father's tongue! At another level, the situation is quite different for children whose home language is Kachchi. These children are expected to go through early stages of school life in a language that is not the language of the home. In the British situation, Kachchi children are expected to make a phenomenal conceptual leap in being literate for the first time in a language that is three times removed from their immediate and personal experience. This is in spite of ample evidence which exists now in support of the importance of the language of early cognition in the acquisition of the language of education (for a summary of research findings see Alladina 1984).

If there was a genuine fusion of languages, as for example between Gujrati and Kachchi, the problem of transition to literacy from an unwritten language to a written language would be less of a hurdle. But Mohan (1984) considers this language fusion a myth. As she so graphically puts it:

> ...predator languages stalk and swallow up the smaller languages in a fusion of population, but not of language form. Languages don't fuse 'democratically'; they give their lives so that the strongest of the group might survive...

PEDAGOGIC IMPLICATIONS

The relationship of diglossia in the cases of most languages has meant that the contribution of a language with oral tradition has been ignored by the mainstream education system which uses the standard form of a language thus consolidating its dominance, giving it prestige and according status to it. In the British context the situation is even more perverse because not only the languages with oral traditions but even the standard forms of languages other than English and particularly non-European languages, are undervalued and marginalised by the school system.

The educational approach to languages in Britain is basically from a monolingual viewpoint. The diversity of languages in Britain is seen as an obstacle. The fact that in the inner London schools alone there are more than 147 languages is often presented as reasons for not doing anything. The solution is sought in initiating 'bilingual programmes' in some of the major languages used in Britain. If education in Britain was truly child centred it should be obvious that the home language of a learner has to be used to build bridges towards the acquisition of the standard form of that language or a related language, and that standard has to be used to teach the language of wider communication or the language of education.

In the specific example of Kachchi and Gujrati, if standard Gujrati is taught to Kachchi speakers, then recognition and validity has to be given to Kachchi language, culture and traditions and the contribution they have made to the wider Gujrati culture. Kachchi poems, stories and songs, and the contribution of the Kachchis to modern Gujarat have to become part of the teaching of Gujrati.

Giving recognition and validity to the ethnolinguistic diversity is unlikely to happen in a world where the relationship between languages is in the shape of a pyramid with English at the apex followed by the prestigious and economically powerful languages often referred to as the 'modern languages' under which come the 'lesser languages', 'minority languages', 'ethnic minority languages', 'new minority languages', 'community languages', 'other languages' and so on. And at the bottom of the heap, come the dialects and languages with oral traditions.

Figure 2

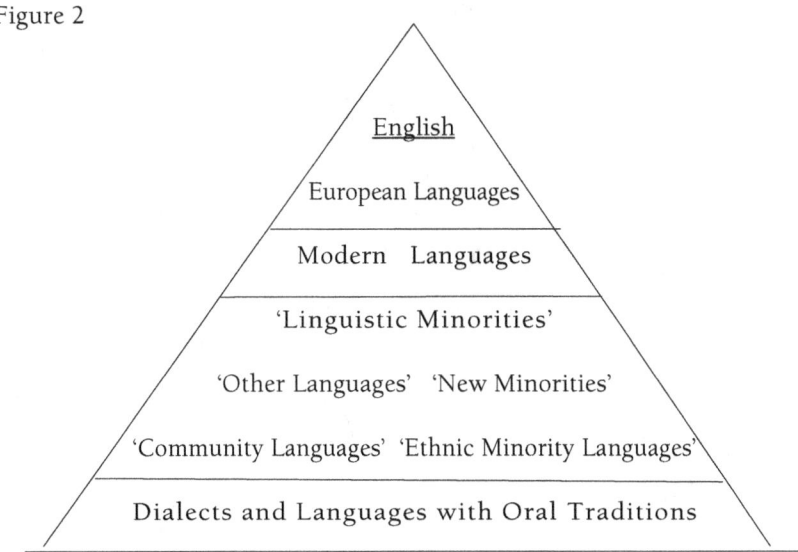

If multilingualism is the norm in the world, the education systems should reflect this by encouraging multilingualism and making school children multilingual and multiliterate. A solution to the tyranny of dominant languages can be found in Mahatma Gandhi's view of world languages which approaches language maintenance organically and not in the either/or and bipolar way. I give you the Oceanic Circle.

> In this structure, composed of innumerable speech communities, 'life will not be a pyramid with the apex sustained by the bottom. But it

will be an oceanic circle whose centre will be the individual', always ready to defend and enrich his mother tongue, each speech community ready to defend and enrich the standard, the superposed or the culture language, each such group ready to defend, enrich and sacrifice for the regional dominant language, and the latter ready to enrich, defend and sacrifice for the link language, national language or language and languages of national and international integration, 'till at last the whole becomes one life composed of individuals, never aggressive in arrogance, but ever humble, sharing the majesty of the ocean circle of which they are an integral unit' (Pattanayak, 1978).

Figure 3

The Oceanic Circle

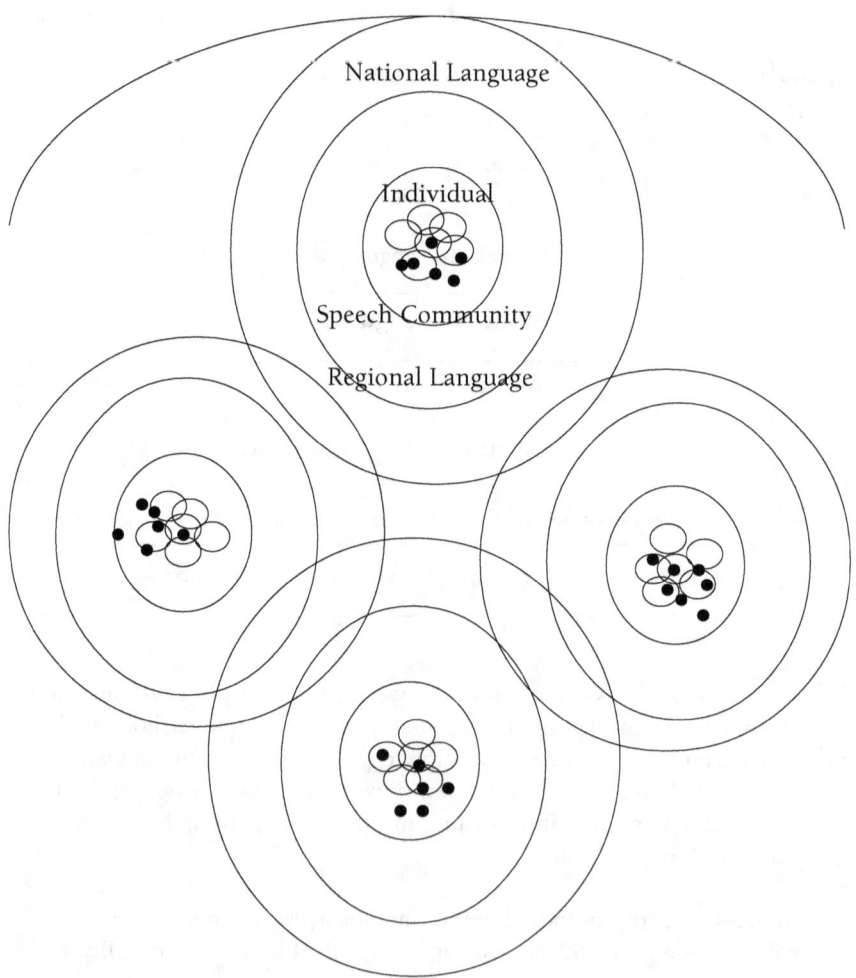

REFERENCES

Alladina S. (1984) *The Positive Interaction Between Languages of Early Cognition and the Acquisition of the Language of Education*. 1983-84 ILEA Teacher Fellow Report to the Multicultural Inspectorate, ILEA, London

Census of India (1961a) *Language Monographs*. Volume V, Part XI-C(1)

Census of India (1961b) *Gujarat Census Atlas*. Volume V, Part IX.

Census of India (1971) *Gujarat*. Part X-CI, Series 5

Census of India (1971) *Language Handbook on Mother Tongue in Census*. Centenary Monographs, No. 10. R.C. Nigam

Commission of the European Communities (1984) *Report from the Commission to the Council on the Implementation of Directive 77/486/EEC on the Education of the Children of Migrant Workers*. CON(84) 54, Brussels, February

Dawsani C.J. and Parchoni, S. (1978) *Sociolinguistic Survey of Indian Sindhi, Central Institute of Indian Languages*. Mysore, India

Dawsani C.J. (1982) *Language Attrition - The Case of Indian Sindhi*. The Third International Conference on South Asian Languages and Linguistics. Central Institute of Indian Languages, Mysore, India

Grierson G.A. (1927) *Linguistic Survey of India*. Volume VIII, Part I, Motital Banarasidas, Calcutta, India

ILEA (1983) *Language Census*. Inner London Education Authority, RS 916/83, London

Kakhar D.P. (1876) *Indian Antiquary*. Volume V, India

LMP (1983) *Linguistic Minorities in England. A Report for the Department of Education and Science, Linguistic Minorities Project*. University of London Institute of Education, London

Mohan P. (1984) 'Two Faces of a Language Death', *India International Centre Quarterly*, II(2)

Pattanayak D.P. (ed.) (1978) *Papers in Indian Sociolinguistics*. CIIL Conferences and Seminar, Series 2, Central Institute of Indian Languages, Mysore, India

Sarkar A. (1964) *Handbook of Languages and Dialects of India*. Kranti Press, Calcutta, India

Language in Communication and the Teacher's Role: The Experience of the Caribbean Communications Project

J. Burke, Y. Collymore, H. Dale, P. Knight and E. Whittingham

The Caribbean Communications Project was an independent Adult Education Centre which operated in West London in the early 1980s. In the course of our work there various definitions and approaches to communication emerged:

> A two-way process in which a message or piece of information is given in a form in which it is comprehensible to the target recipient;

> The means by which we express thoughts, feelings and intentions to others

Communication was seen as vital in both:

1. the transmission between one person or group and another skills socially defined as important, as in formal education or training, and
2. the mutual recognition of Caribbeanness in interaction between people, through Creole language, as part of a culture.

Communication may require the effective use of every code available to human beings: signs, body language, spoken and written language and computer codes. To people of African descent, this will imply a struggle for independence.

Communication can be unsuccessful if the communicators are from different cultural, educational, social or linguistic backgrounds, or different political orientations. Without effective communication between tutor and pupil, learning is inhibited. The tutor of adults must, therefore, develop an awareness of linguistic, social, historical and political dimensions of the student's life, and take these, and the student's 'race' and gender into account in the choice of teaching material and the content and method of lessons.

Attitudes to language have always been influenced by social and political factors. Language has been used to define people in terms of education and social class and used to discriminate against certain groups. People who speak a language form defined by the dominant group in a society as low status, are less likely to feel confident to communicate in that form in situations where they may thereby be judged as inferior, and possibly be discriminated against. Inhibitions may develop about language use not only in that context but in general, lessening the effectiveness of any communication attempted. Negative attitudes to the language of one's home and community may result. Awareness of these factors on the part of the tutor is essential if strategies to overcome them are to be created.

ORAL COMMUNICATION

When tutor and student are from different linguistic backgrounds, there may be differences not only of pronunciation and vocabulary, but also structural differences and differences in nuances of meanings of certain common words. In addition an adult who has had little education, as well as difficulties in reading and writing is likely to have a limited vocabulary and general knowledge, although they may have acquired quite intricate craft skills and a wide experience of life through travel or migration.

Teaching reading to an adult differs from teaching reading to a young child, because the life experience of the adult is so varied. It is possible to teach a group of three or four year olds much the same thing, and progress together in stages through the learning of letters, sounds, whole words and word-building, although the pace will vary according to the ability of the individual children. Adults in a group, however, may have learned the initial stages by different methods; will have reached different stages in their reading development and will have a more varied range of life skills and experiences on which to build. Although they will still have to master the same reading skills as children, the approach to learning, we believe, has to be much more individual. Some will be motivated by wishing to help their children succeed in their schoolwork, others by the wish for promotion at work, or their ambition to pursue a particular course of study or skills training. Such skills may require the use of quite technical and specialised vocabulary, and cannot be acquired by the use of children's reading material. Subject matter related to the interests of the adult learner is essential, in order to maintain interest and motivation and to build confidence.

BLACK LITERATURE AND THE USE OF CREOLE

The adult reader of Caribbean origin inherits a strong oral tradition from the African ancestry of Caribbean people. Storytelling, rhyme, riddles, proverbs and folksongs are all part of this tradition, and can be exploited for the purpose of teaching reading and writing. Caribbean writing is a newer development, and at the start of the Caribbean Communication Project few students (or, indeed, tutors) had been introduced to the wealth of Black written literature now published from the Caribbean, Africa and America. Its educational value is immense. The use of tape and record to bring to the students professional exponents of Caribbean storytelling, such as 'Miss Lou', Louise Bennett, and 'Tim Tim', Paul Keens-Douglas, can stimulate the students' and tutors' own talents.

Discussion is a very important part of the reading lesson, and an equally important stimulus to writing. Topical issues of political and social significance to the student, religious and moral issues, the education of their own children and other daily experience may all be relevant in discussion, leading to further reading and comprehension work. Discussion aids the development of vocabulary and the acquisition of standard English through listening and practice, whilst allowing the free use of Creole and structured Creole work to highlight the differences, and appropriateness for different social situations.

Many tutors are concerned about 'correcting' of Creole structures in speech and writing, and how to deal with non-standard pronunciation, such as the 'aspirant 'h'. We believe there should be a consistent policy on this. Students attempting to speak or write in standard English should be corrected to enable them to acquire the speech patterns and structures they wish. This should be done, however, without suggesting the Creole is in any way inferior or inadequate for learning. Similarly, opportunities should be given for students to see Creole in written form and to use Creole creatively and discuss the distinctions between Creole and standard French, English or Dutch.

Because of the unfamiliarity of written Creole orthographies, and regional variations, students may experience a difficulty in reading Creole inconsistent with their oral fluency. If students are used to giving a Caribbean pronunciation to English spellings then semi-phonetic representations of Creole pronunciations, even in Black literature, such as 'mahn' for 'man', may simply not be recognised. There may also be resistance on the part of students who have developed negative attitudes towards Creole as 'bad language', 'broken English', or 'broken French'.

In reading standard English, the student is likely to read with Creole pronunciation and grammatical interpretation, which does not distinguish certain word endings such as -ed, in the past tense of verbs or the plural -s. The meaning, therefore, may not be clear to the English listener. Questioning will indicate whether the reader has understood. It is then a matter for the tutor and student to decide, in discussion, whether the pronunciation in reading out loud is important to the student, or whether the aim is fluency and comprehension in reading. This will depend on the student's own motivation and ambitions, not the tutor's desire to change the speech of the student.

LINGUISTIC DIVERSITY AND EDUCATION

An important part of the background of younger students of the Caribbean Communications Project has been their experience in the English School system. The first response to the language of Creole speakers in the schools was one of panic. It was a shock to find out that after three hundred years of colonial rule Caribbean children were still not little English men or women. The language of the children was then said to be a block to teaching, and 'West Indian' children were widely seen as educationally sub-normal.

Protests made this view unsustainable, and second language and foreign language techniques began to be used, even though Creole was still not recognised as a separate language, and the problem was identified as one of 'language deficit'. This lack of recognition meant, however, that children were not, as in ordinary foreign language teaching, taught to differentiate clearly, or translate, between their own language and standard English. What came out was not standard English, but something that reflected Caribbean usages. This 'language interference' then reinforced the teachers' notions of Caribbean children's deprivation and 'deficiencies'.

The notion of 'language deficit' is not one which will stand up to any serious scientific scrutiny. As it became apparent that Caribbean Creoles were languages in their own right, so those who had previously sought to turn children's Creole *into* English now saw themselves as eradicating it so that Creole could be *replaced by* English. In contradiction to this, others began to call for Creole to be taught as a language, or even used as a teaching language, in its own right. The conflict between these tendencies continues, even though they are now more subtly expressed.

More recent approaches, locating themselves between these extremes, have been described as 'linguistic diversity' or 'repertoire' approaches to teaching. The idea in these is to give Creoles equal status with other language varieties. The problem is that though this may be linguistically sound, it does not deal with the problems of power, of what is a language and what is a dialect, the fundamental inequalities which mean that Creole is still classified as only a dialect of English. The education system has yet really to come to terms with what Creole is, and the scope for its utilisation in teaching.

The Caribbean Communications Project dealt mainly with adult students. The attitudes of many of these to Creole are crucially ambivalent, veering between positive and negative.

As we have seen, the sources of the negative attitudes are historical, tied up with the whole history of racism against Black people, which created the social reality within which Black people who spoke Creole were poor and oppressed and saw their lack of achievement as caused partly at least by their speech.

It is not easy to detach oneself sociologically from this view. We do have in England at the moment Caribbean youths, who are trying to reassert themselves and have found an identity through taking a more positive approach to Creole. There are some educated people, linguists and white liberals, who take a positive attitude. But the historical experience of Caribbean teachers leads to an ambivalence between these positions; we cannot divorce ourselves from the immediate reality of the links between poverty and Creole, and affluence and English.

Speakers of Creole are emotionally tied to their language; it is their true selves. Those people who have an ear for Creole will hear it all over our society. If you travel on the buses or walk in the market places, or wherever adult or young Caribbean people meet, they speak Creole, sometimes relax and speak Creole only, or they may mix it with English, but always they speak it with a certain solidarity. But even when they are speaking Creole with satisfaction and enjoyment, they are conscious that if they were not among their peers, they could be giving 'a wrong impression'. The dilemma does not go away. English has always been the language of education, of economic and social mobility. There is a conflict between what you are and what you are aspiring to be.

Our strategy was to use Creole language tapes from the oral tradition to highlight distinctions in pronunciation and structure, and with the use of Black literature, stimulate discussions to develop confidence in speaking on topical issues. Sometimes, however, teachers would find a situation where a student opposed the use of Creole. But if you can pacify that person and get them to sit down for a few minutes, they will enjoy your poem, or your story, or your song given in Creole, because that is where their soul still is. It is the striving for something else which is creating the problem. Those of us involved in teaching must try to transfer our academic awareness of the economic and social reality; but we cannot do so unless we understand how differently the choices appear to someone who has yet to master the dominant language variety or escape poverty. We must ourselves be careful and tolerant, or else reassuring students of the validity of their own experience may be heard by them merely as advice to accept their present station in life.

The opposition to Creole may relate to someone else. We found parents worried about their children, and children who worried about their parents. Creole-speaking parents may be distressed because their children, going to English schools, still speak Creole, which they see as the thing which has kept their own generation down. On the other hand we find children who have transferred to standard English being embarrassed by the language of their parents, thinking them stupid, wondering how to relate to them. Both of these situations will benefit from a more positive understanding of Creole.

Before tutors actually start teaching they will not appreciate fully the wealth of skills and knowledge their adult students bring with them. After they started, tutors would be asking themselves : 'If I, who can read and write, still have so much trouble in this racist British society, how is someone who can't read and write going to survive?'

We had illiterate students who had jobs, had bought their own houses, were doing very well, but still had a negative concept of themselves, and wanted their children to succeed in a society where you are judged by 'A' levels and degrees, and came to us for help.

Despite the complexity of the situation, we believe the experience of the Caribbean Communication Project has proven the value of taking a positive approach to the utilisation of Creole in tutoring. That is why the Caribbean Communication Project published occasional papers dealing with language issues, and why we analyse the written and oral work of our students in these terms, and why, in the initial training of our volunteer tutors, there is a large input of Caribbean Creole.

Language in Communication and the Teacher's Role

TEACHING WRITING - CREATIVE AND FORMAL

Teaching writing is more difficult than teaching reading, and the utilisation of Creole in this is more difficult because Creole does not have a written tradition. We start to help new students face up to the problem by dividing writing into two categories for them: 'creative writing' and 'formal writing'; and we take creative writing first.

Even if someone can write a few words, the tutor cannot just sit them down and ask them to write, because their reluctance to write as they speak, in what they think of as 'broken English' or 'broken French', is the core of the problem.

To show our students there are Black writers who command respect we use the stories of these writers on tape as a starting point for discussion. Storytelling is a very important part of Caribbean culture, and stories are always told in Creole, not standard English. If these stories are told on tape by someone well-known, somebody they consider to be somebody, they will accept it. If we then contrast that Creole tape with a standard English version, then, one hundred percent of the time, when you ask the student which version was better, they say the Creole one, because it is something they understood, something they can relate to, and something they now find acceptable.

One Caribbean writer whose work was extremely useful was the Trinidadian Samuel Selven (1979). One of his stories, about a 'village washer' bought to mind the experience of older students of washing clothes by the river, or by wells, because there were no washing machines and no running water. They had no scrubbing brushes so they used corn husks instead. These are not only skills, they are historical things that we need to document before they are forgotten in our modern world of gadgets. Use of this kind of material helps to make younger students reappreciate older people as a learning resource.

Caribbean cooking skills can be used for educational purposes. It is not just a matter of putting up recipes as texts on the wall, but again a question of passing on other skills, for example the use of banana leaves (not only in the Caribbean, but also in India and Africa) as a fore-runner to tin foil, for wrapping food in for cooking. These are the sort of skills that we try to bring out. We make our older people value them and our younger people accept them and be proud.

Another type of teaching material developed by the Caribbean Communication Project were geography packs. One was based on a trip to Norfolk carried out by students and tutors, and utilised photographs taken by students, bus maps, town plans, and student reports of the trip. Another was compiled for students visiting the Caribbean using items like a 24-hour clock, a used plane ticket, a British Rail timetable, and, again maps. One tutor found that some students had not appreciated that blue on the map meant sea, and green meant land. She put together for them maps of the whole Caribbean and of individual islands, and worksheets on the problems of travel to them. When the Grenada crisis came up, the map of Grenada suddenly came to life; we were able to follow events like that, and the path of hurricanes, in detail.

For the tutor creative writing is easier to teach than formal writing. When the student is just trying to communicate their personal experience in a story or a letter to a cousin abroad, you don't have to worry about the sentence structure of standard English.

Formal writing is more difficult to teach. It has been made more difficult partly because our students may in the past have had liberal teachers of various colours and backgrounds, who have felt that spelling is not important so long as the person reading the message knows what you want to say. This may be true, but one of the responsibilities we have as Black tutors to Black students is to help them combat stereotypes of Black people. Those of our students who are parents know this, and if they come to you and say 'I want to write a letter to my child's teacher,' they don't want a letter full of spelling mistakes, because they know the teacher will judge them on what is being presented. Our students see correct writing as a route to social mobility; they don't want to be always at the bottom doing menial jobs. Tutors who are eager to get students writing must not forget that in the outside world you are judged by your colour and qualifications, and if you cannot write a letter you are not going to get much of a job.

This is not to say that we want to teach people who cannot read or write to use great long jargonistic phrases. We give them short clear sample drafts of letters, say, to the gas board or to query a telephone bill. A lot of our older students always want to start their letters with 'Dear whoever, Greetings in the name of our Lord', or 'Blessings upon you'. This is something we do not encourage; the bank manager or British Telecom, or even the teacher may not always be pleased to have greetings from God! Formal writing requires appropriate expressions as well as correct standard English.

LANGUAGE, POWER AND 'INTEGRATION'

How has our own perception, as Black people, of language, been affected by the British response to our presence over the past twenty-five to thirty years since they noticed we might be here to stay?

The British describe us as a 'minority group'. We have to be very careful that we do not let this phrase make us think ourselves permanently into a state of subordination and supposed inferiority. A minority in one society may be a majority in another. Language use may also differentiate within, as well as between, both ethnic minorities and majorities.

The use of particular Creole varieties in the Caribbean may mark speakers as coming from lower social strata. Historically, therefore, a culture has developed which is alienated from the very language which is at the heart of it. Many Creole speakers try to distance themselves from their own language. Those able to use formal education to move out of lower socio-economic strata may try to pretend Creole is not part of their origins. Not until the work of Labov (1977) on 'Black American English' did the dominant intellectual culture of the English-speaking world start to admit the possibility of positive values for such language varieties, and the equality of their forms and structures with those of other language varieties.

Prior to this, negative attitudes to Creole facilitated governmental policies of 'assimilation' in the UK in the 1960s. The Black 'newcomers' were to be absorbed into a culturally and linguistically homogeneous society. People had to get rid of what they came with, in order to fit into 'our' society. The action of the London Borough of Ealing in busing Black children around to disperse them equally between schools was part of this policy.

The assimilationist approach gave way to a 'culturally diverse' approach, classically expressed in Roy Jenkins' (1966) definition of 'integration' as:

> ...not a flattening process of assimilation, but as equal opportunity accompanied by cultural diversity in an atmosphere of mutual tolerance.

Educational programmes began, supposedly, to focus on the special needs of minority groups. The idea that mother tongues other than English should be valued and positively encouraged began to develop. But, even as this emphasis on culture and cultural difference developed, so critics began to point out that it did not of itself deal with access to or denial of economic and social power. The 'cultural diversity' approach conceived of racism as simply a set of mental prejudices held by a few people, which would disappear if we all knew how other people dress and speak. It didn't look at the effects on education of the structural nature of institutional racism.

The 'anti-racist' perspective, to which some of us have moved on, emphasises equality. Mere tolerance of cultural diversity which does not situate culture in the context of people's power and access to power, and their ability to speak and listen about that power, cannot achieve anything. That realisation is the origin of this book.

There are routine customs and practices within our society which mean that Black people and White people stand in different relation to each other in terms of health, housing, education, employment and life chances. But of course the analysis of institutional racism, of customs and practices, must not absolve individuals from looking at their attitudes, especially powerful individuals, the so-called gate-keepers who make decisions over the funding of research, and of voluntary bodies like the Caribbean Communications Project.

This anti-racist perspective also stresses that since we Black people are those who experience the brunt of racism, it is we who are in the best position to articulate and say what it is about, how we see that it should be dismantled. Other people have to listen for a change, rather than take the chair and take the lead. This is a pre-condition for us to share in the power structure in this society.

REFERENCES

Jenkins R. (1966) *Address to a Meeting of the Voluntary Liaison Committee on 23 May 1966.* National Committee for Commonwealth Immigrants, London

Labov W. (1977) *Language in the Inner City.* Blackwell, Oxford

Selven S. (1979) *Turn Again Tiger.* Heinemann, London

Communication Without Writing: Pictorial Art and the Education of Gypsy Children

Éva Pongrácz and Elemér Várnagy

with an introduction by T.A. Acton

INTRODUCTION

The paper by Várnagy and Pongrácz might, at first sight, appear to propose an alternative to multilingualism and mother-tongue teaching. To some extent, this is so; but it must be borne in mind that the Gypsy children to whom they refer belong to a specific group, the Boyash or Beash, whose linguistic situation and history is untypical, but, nevertheless, has wider implications.

The Beash of Baranya County, with whom the work described in this paper was conducted, are among those Gypsies who speak dialects of Romanian, rather than Indian-derived Romani, as their mother-tongue. This is also true of Gypsy emigrants from Romania in the West who call themselves Rudari or Ursari, and Romani-speaking Gypsies use the word 'Boyash' to refer to all these groups - and sometimes to all non-Romani speaking Gypsy groups.

The language of these Beash has been studied by a colleague of Pongrácz and Várnagy (Papp, 1982). As a language, Beash is far from being the same as modern standard Romanian. Dr Papp had established that the Beash spoken in the neighbourhood of Pécs had around 1,800 separate vocabulary items - quite a rich vocabulary. Of these some 40 or 50 words only are shared with Vlach Romani dialects, and all of these are present also in Romanian. In fact, we may say that as far as vocabulary goes, this Beash dialect is virtually identical to Romanian as spoken in the Banat district of Romania some 3-400 years ago. Unlike the non-Romani dialects of some other non-Romani speaking small Gypsy groups, such as Gammon or Jenisch, which contain numbers of Romani-derived words, Beash effectively contains none at all. Ordinary standard English contains three Romani words ('pal', 'cosh', and 'lollipop' besides the numerous loan-words in local varieties of English). How does it come about that we have a Gypsy group fiercely maintaining as its own language a variety which contains less Romani lexical influence than almost any other European language?

Effectively, the explanation that seems to emerge from Dr Papp's researches is that whereas these other varieties - and often Romani itself are 'low' languages of diglossic groups where the national language of the host society provides the 'high' language, Beash must be seen as the old 'high' language of a formerly diglossic group, where the low language (Romani) had to be very sharply differentiated from the high language. The circumstance of this must be sought in Romanian history.

In Romania by the mid-seventeenth century the great majority of Gypsies were reduced to chattel slavery. Romani language, therefore, was the language of someone who ought to be a slave. We may suppose, therefore, that the ancestors of the Beash asserted their right not to be slaves by speaking good Romanian, by consciously and deliberately rejecting Romani, and thus denying that there was any warrant for enslaving them. This would not have worked if there had been any Romani vocabulary used with their Romanian. Papp refers to Weigand (1897, pp.39-40) who says that the Beash goldwashers, living in Romania at that time, would not entertain any suggestion that they were of Gypsy origin, despite the fact that they were a distinct social group, darker in colour than Romanians. Their consequent need to speak a Romanian dialect as a 'high' language may help to explain the conservatism and tenacity with which they now maintain the language. Dr. Papp is now engaged on comparative grammatical analysis to see if he can trace any grammatical influence from Romanes onto Beash.

In the late l9th, and the first half of the 20th century, the Beash, like other Gypsy groups, fled Romanian oppression and disorder. Those Beash who entered Hungary (passing to the part of Hungary furthest from Romania) were no longer, as they may have been in Romania, a relatively well-off Gypsy group. Instead they were the poorest of the poor Gypsies. Because they were migrants, and because they were and are noticeably dark-skinned, Hungarians made no distinction between them and other Gypsies as objects of prejudice, and the Romanian Beash language was as unintelligible as Romani (and was often assumed to be the same). Before 1950 many of the Beash were reduced to living in holes dug out by the roots of trees in the forests. Given that some Gypsies (the Romungri musicians) do enjoy relatively good standing in Hungary, and that policies of at least providing housing were pursued by postwar socialist governments in Hungary, and that Hungarians treat them as Gypsies, and that they do look, physically, like Gypsies, it is not surprising that the Beash who a century ago denied the connection, now acknowledge themselves as Gypsies, and participate in the Romani 'self-governments'. Nonetheless, they remain a distinct and cohesive community, and any attempt to assimilate them to some ideal of pan-Gypsyism would be as mistaken as the attempt to assimilate Gypsies to Hungarian ethnicity.

In this community, then, in which we have linguistic pride born out of an historically necessitated act of linguistic self-suppression, where Gypsy identity has only been re-embraced within living memory, self expression through art - which is a widespread popular movement, as well as a method teachers have come to embrace - may well fulfil deep cultural needs. Várnagy and Pongrácz compare art education for the 'disadvantaged' with work therapy (presumably as practised in the rehabilitation of the mentally ill). Perhaps we may turn that comparison around and wonder to what extent work therapy is itself a substitute for linguistic liberation.

PICTORIAL ART AND THE EDUCATION OF GYPSY CHILDREN

This paper is based on research which took place in the 1970s partly in a school in a traditional small working class town, and partly in a new school linked to the Pécs Centre for Education in the suburbs of Pécs. In both of these schools art education is an important part of the special provision for 'disadvantaged children'. A substantial proportion of the children defined as 'disadvantaged' are Gypsies, with parents at different stages in the process of social integration.

These children face many stumbling-blocks in the world of school. Our purpose in looking at ways of self-expression by Gypsy children through pictorial art is to extend their (and our) awareness of possible choices in human life. We think that such self-expression in creative activity can be a kind of work- therapy. The problems which the children have suppressed and concealed within themselves can be brought out into the open and made explicit. There may be no immediate solution to these problems, but if they are at least formulated openly, then the tension caused by burying them inside of oneself can be lowered.

In our opinion, although of course pictorial art can only be a reflection of what is already part of someone's personality, nonetheless, the very act of creating it at the same time extends the range of that personality. Therefore art education can be a powerful tool for encouraging the personality development of 'disadvantaged' children. Harris tells us that paintings and drawings are spontaneous exteriorisations of the feelings of the child at the moment of their execution (Harris, 1963). We have to look, however, at the work which is produced voluntarily by the children rather than that which reflects the schema of their teachers. We have to put the needs of the children first. They must be creating first of all for their own pleasure, and only secondarily for their teachers.

At the start we worked on the assumption that the level of ability exhibited by Gypsy children would be totally environmentally determined. As the work progressed, however, it became evident that individual children had special talents which could be built upon as their personality development progressed. At the same time we hope that the positive attitudes engendered by achievement in this field can be transferred to other areas of school life. These special talents can also, of course, be found in Gypsy adults, as witnessed by the varied paintings, by Gypsy masters, in the Gypsy museum in the village of Luzsok in Baranya county (the county of which Pécs is the county town).

How exactly do we develop creativity in these children through artistic activity?

In our school art rooms, children are playing as they create, freeing themselves from constraint, and finding immediate rewards in the process of creation. They can celebrate ideals of beauty and justice together with the educator, because their works are spontaneous expressions of universal human values. The configuration of Gypsy children's paintings is like that of expressionism and surrealism. These children often scorn all convention in their uninhibited expression of their private and interior experience. We may describe the style which results from this as a 'psycho-realism'. In fact, in encouraging the expression of these drives we put ourselves on a basis of equality with the children, abandoning the subordination of the child to the teacher.

We give the children non-directive advice, but they do not have to accept it. Often the children re-discover for themselves old techniques. Even the art classes themselves are not compulsory, and the children can come and go freely during them. There is a communal framework to their activity. They imitate each other and spend time in looking at and criticising their work.

Various emotions come through in the children's paintings: desire, a sense of belonging to this or that, affection, dislike, etc. Often they seek to express an internal surrealist world which in fact is derived from their environment, that is to say from their own culture which developed as a socio-cultural generation during their recurrent migrations. Perhaps we can grasp the aesthetic substance of these works all the more vigorously because they are not limited by stereotypical conventions in their creation. No externalised model of reality can reduce them to a mere imitation of anything. No technical system restrains their fantasies. Their configurations visually represent ideas; one may speak of an intellectual realism, in which Gypsy children do not so much represent what they see about a thing as reflect what they *know* about its characteristics. It is interesting that taught methods do not constrain the work of adult Gypsy painters either. They do not like technical systems either. Visual reality and their own internal world are reflected together in their canvasses. Thus the conservation of valuable Gypsy cultural traditions is assisted.

An American investigation (Alschuler and Hattwick, 1947) of children aged between 4 and 6 found a close correlation between the attitudes of the children and their choice of colour in artwork. For example the use of red, yellow and orange was said to signify an open and affectionate nature, while those who used blues and greens tended to be calm and undemonstrative. Black, brown and purple could be marks of emotional stress. These findings were echoed by a Hungarian study (Turóczi, 1980) of a sample of 5,000 individual using 24 different colours).

We found ourselves most frequently able to place Gypsy children in the first category. In our research in 1976-77 we found that some 70 per cent of the Gypsy children we studied preferred a warm colour - either red, or something between red and pink. We take this as a manifestation both of their desire for enfranchisement, as full members of society, and of the lyricism of their own culture. Their choice of paired complementary colours was also significant. Various shades of green betray impulsiveness, an ambition to make one's mark. The following were the most frequent choices by Gypsy children for pairs of colours: bright pink and green; yellow and violet; orange and blue.

Generally also, the Gypsy children's paintings made use of many ornamental or decorative motifs which show a rich emotional life.

We must conclude that an educational process, which includes pictorial art, is bound to be more effective in enabling Gypsy children to express themselves, and thus to develop their personalities, than one that relies solely on verbal communication.

REFERENCES

Alschuler and Hattwick (1947) *Painting and Personality*. University of Chicago, Chicago

Harris D.B. (1963) *Children's Drawings as Measures of Intellectual Maturity*. Harcourt, Brace and World, New York

Papp G. (1982) *A Beás Cigányok Román Nyelvjárása / Beás-Magyar Szótár*. Gypsy Research Series Volumes V & VI. Janus Pannonius University Pedagogical Department, Pécs

Turóczi M. (1980) *A Szinek Világa és a Személyiség* (The World of Colours and the Personality). Györ, Szerzö kiadása

Weigand G. (1897) *Kórósch und Marosch-Dialekte*. Leipzig

Adult Literacy and Oral History

Jane Mace

In the last quarter of the twentieth century, while the study of literacy in adult life has grown and changed, there has been a persistent recognition of the expressive power of the spoken word as the basis for writing development (Mace 1995). Despite the increased pressure in adult basic education funding patterns to show measurable learning outcomes, there is evidence that teaching approaches which maintain a dynamic between the oral and the written are as alive now as they were in 1978 when one of the first publications by adult literacy students included this text:

> When you take away the block -
> the fear of mis-spelling -
> it's like a door being opened.
> Putting words to paper
> and building a picture out of your mind
> without the fear of spelling mistakes,
> this creates a part of your mind
> that you've never experienced -
> to write what's in your mind
> and express feelings and hopes
> which you wouldn't before.
> You look at your writing and say
> 'Did i write that?'
> Everybody's thinking about something
> i went round a word like enormous -
> i would write big.
> As soon as i stopped bothering
> i were off! (Kevin 1978)

There are differences between oral history practice and adult literacy education. The first is concerned with collecting the oral account of an individual, which sometimes (but not always) is later transcribed, edited and extracted for publication. The second is concerned with working with the oral language of individuals in a group and finding ways for the warmth of speech to be set on paper in such a way that the speaker can grow in their literacy skills through seeing value and connection between what they say and what they read and write. The two practices meet at the point where ideas about 'making history' come alive in the creative interplay between talk and writing. Kevin's text was the result of such a process - in this case, one which took place during a residential weekend bringing together literacy learners with literacy tutors. It was published in a book, and laid out in the way you see it here, not because it was written as a poem but as part of the deliberate practice which was evolving at that time known as 'line-breaking'. (Each line breaks at a point of sense. For the cautious, slow or uncertain reader, this gives them a greater chance of taking in meaning as well as decoding words, than the usual conventions of typesetting to a justified margin).

I have been teaching in adult literacy work for twenty-eight years, on and off. For ten of those years I was a member of the collective which edited and produced a national paper entitled *Write First Time,* printing writing by adult literacy students in Britain, funded by the Adult Literacy and Basic Skills Unit from its first issue in April 1975 until April 1985 (when it stopped publication after the withdrawal of grant-aid). The collective was composed of both tutors and students, with production workshops taking place for each of the three issues per year in a different part of the country. Many of those literacy students had been 'bothering' (and bothered) by fears of expressing poor education in their writing for most of their lives before joining literacy study groups. Literacy education, which is about strategies to reduce or eliminate such fears, is very much a social and political process.

For any of us, writing is an activity which concerns thinking. At times, it is the only means by which we can get a difficult bit of thinking worked out. Yet, becoming literate has too often been perceived as becoming capable of dealing with *other people's* written work: learning to read. Leaving out the potential for writing means leaving out what Kevin describes as the power to 'create a part of your mind/that you've never experienced'. When a group of adult literacy tutors sat round one afternoon in 1974 and discussed the production of a regular newspaper of writings by literacy students, it was some time before we recognised the force of this idea. The titles we tried to find for this paper all concerned filling a 'reading gap' generally agreed to exist for adult new readers of English. Late on, in the tiredness of the meeting, the word 'writing' was suggested as needing emphasis. As the title of the paper soon emerged, so the discussion revived its energy.

Who, in any literacy programme intending to 'make literate' in their own language a large number of people, are the individuals best qualified to write the texts for reading? Who will write the primers? How will they get published and distributed? These are the questions that we felt needed to be answered, if we were to talk about creating written traditions with any kind of dynamic relation to oral language.

In the fifteen years before 1985 in this country, an exciting renaissance of working class writing and community publishing has taken place, which to a large extent has helped to provide an answer. Written in the rhythms and varieties dictated often by the tape transcript of the author's spoken language, many of these autobiographical and reflective pieces of writing disturbed the understandings and expectations that readers of English brought to the written forms of our language. This publishing activity has brought together literacy practice and oral history techniques. During its ten year career, *Write First Time* produced over thirty issues, distributing some 6,000 copies of each issue nationally to organisations where working class students in adult literacy groups and projects meet. Its work is still accessible in the archive at Ruskin College library, Oxford.

In the same period, other writers and 'people's history' projects, encouraging elderly people to reflect on their memories in writing and discussion, up and down the country, have produced publications of written work, mixing oral transcripts from taped conversations with first person narratives and poetry. The Federation of Worker Writers and Community Publishers first concerned in 1976 (FWWCP 1982). By the time Write First Time had fallen victim to the Conservative cuts in 1985, the Federation was linking together some 26 local writers' workshops and publishing groups across the country. In 1998 it was still going from strength to strength.

Since the mid-1980s, the most encouraging development for the kind of work outlined in this paper has been the foundation, in 1984, of a national network bringing together two traditionally separate fields into the Research and Practice in Adult Literacy (RaPAL) network. That year, too, saw the first of several publications by the anthropologist Brian Street, heralding what he came later to call 'the new literacy studies' (Street 1984). RaPAL has gone on to fertilise much exciting interchanges between teaching and researching, to be found in, for example, Barton and Ivanic (1991) and Hamilton, Barton and Ivanic (1994), and proponents of the new literacy studies have developed useful conceptual tools with which to reframe narrowly functionalist views of what literacy education is for.

Meanwhile there are changes to the practices of publishing writing by literacy learners. As I suggested at the beginning, there has been a persistence in these practices, despite the changes in funding cultures in the intervening years since Kevin and others found their way into print. RaPAL bulletins regularly publish details of writing projects and small-scale publications produced out of educational practice in adult and further education colleges. There have always been questions about the validity of such work. How much does reading texts of this kind help or hinder individual literacy growth? Or might it even hinder it? What are the problems of conflict between the vitality of oral language and the conventions of 'proper English'? Most honest literacy teachers would agree that we know more of the problems than the benefits - as far as the author's individual 'progress' is concerned. For, like many of the students of literacy that we work with, we often find ourselves trapped in a narrowly defined notion of what progress in reading and writing actually is: the notion of a measurable, linear journey along graded stages of vocabulary, syntax and grammar; a series of conquests in the battle with English spelling and punctuation.

Writing, however, like any other art, is concerned as much with context as with form. Smith (1982) offered important insights to the bate on oral and written language, in particular, his distinction between 'composition' and "transcription' within the writing task. The literacy tutor working as a scribe or secretary with a student/author is collaborating in, and being a servant to, the author's written composition. The important of this 'language experience' was one of the starting points of my own practice (Mace 1979). The author (or literacy student) is not 'cheating' or being cheated. The words on the paper are theirs, and provide a draft. Such drafts are not dictated - they are noted down from the warmth of dialogue and narrative, to be read back, redrafted, edited, 'polished', and shared with other readers and writers in the literacy group.

Meanwhile both Black and white working class adults, taught to deny their own speech as inferior to, or a deviation from the 'standard' forms of English, are well aware of the transactional value of grammatically orthodox prose, 'correctly' set out. The demand for teaching the techniques necessary for this kind of writing must not be ignored - least of all by teachers who themselves have acquired such skills and benefited from other recognition (in publications like this one, to take just one example).

But it would be a mistake to see the practice of oral history and literacy work, that validates oral language in writing, in opposition to the kind of teaching that develops those skills. Every writer struggles to find his/her own voice; and gains courage from listening, to, and reading, the words that speak in a vocabulary and rhythm that have meaning for him/her. The evidence from the growing body of published writing produced by writers' workshop, literacy projects, and people's history groups is that a large number of people are learning to reclaim their own language, and, with the writer quoted at the beginning, to 'stop bothering'.

NOTES: USEFUL ADDRESSES

RaPAL (Research and Practice in Adult Literacy): Membership Secretary, Margaret Herrington, The Old School, Main Street, Tilton-on-the-Hill, Leics LE7 9LF
FWWCP (Federation of Worker Writers and Community Publishers): 23 Victoria Park road, Tunstall, Stoke-on-Trent ST6 6DX. email: fwwcp@mcmail.com
Jane Mace, Centre for Continuing Education and Development: South Bank University, 103 Borough Road, London SE1 0AA. email: maceja@sbu.ac.uk

REFERENCES

Barton D. and Ivanic R. (1991) *Writing in the Community*. Sage London
Federation of Worker Writers and Community Publishers (FWWCP) (1982) *The Republic of Letters: Working Class Writing and Local Publishing*. Comedia Publishing Group, London
Hamilton M., Barton D. and Ivanic R. (1994) *Worlds of Literacy*. Multilingual Matters, Clevedon, Avon
Kevin (1978) 'The Way To Be' in Write First Time Collective (eds.) *Let Loose*. Write First Time, Manchester
Mace J. (1979) *Working With Words: Literacy Beyond School*. Writers and Readers, London
Mace J. (1992) *Talking About Literacy: Principles and Practice of Adult Literacy Education*. Routledge, London
Mace J. (ed.) (1995) *Literacy, Language and Community Publishing: Essays in Adult Education*. Multilingual Matters, Clevedon, Avon
Mace J. (1998) *Playing With Time: Mothers and the Meaning of Literacy*. UCL Press, London
Smith F. (1982) *Writing and the Writer*. Heinemann, London
Street B. (1984) *Literacy in Theory and Practice*. Cambridge, Cambridge University Press

SECTION FIVE

Education and Language: Practice and Politics

Introduction

We begin this section with two papers that get down to the nuts and bolts of preparing classroom materials in languages without a written tradition. The situations described in the papers are different. Kephart deals with a Caribbean Creole that was the majority language of the community in which it is spoken. Zatta deals with a variety of Romanes belonging to an ethnic group which is a minority not only compared with the Italian host society, but also within broader Gypsy society. Yet there are obvious parallels. Both papers are the work of enthusiasts; both have had to have the wealth of material illustrating them savagely cut to bring them within the compass of this book. They show just how much work is involved in making the multilingual school a practical reality; but at the same time they show that work is both possible and worthwhile.

The paper by Müller and Szabo presents an instructive contrast to that of Zatta which must be set in context. It concerns adult literacy work in German with sedentary or semi-sedentary Sinti Gypsies living in Germany. At first sight it might appear anomalous to include in this volume a report of an adult literacy project which explicitly eschews the use of the oral language of the students. If, however, we listen to the silences and omissions of this paper we may find them more eloquent than any amount of advocacy of multilingualism.

Müller and Szabo and their Bremen colleagues are not opposed to the use of Romanes in education. They would deplore the kind of prejudiced attitudes shown to be present in some teachers by Zatta every bit as much as does Zatta herself. Their abstention from the use of Romanes is in deference to the views of the Sinti Gypsies themselves. As the paper by Papenbrok tells us, the German Gypsies were extensively studied by ethnologists and linguists in the period before 1939. In particular a female anthropologist known to the Gypsies as 'Loli Chai' ('The redhead') collected extensive genealogies, using the Sinti Romani language. She and other academics then collaborated in the rounding-up of Gypsies (including assimilated house-dwellers not known to their neighbours as Gypsies) for the Nazi concentration camps, in which a quarter of a million Gypsies died (Kenrick 1999). It is therefore hardly surprising that German Gypsies remain more than usually suspicious of academic attempts to document their culture. In particular one leading German Gypsy organisation, the Verband Deutscher Sinti, in contrast to most other constituent groups in the World Romani Congress, has a firm policy that the Sinti variety of Romani spoken by most of its members should remain a secret language, and should not be generally written or used in education. The Sinti-Haus Bremen Project was politically close to the Verband Deutscher Sinti and properly respects this view, which is shared by the majority of Sinti.

Whatever the motivation, however, the decision NOT to use the mother-tongue has a profound effect on the educational project. Consider the image of the Rom Sloveni Gypsy group that emerges in Zatta's paper. They appear as the bearers of a rich culture, and extremely articulate and able to cope with a hostile environment. By contrast the Sinti Gypsies in Müller and Szabo appear as literally dumb, terrified even by going shopping or visiting the doctor. In Zatta the Rom Sloveni appear as in control of their destiny through the wisdom that is passed down from generation to generation in their true-story-telling tradition. But how does a Gypsy appear in Müller and Szabo? As 'a slave ... an animal forced to work ... a poor devil'.

In Zatta the Rom Sloveni appear sharply defined in the individual contours of their own group, defined as much as anything else by their differences from other Gypsy groups, their disdain of the conventions of fiction, their stubborn attachment to horsetrading as distinctive as their dialect. The Sinti in Müller and Szabo, however, are empty generalised figures. They are not defined by their Gypsy specificity, their position in the continuum of Romani culture. Rather they are defined only by the inadequacies in their participation in German culture. They are not defined by their Gypsy-ness, but by their un-German-ness. Müller and Szabo do not even discuss the specific historical factors which have led the Sinti to reject mother-tongue educational work. They can only allude to it in to closing paragraphs of their paper in the most veiled and ambiguous fashion.

This difference cannot be attributed to any generalised cultural advantage of the Rom Sloveni over the Sinti; indeed by reputation as an ethnic group the Sinti possess a rather larger stratum of renowned professional musicians and artists. Nor can it be attributed to any ideological superiority on Zatta's part; the writers of both papers are equally anti-racist. The difference has to be attributed to the brute fact that Zatta and her fellow workers share in the Romani language and use it, while Müller and Szabo do not.

One can argue - some Gypsies do argue - that this does not matter. It does not matter what non-Gypsies think of Gypsy culture, for it is only the opinion of those who actually participate in the culture that really counts. People should not have to prove their *folklorique* authenticity in order to be given their human rights. Indeed liberal sympathisers may be more helpful if their vision is fixed on the problems rather than the strengths of the Gypsy way of life. And if the strengths do become well-known, who can deny, in the light of the Nazi era, that such knowledge may make control, or even genocide of the Gypsies easier ? Ian Hancock sometimes goes so far as to suggest (though not wholly to endorse) the idea that the maintenance of illiteracy could even itself be a strategy for ethnic defence. There do exist wealthy Gypsies who actively oppose the idea of their children learning to read and write. If they pay mechanics to mend engines, labourers to hump materials, lawyers to speak in court, why not pay secretaries to read and write for them. Everyone knows, after all, that learning to read ruins your memory. One cannot dismiss this point of view as irrational.

Perhaps indeed a Gypsy child brought up in the bosom of a secure and economically self-sufficient family, isolated from school and non-Gypsy prejudice, 'knowing' people of other cultures only from the outside as far as is economically necessary, may have a rich and satisfying life. But what of the many under economic threat ? What of the thousands brought into the non-Gypsy school system, the strength and pervasiveness of whose culture parents who have not themselves been to school can only guess at. It must become harder and harder for Gypsy children to preserve their self-respect without also demanding an informed respect from non-Gypsies - that is to say treating non-Gypsies as also human beings. We must not forget that Europeans have not, and often still do not, behave like human beings to Gypsies; but there may be situations - the school in particular - in which the only way forward is to give them the chance. Perhaps the Verband Deutscher Sinti ought to consider at what point their opposition to mother-tongue teaching ceases to be a valid defence against non-Gypsy persecution, and becomes instead a self-mutilation which only compounds the effects of that persecution?

The papers by Jones and Levinsohn represent a further stage in the development of mother-tongue teaching. They are writing about the situations in Sierra Leone and Colombia where the arguments about the practicability and desirability of mother-tongue teaching have been won sufficiently to permit government or church support, which enables the work to go on in the ordinary school system, and their papers deal not with the initial problem of developing pedagogic technique and materials, but with the administrative changes to allow the new techniques to be generally applied. At the same time setting up such administrative structures can only reveal the need for a great deal more curriculum development - a vast elaboration within the universities of the kind of pioneering work done by Kephart and Zatta.

The linguistic and bible translation activities of Christian organisations among ethnic minorities in South America have been subjected to vigorous criticism by the German Human Rights organisation, the Gesellschaft für bedrohte Völker (Gesellschaft für bedrohte Völker 1979). Ironically, this organisation is also the main non-Gypsy supporter of the Gypsy organisation, Verband Deutscher Sinti, mentioned above. They make allegations of uncritical support and help to US imperialism and right-wing dictatorships in South America. They argue that the function of developing writing and translations in the minority languages is to implant an obscurantist and conservative ideology which hinders the absorption of the Indians into the struggle for the creation of genuine national independence in Latin America.

Reassessments and changes of practice in the field as described by Stoll (1982) might be thought to acknowledge the past validity of some of the criticisms. The critics, however, have often presented their own rejection of Christian ideas as though it followed that missionary activity was ipso facto oppressive, building on specific examples of malpractice to erect an argument which if taken to extremes would condemn all attempts by minorities to persuade other people to their own views or even cultural diversity itself. One might counter that to visualise South American Indians just as blocks of humanity to be incorporated into someone else's nationalism, into a monolithic Latin American resistance to the United States, can also be a form of cultural imperialism.

The developments described by Levinsohn seem to us be of a piece with those described by Zatta and Jones. There are similar problems, similar solutions and a similar rejection of the lack of vision of monolinguals. The ultimate purposes and perspectives may vary, and may or may not possess the explicit commitment to the equality and autonomy of ethnic minorities made by the Sinti-Haus Bremen. But it is clearly arguable that the Inga of the Putamayo are receiving as great a contribution to the possibility of ethnic and personal autonomy as the Sinti of Bremen from the work described in Section Five. Perhaps the development of mother-tongue literacy *in a multi-lingual context* has its own logic of liberation which is independent of the ideology and motives of those who bring it about.

These linguistic activities do not, however, take place in a vacuum, and the political issues have been raised again and again in our own debate, particularly by those who are themselves speakers of languages without written traditions. The Caribbean Communications Project encountered a range of successive various ideological stances towards Creole languages and the education of Caribbean pupils in British schools. The paper by Brandt analyses the effects of these ideological stances in terms of linguistic and educational politics with particular reference to the language of politically alienated and disaffected Black British Youth and their variety of Creole: British Youth Caribbean Creole, a term which he prefers to 'Black English' or the 'London Jamaican' described by Sebba (1993). In discussion, members of the Brent Asian collective suggested that racism also disadvantaged the speakers not only of Asian languages without a written tradition, but also of literary languages like Gujerati, which were held in equally low esteem by head teachers. Where Brandt felt, however, that British Youth Caribbean Creole could be effective as a vehicle of protest against racism partly because of its divorce from the school, the Brent Asian collective argued that Asian languages should be used in council offices and banks as well as in schools where mother-tongue teaching should be part of the mainstream curriculum and linked to racism awareness teaching. This difference of approach to some extent mirrors that between Zatta and Müller and Szabo discussed above. It reminds us that the official utilisation of minority languages does not come to pass without a political price. The price may be one that the community is prepared to pay, of political incorporation; but within our own time the price has sometimes been political segregation or even genocide.

REFERENCES

Gesellschaft für bedrohte Völker (1979) *Die frohe Botschaft Unserer Zivilisation - Evangelikale Indianermission in Lateinamerika.* Gesellschaft für bedrohte Völker, Göttingen

Kenrick D.S. (ed.) (1999) *In the Shadow of the Swastika - The Gypsies During the Second World War.* University of Hertfordshire Press, Hatfield

Sebba M. (1993) *London Jamaican.* Longman, Harlow

Stoll, D. (1982) *Fishers of Men or Founders of Empire?* Zed Press, London

Using Creole to Teach Reading in Carriacou

Ron Kephart

Children in Creole-speaking communities where the official language is English face a double hurdle in learning to read. First, like all people learning to read English, they face an orthography and spelling system which are not designed for English, but rather adopted piecemeal from a variety of sources, (Pitman 1966) and which do not present a coherent system from which learners can easily build an internal model of the reading process. Second, and even more serious, they have to deal with the fact that their language, which resembles English superficially, nevertheless operates with fundamentally different underlying grammatical categories. The surface similarities between Creole and Export English (the prescribed, idealised form to which education in the 'English-speaking' world aspires, and which is typically exported from one of the metropolitan centres) have, for many years, led to a deficit mythology in which Creole is seen as simply ungrammatical or 'broken' English. Children who failed to learn Export English were simply labelled 'dunce' - a classic case of blaming the victim. In this way, in part, the elite in Creole-speaking societies have over the years controlled access to the metropolitan language and thereby helped maintain the social stratification that is present in most of these societies.

Reading is a skill which is central to education as we know it. Reading has been shown to be a psycholinguistic process, an active interaction between readers and print for the purpose of extracting meaning (Goodman 1970; Spiro et al. 1980). Fluent readers do not simply 'decode' printed material in a linear fashion, nor do they impassively soak up what is on the page. They bring to the material all they know, conscious or not, about their language, and the topic, and all their other experiences. As they read, fluent readers use this knowledge to construct hypotheses or 'schemata' of the meaning of the print, which they continually accept/reject/refine based on what they encounter on the page.

This model holds for languages other than English, as for example, Spanish (Hudelson 1979). Reading, as a process, is not tied to a specific language, and should be transferrable, somewhat the way learning to play one stringed instrument makes learning the next one easier. Furthermore, if fluent reading is a psycholinguistic process, the native language of learners should be the most efficient medium through which to build a first model of this process, that is, to learn *what reading is* (Pike 1983; Downing 1979).

This paper draws on research in Carriacou, Grenada, testing the hypothesis that learning to read Creole English will help children in their reading of

Export English. A group of twelve-year-olds classified as poor readers by the educational system were given access to literacy through Carriacou Creole English (CC), using a phonemic orthography developed from the author's analysis of the language (Kephart 1980). An eclectic 'language experience' approach was used. At the same time their ability to read Export English was continually assessed and compared with that of a control group.

Carriacou may be considered a bilingual community (Kephart 1983) in which the native language of most people is a variety of Lesser Antillean Creole English (Hancock 1977) which differs somewhat from that of other nearby small islands in being strongly influenced by Lesser Antillean Creole French, locally called Patwa. Many Carriacou people exhibit varying degrees of bilingualism in Export English (EE), and many also have some facility in other Caribbean languages like Spanish and Creole French, which used to be spoken widely in Carriacou.

The problem of writing down a Creole language is not from a linguistic viewpoint, different from that of providing a writing system for any previously unwritten language. The complication arises from the fact that most of the world is controlled by an elite with a heavy emotional and economic investment in whichever metropolitan or export language happens to be the 'official' language and writing system of the area. Compounding this is the deficit mythology which generally surrounds folk languages. The end result is the tendency to metropolitanise the folk language in writing, usually distorting it in the process (Layme 1980; Valdman 1970, pp.8-9).

A number of linguists have directly addressed the issue of providing orthographies for unwritten languages (Pike 1976; Hall 1966; Hardman and Hamano 1984). A common theme running through these discussions is the need to balance the practical limitations of typewriters and typefonts available in the country with the desirability of a 'one phoneme = one grapheme' correspondence. Unfortunately it is not always clear to educators just why a phonemic orthography is desirable, and to make matters worse, some writers appear to confuse *phonemic* with *phonetic* transcription, two very different enterprises (Berry 1970). A *phonemic* writing system seeks to represent only the phonological contrasts necessary for native speakers to reconstitute print into language. A writing system in which graphemes parallel the organisation of phonemes in the oral language into meaningful words, phrases and sentences will be psychologically real for native speakers and therefore easiest to learn (Hockett 1960; Sapir 1949; Hyman 1975).

It may be worthwhile, nevertheless, to look at some of the other options available for writing CC, some of which have been used at various times. One, of course, is to spell everything in EE orthography, a relatively easy solution since most CC words have cognates in EE. For those that do not, spellings have to be invented, e.g. *dey* for /de/ 'to be present'. This is essentially the method used in the *Marryshow Readers*, a series of primary school readers developed in Grenada during the revolution. The problem with this series, which is excellent in cultural content, is that children still have to face EE orthography, which makes little sense for English, and even less for Creole.

Another approach to writing Creoles, perhaps the most common one in use, is sometimes referred to as 'eye-dialect'. Here variation from traditional spelling is used to signal perceived pronunciation differences. Often an apostrophe is used to show a 'missing sound', e.g. *an'* for /an/ 'and'. One problem here is that various writers may not agree on which pronunciation differences to emphasise. Another is that Creole written in this system ends up looking like a distortion of English, thereby upholding the deficit mythology. Yet another problem with eye-dialect is that it presupposes a thorough knowledge of the export language's phonology and spelling system - an unrealistic expectation for most Creole speaking children. Still, this is the most widespread way in which Caribbean Creoles have been written.

Once a phonemic approach is decided upon, there is still the question of what symbols to use, and how to assign phonological values to them. The IPA symbols, which are recognised internationally, are available but impractical for everyday use. For the Carriacou project an *ethnophonemic* system was decided upon (Hall 1966, p.41) in which as far as possible only symbols found on a standard English typewriter were used. At the same time, I tried to assign values to the symbols which corresponded, when such correspondence exists, to approximate values in EE, in order to assist in transfer. I did not, however, feel that transfer was worth distorting the structure of CC for, especially as transfer of *process* rather than *detail* was the goal.

The consonants of CC and EE are relatively similar; the CC consonant system looks like this:

p	t	č	k
b	d	ǰ	g
f	s	š	h
v	z	ž	
m	n		j
w	l	y	r

The ethnophonemic CC system looks like this:

p	t	ch	k
b	d	j	g
f	s	sh	h
v	z	zh	
m	n		ng
w	l	y	r

The only 'new' symbol is zh; all others share at least their (approximate) Creole values with EE, though some have additional values in EE as well. Note that some are digraphs.

CC contrasts more radically with EE in the vowel system; as a result the vowels were much more difficult to handle. There are only five vowel symbols on a standard typewriter, and CC has a seven-vowel system. (Actually, [ ] (/r/) is also a central retroflex vowel, but in CC it occurs only in positions occupied by consonants, i.e. before a vowel, and therefore it is analysed phonologically as a consonant.)

```
    i       u
    e       o
    a
```

The problem is in the contrast between the mid and mid-low vowels, both front and back. I tried *ei, ie, ee, ey* for /e/ and *ou, uo, oo, ow* for /o/, but none of these were satisfactory. All imply a glide when what is being represented is a simple vowel. I finally settled on an acute accent, giving é and ó for /e/ and /o/. Of course most typewriters there do not carry an acute accent (lingocentrism is everywhere!) but later with the help of the children we found that a bar (raised hyphen) was just as good and most machines are capable of at least that. So we end up with the following alternative systems:

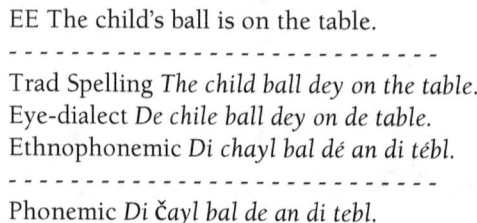

With this as a basic system to work from, the three glides of CC were easy: *av, ov, ow*. The only problem left was the words shared with Creole French; some of these contain contrasts which do not usually occur in CC. For the nasalised vowels, I used the tilde giving ã, ẽ, õ for words like *tetshe* 'tree boa' and *sukuyã* 'vampire'. I also added the glide *ey* for /y/ in words like *soley* 'bigeye fish'.

At this point we might compare the various approaches to writing CC that have been discussed.

EE The child's ball is on the table.
- -
Trad Spelling *The child ball dey on the table.*
Eye-dialect *De chile ball dey on de table.*
Ethnophonemic *Di chayl bal dé an di tébl.*
- -
Phonemic *Di čayl bal de an di tebl.*

Notice that the ethnophonemic system, while based on the structure of the language itself, uses symbols found in the children's environment, with about 85 per cent of the symbols transferable to EE. The vowels transfer less than the consonants but they are within the mainstream of European and African alphabetic tradition, which is more than can be said for traditional English orthography.

Between January and April 1983 the first exposure the children had to their native language written was a mimeographed primer which I called *Karyaku Wod Buk (Carriacou Word Book)* (Appendix 1). The primer used simple line drawings to illustrate sample words; I was careful to use only things which occur in the children's environment and which, presumably, they were familiar with. I tried to illustrate each grapheme in all its possible environments, i.e.

initial, medial and final position.

We began going through the primer, introducing each grapheme and the sample words, and then having the children offer new words which they felt contained the same sound. This led to some refinement of my phonological analysis, as the children's reaction convinced me that the long vowels */ii/ and */aa/ were a figment of my own emic grid. As we progressed through the primer, I made flash cards with all the words in the primer plus all the words contributed by the children. These were subsequently used as a warm-up at the beginning of each class session.

As soon as we had finished going through the primer, we began collecting 'language experience' texts from the children. The first of these was a series of sentences telling us what had happened the previous weekend:

Pipl kil pig 'People killed pigs'
A bék bred Satodé I baked bread on Saturday'
A bin an fishin an a en-kech notin 'I went fishing and I didn't get anything'.

These sentences, and others like them were first written on the board, and then bound into a booklet with a drawing illustrating each sentence; the booklet was then used in class as a reader.

I had a number of folk tales and personal anecdotes collected during field research in Carriacou in 1979. One of these was a story about a *lajables*, the woman with one cloven foot who lures men into the bush and 'scrambles their brains'. This became the second booklet. After this I began collecting stories in the class, either taping them for later transcription or sitting with a small group and writing the story as they dictated it. We soon had enough of these booklets so that all children in the class could be either reading to one another or drilling each other with the flash cards. We also made sentence strips of all the stories so that the children could practice putting the stories back together.

After about six weeks of exposure to written CC I gave the children a word recognition test, in which the task was to circle one of several CC words which correctly corresponded to an adjacent drawing. They surprised me by getting a mean score of 82 per cent (on 20 items), about how they had performed on a similar test in EE. Some observers of the project had predicted that my spelling would 'confuse' the children, but apparently this was not the case.

Towards the end of the 13-week term, some of the stories we had read were collected into a reader and printed on the mimeograph machine so that each child could have a copy. This reader was titled *Kom Le Wi Rid (Let's Read)* and optimistically given the number one.

During the May-July 1983 term a group of children considered to be good readers was added to the project to test their reaction to exposure to their native language. The results were startling. After two days I walked into class and found them reading, fluently, a story accidentally left on the board from the day before. This was not a folktale that 'everybody knows', but rather a personal anecdote. After this I began trying out the system on other already literate Creole speakers. They rarely took more than a few minutes to grasp the new system; some actually told me it was easy to read because it 'feels right' or 'this is the way our language ought to be spelled'. On the other hand, written CC is opaque to most non-Creole speakers, as expected. During this term tests on word recognition, sentence completion, and passage comprehension were all done in CC. Far from being 'confused' the children performed as well or better than they had done in EE. Also their on a reading inventory in EE improved significantly (at the 0.001 level). The September-November 1983 term was to have been the last of the project. It began well. I enlisted the assistance of a local teacher, Ms. Bartholomew, who had impressed me by the ease and fluency with which she was able to read CC after looking at it for only a minute or two. Each day I gave her a rough outline of what I wanted to accomplish, and then observed the session as she carried it out.

It had become obvious by now that some of the children didn't have even the beginnings of an internal model of alphabetic reading. To try to develop this we started off with a heavy dose of phonics drills. At the same time we developed a second mimeographed *Kom Le Wi Rid*, this time with some crossword puzzles and songs as well as two stories in CC and a page of *Patwa*.

One of the stories in the reader was an encounter with a supernatural goat (Appendix 2). On October 18 we began introducing the children to the words they would need to know to read the story. The next day, school children in both Grenada and Carriacou stayed out to protest the house arrest of the Prime Minister, Maurice Bishop. That morning the massacre at Fort Rupert took place, followed by the coup and curfew, followed in turn by the intervention of the US and Caribbean armed forces. School re-opened on 31 October, but the next day US Marines occupied Carriacou. The school grounds and adjoining area were used as a landing field and camp site, and it was impossible to hold classes.

Finally on 8th November, classes started up again, and for the next two weeks or so life was almost normal. We capitalised on the children's new experiences to spell words like *elikapta, marin, jet, parashut*. We continued working through the second reader and for the first time I gave them written questions on the stories. Also in collaboration with a visiting musicologist we produced a booklet containing folk and nation (big drum) songs, in EE as well as CC and *Patwa* (McDaniel and Kephart 1983).

When I was called home to the US in late November, the project was still unfinished, but some tentative conclusions can be still be drawn.

First, based on results of the post-test given at the end of the May term, there is some evidence that learning to read CC was helping the children in their reading of EE. Their improvement was significant at the 0.001 level, while the control group's improvement on the same test was only significant at the 0.1 level.

More important, in my opinion, is the fact the learning to read Creole was not confusing the children; they continued to improve *both* in CC and in EE right through to the end of the project. This runs counter to some of the strongest criticisms of the project by educators who were certain the children would be permanently handicapped by reading Creole English. Just how people could be handicapped by learning to read their native language was (and still is) a mystery to me, but I believe some of the criticism was/is motivated by professional jealousy. Of course there is also sincere concern for the welfare of the children, but when that concern for the children translates into an underestimation of the intelligence and ability of the children to handle information, then it is misdirected.

The role that the prevailing language mythology plays in all this is important. A Grenadian school principal told me her students, who attended a prestigious high school, did not speak Creole even on the street, and furthermore they would not be able to read Creole because their education had moved them too far away from it. I followed some of these students on the street after school and heard them speaking Creole. Then, one afternoon, one of the top first-formers, a 12-year-old girl, was waiting near the office. I gave her a reader to look over, which she did for five minutes or so, and then I asked her if it was easy to read. She said yes. Then I called the principal over and gave the girl a text, which she hadn't seen, and asked her to read it. She did so quite easily and fluently. The principal was surprised, to say the least.

Professional educators, especially English teachers, are sometimes fooled by surface similarity into assuming that they know what a sentence in Creole English means - again, this is a function of the deficit mythology about the nature of Creole English. I once visited a class of 5th-formers and wrote 'They go in the store' on the board, and asked the students what it meant. The teacher, a visitor from England, was quite startled when they told her it was 'they've gone into the store and they're still inside'. The teacher had assumed that CC structure was simply EE without the frills.

Anther point the project tried to make was that it is possible to produce written material from the children's context with equipment generally available in the 'Third World'. The results, of course, are not as slick and colourful as those emanating from the large metropolitan publishing houses. Still, the children enjoyed them and even children not involved directly in the project were constantly asking me for them.

This research hints that giving children in Creole-speaking societies access to literacy through their native language might enhance their education by making it easier for them to construct an internal model of the reading process, which they can then utilise in their encounters with the metropolitan or 'export' language. Of course this is not, ultimately a purely scientific question (Craig 1980). At one level, some of the strongest critics of such an approach are educators who appear to feel threatened when linguists, anthropologists and others venture onto their turf. On another level the assumption that it is a good thing for all people in such societies to learn to read fluently challenges the very foundations on which social stratification and the privilege of the elite class are built.

ACKNOWLEDGEMENT

My interest in Carriacou began as a Peace Corps Volunteer there in 1971-4. The research reported here was supported by two fellowships from the Inter-American Foundation, 1979 and 1982-4. The project would have been impossible without the help of many Carriacou people, who have always made me 'feel homely', but especially the children in the project group, Mr Patrick Compton, the Principal, and the teachers. Of course I must claim full credit for any errors contained herein.

REFERENCES

Berry J. (1970) 'The Making of Alphabets' in Fishman J.A. (ed.) *Readings in the Sociology of Language*. Mouton, The Hague, p.737

Craig D.R. (1980) 'Models for Educational Policy in Creole-Speaking Communities' in Valdman A. and Highfield A. (eds.) *Theoretical Orientations in Creole Studies*. Academic Press, NY, p.245

Downing J. (1979) *Reading and Reasoning*. Springer Verlag, NY

Goodman K. (1970) 'Reading, a Psycholinguistic Guessing Game' in Gunderson D.V. (ed.) *Language and Reading: An Interdisciplinary Approach*. Centre for Applied Linguistics, Washington, p.107

Hall R.A. (1966) *Pidgin and Creole Languages*. Cornell UP, NY

Hancock I.F. (1977) 'Repertory of Pidgin and Creole Languages' in Valdman A. (ed.) *Pidgin and Creole Linguistics*. Indiana UP, Bloomington

Hardman M.J. and Hamano S.S. (1984) *Language Structure Discovery Methods*. Gainesville, dup.

Hockett C.F. (1960) 'The Origin of Speech', *Scientific American*, 203(3), pp.89-96

Hudelson S. (1979) 'Spanish Reading for Spanish Speakers: A Theory and Classroom Implications' in Schafer R.E. (ed.) *Applied Linguistics and Reading*. International Reading Association, Newark, Delaware, p.129

Hyman L.M. (1975) *Phonology, Theory and Analysis*. Holt, Rinehart & Winston, NY

Kephart R.F. (1980) *Preliminary Description of Carriacou Creole*. University of Florida MA Thesis.

Kephart R.F. (1983) 'Bilingual Aspects of Language in a Creole Community' in *Bilingualism: Social Issues and Policy Implications Proceedings of the Southern Anthropological Society*. University of Georgia Press, Athens

Layme F. (1980) *Desarollo del Alfabeto Aymara*. ILCA, La Paz

McDaniel L and Kephart R.F. (1983) *First Carriacou Children's Songbook*. Carriacou, dup.

Pike K. (1976) *Phonemics*. University of Michigan Press, Ann Arbor

Pike K. (1983) 'Conversations with Kenneth Pike', interview by Blair B. in *Languages for Peace*. 1

Pitman Sir J. (1966) 'The Initial Teaching Alphabet in Historical Perspective' in Mazurkiewicz A.J. and Hofstra U. (eds.) *The Initial Teaching Alphabet and the World of English*. The Initial Teaching Alphabet Foundation

Sapir E. (1949) 'The Psychological Reality of Phonemes,' in Mandelbaum D.G. (ed.) *Selected Writings of Edward Sapir*. University of California Press, Berkeley, p.46

Spiro R.J., Bruce C.B. and Brewer W.F. (ed.) (1980) *Theoretical Issues in Reading Comprehension*. Lawrence Erlbaum Associates, Hillsdale, NJ

Valdman A. (1970) *Basic Course in Haitian Creole*. Mouton, The Hague

Appendix 1
Sample pages from the primer *Karyaki Wod Buk*

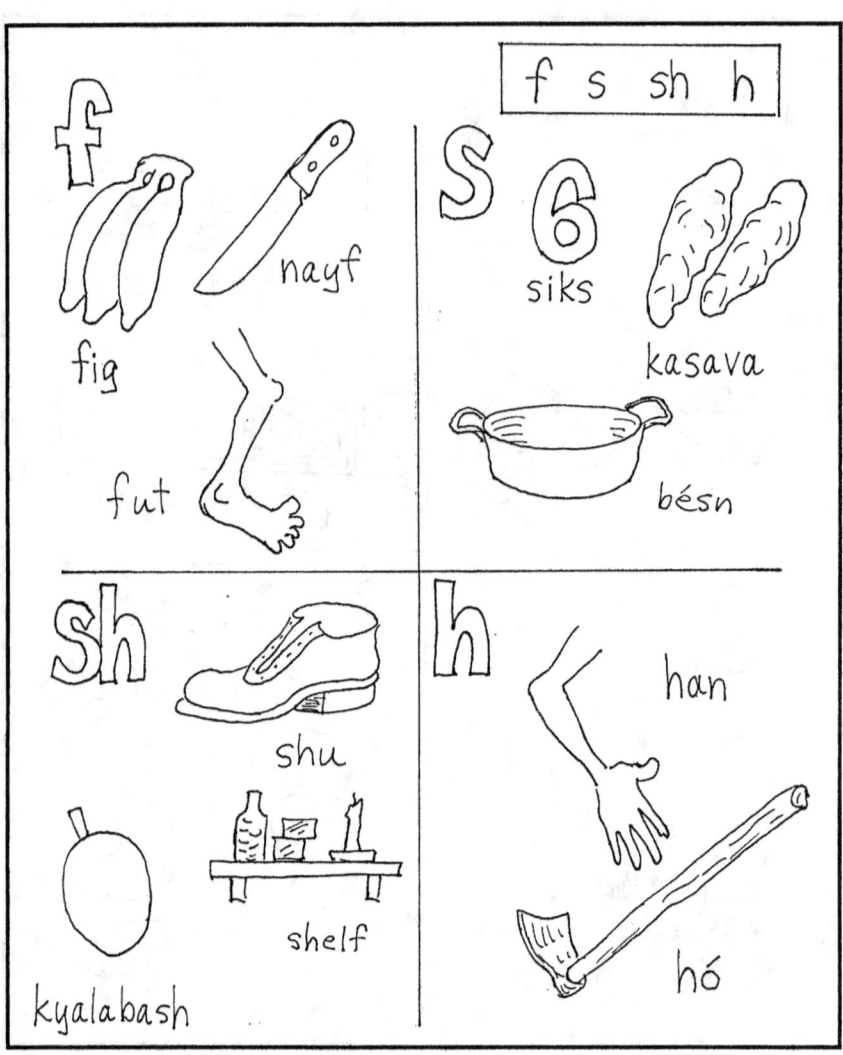

Appendix 2
Story from the second in the series of readers *Kom Le Wid Rid*.

Di Gót

Wan dé, Padli an Móna
kom-owt in skul in Leste.
An di wé hóm dé pas an di bich
an pik gréps.

Wen dé mit bay di gréps-tri
dé mit a big gót.

Di gót sé

"Du yu si big byeds layk diz?
Du yu si big byeds layk diz?
Wen a kot am dé gó wanga ya!
Wen a kot am dé gó wanga ya!"

Dé ron ontil dé mit
in di kras in tong.

-4-

Den dé mit di sém gót agen!
I sé

"Du yu si big tit layk diz?
Du yu si big tit layk diz?
Wen a kot am dé gó wanga ya!
Wen a kot am dé gó wanga ya!"

Den dé ron ontil dé mit hóm.
Dé fal-dong spichles
infront di dó.
Den di granmoda
rob dem dong
wit spirit an laym
an dé tel shi wat apn.

-5-

The Use of Romanes in an Italian School

Jane Dick Zatta

The experience herein related is that of a small group of Gypsy children who attend a public primary school in the village of Piove di Sacco, Padua, Italy. These children were first enrolled in the Italian school system in the year 1970-80, and the introduction of Romanes into their school curriculum dates from 1981-82 (Zatta, 1983). The families of these children belong to the Rom Sloveni group of Gypsies, found primarily in northern Italy and the Slovenia region of Yugoslavia. The Rom Sloveni and other similar Rom groups presently living in Italy, known as Istriani and Hravati, arrived from Yugoslavia about forty years ago as the result of the Nazi-Fascist persecutions of the last war and many of them were confined in concentration camps (Kenrick and Puxon 1972).

Before arriving in Italy, these Rom groups inhabited very well-defined areas of the Slovenia and Istria regions of Yugoslavia, where they lived a semi-nomadic existence working as horse-traders and breaking gravel for road beds. The Rom Sloveni (whose last names are mainly Hudorovich and Braidich) were found in a precise geographical area lying between the rivers Kolpa and Krka from Ljubliana to Vinica, where many of them still live. Their area extended up to, but did not include Karlovacs, which is considered 'nai du maro them'. Their presence in that area dates from at least the first part of the 19th century. Strukelj (1980) cites birth and marriage registers from the first part of the 19th century which refer to the Hudorovich and Braidich as horse traders and healers.

The dialects of Romanes spoken by these groups are related to that of the Arlija in Turkey, and are very similar amongst themselves. In fact they are really varieties of the same dialect rather than separate dialects, in spite of the fact that the Rom themselves consider the various groups absolutely distinct. The differences in the dialects consist in some difference in lexis and slight discrepancies in tense formation and prepositions. Often the differences with regard to vocabulary concern Slavic loan words.

Both the differences and the similarities are ascribable to the situation of the Rom in Yugoslavia, where the groups of Rom in question were distributed in very small and strictly defined geographical areas. The rigid and long-standing segregation of the different groups in very small areas allowed for the groups to develop difference amongst themselves even though they lived in close proximity to one another.

When the Rom came to Italy they tended to confirm their preference for a strict territorial division. After an inevitable initial period of confusion and overlap, they sorted themselves out into various distinct geographical areas, and the itineries covered by these groups are anything but haphazard. Certain zones are typical of certain family groups. For example, Piove di Sacco is Hudorovich territory while Codevigo, which is only three km distant, is Stoiko (Istriana) territory. Thus certain terms, although they are understood by the Hudorovich, would never be used by them and are considered to be Istriani, while other terms are not even understood. In addition there is a certain 'grey area' of words which are considered more or less suitable to one language but are nevertheless used by the other group. This is also the inevitable result of intermarriage, in addition to other factors. For example, the word 'murdari' (to kill) is considered to be Histriani by many Rom, and the Sloveni prefer 'nasali' or even 'mari'. However 'murdalo' crops up in their speech as an adjective. The Rom Sloveni (and similar groups) have preserved extremely insular and fragmented life-styles. The typical group structure consists of clusters of nuclear families living in close proximity to other members of the extended family. Thus certain malapropisms come to characterise particular family groups. Examples within the group in Piove di Sacco are: *goccia* (for *doccia*) and *lenamento* (for *allenamento*).

The history of the Rom Sloveni living in Piove di Sacco is typical of the Rom Sloveni in Italy. The group is composed of an elderly 'phurano dat', Rave (Antonio) Hudorovich, 66 years, his wife Tsiko (Angela), 65 years, and their nine children with their respective families which include 26 grandchildren and two great-grandchildren. In addition to the Hudorovich clan, there are frequent visits (called 'gal ladi') from other members of the extended family, which typically last from a few weeks to a few months. Rave and Tsiko were among the Rom brought to Italy in 1942 and interned in the concentration camp at Tossicia. After escaping from the concentration camp following the Italian armistice in 1943, Rave and his family made their way back to northeastern Italy where they travelled between Milan, Ferrara, Bologna, Udine, Bolzano, Verona, Padova, and Venice, following the calendar of the local markets. The conditions of Italy immediately following the war were well-suited to the traditional life-style of the Gypsies. In a prevalently illiterate, agriculturally-based society (where economic transactions were direct and unburdened by bureaucratic regulations) their profession as horse-traders, in which their fabled ability is no myth, made them useful participants in the society of the time. The slow, wandering pace of the journey in horse-drawn wagons meant that no economic investment was necessary for this activity, and horses were simply left to graze by the side of the road, or turned loose in farmers' fields at night. The physical configuration of the landscape with abundant open spaces allowed the Roms to make their camps at a certain distance from inhabited areas, a fact which, together with the temporary nature of their presence and the usefulness of their occupation caused them to be tolerated by the Gaje, with whom the Rom had achieved a certain equilibrium.

Urbanisation and industrialisation in the past forty years have however profoundly changed society, causing crisis in the Rom culture, in spite of its tremendous vitality and historical ability to adapt. The advent of the motor car, which quickly monopolised the roads, marked the end of the horse-trading economy, not so much because automobiles and tractors made the horse obsolete (there is still a market for horses as meat animals, and recently there has been a great increase in the interest in horse-racing) but because the impossibility of a leisurely journey in horse-drawn wagons meant that the Rom had to own land on which to keep their horses.

The increase in the general level of education, a process from which the Rom were excluded, corresponded to an increased regulation and complexity of economic relations. The impossibility of obtaining necessary permits, and of meeting the bureaucratic requirements of private ownership are important factors which prevent the Rom, almost 100% illiterate, from engaging in various independent commercial activities. In addition the open spaces once available to the Rom for their campsites were swallowed up by spreading urbanisation, causing the disintegration of family groups with the consequent lack of social control, fundamental condition for the conservation of values and norms of behaviour upon which the Rom society is based.

The situation of the Hudorovich clan in the area of Piove di Sacco is typical of the problems faced by the Rom in Italy. Rave and his family are one of the few Rom groups who have stubbornly preserved the traditional profession of horse-trading, in spite of the difficulties that this involved. Rave first began visiting Piove di Sacco in the 1950s, drawn there by the presence of a bi-weekly livestock market, one of the largest in the province. He began to gravitate more or less permanently to the zone of Piove di Sacco in the 1970s. Rave, who has never learned to drive a car, had come to a tacit agreement with the mayor of Piove di Sacco who let him keep several horses within the area of the livestock market, and allowed Rave to camp in the vicinity. His children, however, were never tolerated for long, and like most Rom in Italy who still cling to a traditional life-style, they were forced by threats and eviction notices to move about continually. Piove di Sacco, which was once the heart of an agricultural district, is typical of the process of urbanisation. Agricultural activity had declined, while undisciplined construction of blocks of flats and small industries has radically changed the landscape. The economy has changed from agricultural to commercial as Piove di Sacco has increasingly become a dormitory town for Padova. These changes brought about a dramatic worsening of the relationship between the Rom and the Gaje. The Rom were forced to split up into small groups of one or two caravans because of the difficulty of finding a campsite. The new configuration of the landscape meant that the Rom must inevitably camp in close proximity to the Gaje or resort to dangerous and undesirable locations such as refuse dumps. Deprived of a useful function in the society, and of a valid means of economic survival, the younger Rom relied increasingly on importunity and petty thievery for survival. No longer necessary, they were viewed by the Gaje as a nuisance and the arrival of a caravan was swiftly followed by the arrival of the carabinieri with an eviction notice. The Rom then moved to a new location where the process was repeated.

In 1970, several people sympathetic to the problems of the Rom began to press the administration to recognise the right of the Hudorovich family to stop in Piove di Sacco, and to create a campsite for them. In spite of numerous problems including a widespread and deeply-rooted hostility on the part of the local population towards Gypsies, as of 1980 members of the Hudorovich family were no longer evicted from the territory of Piove di Sacco, while the camp became a reality in 1981. At the present in the territory known as 'Piovese' there are three camps besides the one in Piove di Sacco (a fourth, at Codevigo) has been under discussion for the past three years). Rom children are enrolled in schools in four different communities. In addition the Veneto Region has just passed a law in favour of the Rom, the first in Italy, which recognises the right to the preservation of their culture, to nomadism as a way of life, and provides financing for the creation of campsites. The proposal for this law was written by my husband, Dr Paolo Zatta, and dedicated to the memory of Derek Tipler.

It was in this context of rejection, economic distress, and the risk of progressive internal destabilisation due to the dispersion of the family group that the education of the Rom children in Piove di Sacco was begun in 1979. On a national level the education of Gypsy children is most notable for its failure. In 1981 a study carried out by the Opera Nomadi for the Lazio Region revealed that 75% of Gypsy children did not attend school at all during the school year 1979-80, that only 8.02% of Gypsies completed the first five classes, while a mere 1.34% had completed compulsory education which in Italy is eight years, divided in five elementary classes and three middle school classes, covering ages six to fourteen. Another study completed by the Opera Nomai in 1984 looked at 1176 Gypsy children enrolled in the school throughout Italy for the school year 1982-83.

This study showed that 36.9% of the children were enrolled in the first class, 21.43% were enrolled in the 2nd class, 15.31% in the third class, 12.41% in the fourth class, and 12.24% in the fifth class. Another 1.7% were enrolled in some sort of special class, while there was no significant presence of the Gypsy children in either the pre-school (ages 3-6) or the middle school (Zannatta, 1984).

Recently there has been growing recognition of the fact that the main responsibility for this failure lies in the inability of the educational institution to mediate between the cultural system of the Rom and that of the Gaje, making the Gaje culture with its emphasis on the symbolic and the abstract inaccessible to the Rom, and at the same time recognising the reaffirming the value, point of view, traditions, language and history of the Rom. On the one hand, the school is not able to guarantee sufficient scholastic achievement to hypothesise a real economic alternative for the Rom, and on the other hand one of the main reasons why Gypsies resist the education of their children is that it is seen by them (correctly) as a menace to the survival of their own culture.

Mirella Karpati (1982) pointed out that the education of Gypsy children is most widespread in those contexts where the Gypsy children's culture has been almost totally destructured, and the Gypsies amalgamated into the lowest levels of urban ghettos (with all the negative connotations that this implies) while the Gypsy groups which have maintained the social structure solidly intact, where traditional values are still strong, are the most reluctant to send their children to school, although they would be willing to have a school at the camp under their supervision. At the National Residential Course for Elementary School Teachers of Gypsy Children, many teachers reported the fear expressed by Gypsy parents that allowing their children to attend the Gaje school would cause them to grow up as Gaje, and renounce their identity as Rom. This rejection by the Rom of a school they feel threatens their culture is extremely encouraging and a sign of the vigour which the Rom culture in Italy still possesses, in spite of profound economic crisis. In recent years the Opera Nomadi has recommended that teachers for Gypsy children be specifically trained in the Rom culture, and this recommendation was partially recognised by the convention signed between the Opera Nomadi and Minister of Public Education in 1982 which recognises the Gypsies as an ethnic minority with the right (in principle) to specifically trained teachers.

Such training is necessary, if affirmations of the rights of ethnic minorities to the preservation of their culture are to be given any consideration other than declarations of principle. A teacher who is ignorant of the language, culture and history of the Rom tends to approach their education with the aim (even if unconscious) of wiping out all previous learning, including language, viewed as 'wrong' in the context of Gaje culture. A teacher for example, with no training in Romanes, an oral language where the phenomenon of metathesis is common, is unable to distinguish between learning difficulties such as dyslexia and dysgraphia, and problems caused by interference between two different language-codes, common to all bilingual children. Moreover, he is blind to the products, characteristics, values and modes of transmission of a culture of which he knows nothing. Every deviation from the norm (a word to which an ethnocentric interpretation is given) is deplored and related to common negative stereotypes of Gypsies. The children who experience this type of education are the victims of double rejection, once because of the social conditions in which they live, and secondly within the school which treats their cultural identity with scorn, presents the Gaje models and roles as the only ones possible, evaluates the children in terms of their failure to reproduce these models, and teaches them the inferiority of their origin and way of life. The year-end report of one auxiliary teacher responsible for the first school experience of ten Rom Sloveni (or Istriani) children ranging in age from 6-14 illustrates the absolute necessity of, in the first place, a knowledge of at least the most basic notions of Rom culture, history and language in order to present the children with a positive sense of their own identity, reaffirm the essential traits of this identity, and teach new skills by building on those abilities the children already possess. The teacher displays negative attitudes towards Gypsies typical of many teachers, as well as ignorance of Rom language and culture:

> The life-style [of Gypsies] negatively influences the scholastic achievement of their children, who seem in fact to be maladjusted. By scholastic maladjustment is meant the incapacity of children to observe the most common norms of conduct required by the scholastic community, and to acquire the basic learning taught by the school. This maladjustment derives principally from their social origins.
>
> In the nomad group the level of aspiration is low, the attitude towards culture and towards the school is indifferent, producing in the children insufficient motivation for learning.
>
> All of these negative factors observable in the group of nomads have created disadvantages for the children. At school the children are easily distracted, they have trouble learning, they have difficulty in acquiring the various skills, they have trouble conceptualising, exemplifying, expressing opinions, making comparisons, drawing conclusions from data examined.
>
> Other examples typical of maladjusted children are: aggressiveness, shown as opposition towards the teacher and towards discipline in general; they were in fact rude, disobedient, at times insolent; their unstability was shown by their incapacity to pay attention, they are in fact always nervous, in constant movement, unable to control themselves; apathy, which consists in being unresponsive to external stimulation - they showed no reaction, they were mentally absent.

The severer the rejection of the Rom, the more necessary is the introduction of specific cultural material. As this report shows, the material and objective problems, as grave as they often are, are the most easily solved. Far more difficult is creating a learning environment which is friendly, positive, encouraging and motivating, and it is this lack which bears the largest responsibility for the failure of the Gaje school to interest the Rom.

LANGUAGE AND LANGUAGE USE AMONG THE ROM SLOVENI

The use of Romanes involves children in all five primary school classes. Twelve Rom children have been involved. None have dropped out, although one moved to a new location within the area of Piove di Sacco just distant enough to mean attending a different school. Another child completed the requirements for an elementary school certificate last year while one who completed the elementary course this year plans to attend the middle school. Preliminary contacts have already been made in the hope of continuing the experience on the middle school level. The interest in the experience of Piove di Sacco has led to its repetition with Gypsy children enrolled in primary schools in Vicenza. Another elementary school in Piove di Sacco, where no

Gypsy children were enrolled, used some of the material produced in the context of a research project dedicated to the Gypsies as a part of their history program. This project, carried out by two fourth classes, involved, among other things, interviewing more than four hundred people in Piove di Sacco and inviting a Rom Kalderash to the school to give a demonstration of copper-working and answer questions about the language, traditions and history of the people.

The use of Romanes material was differentiated according to class level, but it was normally used in two situations: both in class, in the Italian version, and in Romanes in the group of Rom children who are reunited three times a week for half an hour sessions dedicated to Romanes. The objectives of the use of this material are both cultural and technical, addressed to the Gaje and the Rom. As has already been pointed out, promoting a positive attitude towards the Rom culture both in the eyes of the Gaje and the eyes of the Rom children is a top priority in the education of these children. When the Rom children first came to school, even the smallest were well aware of the status of the Rom within the community and showed marked signs of insecurity in the Gaje school. They adapted defensive strategies which in the littlest ones consisted of trying to escape notice as much as possible while the older ones reacted with aggressive behaviour. One child tried to 'camouflage' herself as a Gaji, refusing to go home after school, refusing to play with her fellow Rom, spending as much time as possible at the homes of classmates or teachers, and refusing to let her schoolmates visit her at the camp. Positive, credible models, were necessary to offset the negative stereotypes and reflect the lives of the Rom in terms of the problems they face, their feelings, fears, joys hopes and so on. Generally this sort of insight is provided by literature but the Gaje literature regarding the Rom is almost exclusively negative or fantastic-folkloristic. The latter is if anything even more harmful than the first, since the aspects seen as 'positive' are exactly those which are the most unrealistic and the underlying unspoken message is that nothing can be said for real Gypsies. The Rom children needed to be shown that the values and actions of their culture can be respected by the Gaje too. In addition the Rom children needed motivating, meaningful material from which to acquire basic language skills including reading and writing. The most authentic, reliable and by far the most interesting material of this nature could only be provided by the Rom themselves.

Another objective was to point out to the Gaje children the multiplicity of human experience, expressed in a wealth of different languages and cultures, evidence of the richness of human nature. Exposing the children to the at times complex conventions of the oral tradition of a culture apparently without 'culture' made them reflect on the reasons behind certain conventions in their own language. The children were encouraged to see that no culture is 'better' or 'worse' than another, but that every culture represents another facet of the inexhaustible resourcefulness of the human spirit, and that the diversity of human expression is an enrichment for everyone. As a consequence, the children were brought to realise that prejudice and hostility were the fruits of ignorance (as was shown by the research project the children carried out). These experiences were then plugged back into the school curriculum, and used to help the children understand the reasons behind certain historical events.

From a technical point of view the Gaje children were given a few elementary notions about languages: that languages involve not only different 'words' but also different structures, and above all represent different points of view. Some of the characteristics of the oral tradition of the Rom were pointed out and their function in an oral literature were explained (especially as regards the use of verb tenses). To give the children the chance of seeing these features many of the grammatical and syntactical particularities of the Rom stories were translated literally in the Italian versions, and the children, once they had become aware of some of the characteristics of the Rom tradition, were asked to identify instances in other stories. This experience, which was limited to the fourth and fifth classes was in the context of the language education program, where the children were often asked to analyse the techniques used to create a certain effect, attempt themselves to write for a specific purpose, and analyse the reasons for the success or failure of that attempt. It is important that the presence of Rom children in the classroom be seen as a cultural resource for the Gaje children, where the process of learning is one of exchange and mutual enrichment, and not simply viewed as an intellectual handout that the Gaje concede to the Rom.

From the point of view of the Rom, linguistic education has two objectives. One is obviously the development of a degree of competence sufficient to enable them to communicate effectively with the Gaje society, both on an oral and a written level. Many times the Rom themselves diagnose their needs simply in terms of knowing how to read the write, without realising the degree of linguistic competence necessary to, say, fill out an application for public housing, enrol in the public health service, obtain a licence for a commercial activity, write an effective letter of protest, and so on. Language education is however the area in which Rom children have the greatest degree of difficulty. In the previously mentioned study carried out by the Opera Nomadi for the M.P.I. in 1981 70% of teachers interviewed cited language as the area where the Rom children had the least success. Insufficient language competence precludes the study of other subjects such as history or science, where language is not the subject but the vehicle of learning, and failure in this area is one of the main reasons that Rom children fail to reach higher than the first few classes of the elementary school.

At the same time, Italian must not be acquired at the expense of the children's mother tongue, but on the contrary, education should reinforce, not destroy, the children's abilities in their own language. The Rom Sloveni, who have no tradition of anything that could be called fiction, nevertheless have an oral tradition with a particular function and role within their culture which is governed by a series of very precise norms. The attitude of the Rom Sloveni towards the narrative function of language differs profoundly from that of Western tradition, both from the point of view of the purpose of narration, and from the point of view of the stylistic and linguistic elements by which that purpose is achieved. Thus the Romanes speaking children who attend the Italian schools must cope not only with interference deriving from the grammatical differences between Romanes and Italian, interference which reveals itself at the sentence level, but far more importantly, with the different concepts of the purpose and characteristics of narration. As would be expected, the linguistic and stylistic features of an oral language are vastly different from those of a written one. Carry-over of Romanes characteristics in Italian causes problems in communicating correctly in Italian, while at the same time imposition of Italian standards causes backlash interference, corroding the child's linguistic abilities in his native tongue. From the technical point of view then, Romanes was used as the basis for contrastive analysis with Italian, pointing out to the children the different characteristics of the two language codes. Romany oral texts provided by adult relatives of the children were recorded, transcribed, translated into Italian and used as the basis for discussion, composition and grammar work, both in the Romanes version in the time dedicated to Romanes, and in the Italian version with the whole class.

From the point of view of Italian, the main areas of difficulty which the Rom children encounter are in syntax, the sequence of verb tenses, the use of prepositions, problems in lexis caused by the codification of certain Italian malapropisms which the children are then unwilling to change and misuse of other vocabulary due to Romanes interference. Other problems of conventions of style arise at the text level, which will be treated later. From the point of view of Romanes corruption of vocabulary results from the facts that sedentarisation has a detrimental effect on the oral tradition and that prolonged exposure to the Gaje language in the school causes the children to substitute even basic vocabulary items with Italian. For example, it was found, during work on the stories in Romanes, that the children did not know the Romanes words used in the stories for 'forest' (veš, and 'wolf' (ruv). Forests and wolves were part of the experience of the grandparents in Yugoslavia and are not part of the experience of either the parents or the children. However the parents know these words and were quite surprised to find that their children did not. In fact, in the past story-telling was often sparked by the meeting with other Rom during the journey, moments in which the entire group would gather together. Sedentarisation has drastically reduced travelling and thus also encounters with other groups, to the detriment of the oral tradition and thus to the language. In addition even words which the children know are sometimes substituted in Italian.

THE LANGUAGE

This Romany dialect is considered by some scholars (Giulio Soravia and Rade Uhlik) to be among the most interesting and archaic of the dialects of Romanes spoken in Europe. All eight noun cases, including the vocative, are normally used, and pronominal and adjectival modifiers including demonstrative adjectives and indefinite articles, are always fully inflected.

The following is an example of the declension of a noun:

Singular

rom (man)	romni (woman)
nom: rom	nom. romni
gen: romeskero	gen. romniakero
dat: romeske	dat. romniake
acc: rome	acc. romnia
voc: same as nom	voc. same as nom
abl: romestar	abl. romniatar
loc: romeste	loc. romniate
instr: romeha	inst. romniaha

Plural

nom: roma	nom: romnia
gen: romengero	gen: romniengero
dat: romenge	dat: romnienge
acc: romen	acc: romnien
voc: romale	voc: romniale
abl: romendar	abl: romniendar
loc: romende	loc: romniende
instr: romenza	instr: romnienza

The locative case is used as basis for the circumlocution for the verb 'to have' - *mande hilo, tute hile, leste hilo*, etc., which means literally 'to me there is' and is also the basis for other expressions such as 'to be afraid', 'to be ashamed', etc. In addition the locative case is used after prepositions, when these are followed by a pronoun. However when these same prepositions are followed by a noun, the nominal case is used.

Many times the locative case is used interchangeably with the accusative: *mre čave aven mande hiken; mande hine dar ti avar roma mande na maren*. In other cases these same verbs take the accusative case: *marja le pudiniaha, hikia la*, etc.

The dative case is used for the indirect object, and also for an impersonal construction which replaces the genitive especially for parts of the body: *činja leske men* (it cut his throat); *gajake peli tele borsa* (to the woman the bag fell down).

The instrumental case means 'with', both means and company. *Kame jas dade'ha?* - 'Do you want to go with Daddy?'; *čave gele pu drom kolinza* - 'The children went on the road with bicycles'.

The ablative case means 'of' or 'from' but is not used to express the partitive. *Meru trusatar* means 'I'm dying of thirst' while *kastestar kerdo* means 'made of wood'. It is also used as the second term in comparisons without 'neko' (than).

The accusative case is used for the direct object with animate nouns. However the nominative rather than the accusative is often used even in the case of animate nouns when they are Slavic or Italian loan words. In fact the accusative tends to be reserved for pronouns and for a limited number of Indian origin animates.

The Use of Romanes in an Italian School

The genitive case is used to indicate possession as are the personal pronouns and is usually interchangeable with them. Possessive adjectives are inflected to form possessive pronouns.

The vocative is used for addressing people in the plural. *Ehi čavale! Po miro!* ('Hey children! Be still!') *Ehi romale! Kai hinien?* ('Hey, everybody! Where are you?')

The use of prepositions substituted in many cases by inflections in Romanes is a cause of interference. Children tend to use verbs with prepositions that correspond to the case the verb requires in Romanes. For example the verb 'to ask' in Italian requires the preposition 'a' while in Romanes it takes the ablative case, corresponding to the preposition 'di' (of). Thus the Rom children say 'chiedere di Nino' (which actually means 'ask about Nino') instead of 'chiedere a Nino'. Other times inappropriate prepositions are used. In Romanes the preposition 'near' *paše* is also used to express 'at' in the sense of 'at someone's house'. The corresponding preposition in Italian is 'da'. The children say 'I left my sweater near Nita' instead of 'I left my sweater at Nita's'.

Experience has shown that simple exposure to Italian at school is not sufficient to correct these mistakes, also because the children are continually exposed to the same mistakes in the speech of their parents. Therefore it is necessary that the mistakes be pointed out and the correct use of troublesome prepositions practiced. On the other hand the case system is the aspect of Romanes structure which is the most vulnerable to prolonged contact with the Gaje language. There is a notable difference between the use of inflections by adults and the children who have been in school for several years, who tend increasingly to substitute Italian prepositions especially for the ablative, genitive and instrumental cases.

In comparison to other Romanes dialects, the Sloveni dialect has a rich tense system. It contains in fact five verb tenses: present, past, imperfect, and conditional. The use of verb tenses is one of the most complex problems the Rom children have, especially when writing Italian, but this depends more on customs of usage in Romanes than lack of correspondence with Italian tenses. In general the sequence of tenses is not the same as in written languages, and there are frequent tense switches within the same text. It is possible to make several observations about Romanes tense sequence. 1) In narrating past events, generally the 'scene is set' by beginning the story in the past. Thereafter the tense frequently switches to the present to heighten the dramatic event. 2) After the conjunction 'ti' (introducing a dependent clause) the verb occurs in the present tense. 3) Tense switches usually regard single sentences rather than passages. Usually the first verb is in the past the second in the present tense. This characteristic enlivens and narrative without causing confusion.

One exception to this is the formation of the conditional in and the subordinate clause, literally 'If I wouldn't have loosened the harness the horse would have drowned'. In Italian the verb in the subordinate clause should be in the subjunctive, whereas the Rom children use the conditional twice. Some problems are caused by the missing tenses, especially the use of the past perfect in indirect speech, which is not used in Romanes. The following is an example of the conjugation of a verb:

Cini (to buy or to cut)

Present	Imperfect
meni činu~	meni činave
tuni čine	tuni činse
ov/oi čini	ov/oi činie
ame činan	ame činane
tume činen	tume činene
oni činen	oni činene

Future	Past
meni činava	meni činjum
tuni činsa	tuni činjas
ov/oi činia	ov/oi činja
ame činana	ame činjamo
tume činena	tume činde
oni činena	oni činde

Conditional
meni činjome
tuni činjese
ov/oi činjele
ame činjeme
tume činjene
oni činjene

Rom Sloveni also has several irregular and defective verbs such as the verbs that mean the affirmative and negative of 'can' in addition to several verbs such as 'to like', 'to love', 'to dislike' and 'to need' which are expressed with impersonal or adverbial forms. In addition the Rom Sloveni dialect has several verbs which change their meaning when followed by a prepositional or adverbial particle, as is the case with English phrasal verbs: 'pick up' (*lel upre*), 'fall down' (*peri tele*), 'clean out' (*koöi avri*), 'turn out' (*avi avri*), 'look like', (*hiki sar*), and 'look after' (*hiki palal*) are all phrasal verbs that Romanes shares with English. Other examples are 'kedi tele' which means 'to pick' (while kedi alone means 'to read') and 'hik
' which means 'to see' while 'hik nu' means 'to look at'. The existence of phrasal verbs greatly increases the expressive range of a limited number of lexical items: in Italian specific verbs are used in each case. The children translate these forms directly into Italian where they either have no meaning or a literal one. The Italian translation of 'look after' literally means 'look behind'.

Undoubtedly the most problematic area of Italian grammar for Rom children is syntax. Owing to the extensive case system in Romanes, word position in the sentence is not essential to understanding relationships and word order is extremely variable. The most usual sequence is SVO which occurs approximately twice as often as SOV. However, SOV syntax accounts for at least one third of the sentences. In general adjectives precede nouns and adverbs precede the verb, even displacing the direct object, which results in sentences like this: 'Me le pu dume piralave' ('I him on my back carried.') The direct object can occur anywhere in the sentence, and its position does not depend on whether it is a noun or a pronoun. Sometimes the direct object even precedes the subject: 'Joka le oni lindíupre' - 'So it they picked up.'

When there is an indirect object, it can often precede the subject: 'Onda menge gaje dene' (Then to us the Gaje gave). Although in some cases the direct object is found in the locative case rather than the accusative (and occasionally it can be found in the dative: 'kere leske sar kolo' - 'make it like a wheel') this does not seem to depend on the position of the pronoun in the sentence. For example, 'late haia pu pro' and 'haia late pu pro' are equally acceptable, as are 'aven mande hiken' ('they come to see me') or 'Tu na trome tra daia hike' ('you must not see your mother').

When there is an indirect object, it precedes the direct object in most cases: 'habe ˇcavorenge mangave, grasteske kas' ('Food for the children I asked for, for the horses hay'); - 'čivle lake pro pu per' ('he put to her the foot on the stomach') - 'motavu tuke storia di mro dat' ('I'll tell you a story of my father'), 'na kerle čavoreske nici' ('he didn't do the boy anything').

However the most characteristic feature of the syntax is the position of the adverb, which almost always occurs at the beginning of the sentence, preceding the verb, which is often the last word in the sentence. 'Su pre romen astarle' ('By the feet the Rom [he] seized'); 'čes nakia' ('by he passed'); anu iama peium ('in a hole I fell'); 'Kote ka habe andre hilo' ('there where the food inside is'); 'pu koa baro stolo gaje tarjoven ka kossen doa praho, du angole maren' ('on the tall chair the Gaje stand when they clean that dust, in the corners they clean.') The syntax used by the children reflects Romany preference for placing adverbial qualifiers at the beginning of the sentence. Statements such as 'Tu con me non mai giochi' ('You with me never play.') and 'Fuori tutto hanno preso' ('Out everything they took') are common.

Another feature of the syntax is the omission in certain cases of the verb and of the direct object when these can be inferred. Although the verb most usually omitted is 'to be', other verbs are also occasionally omitted. In the sentence 'ov nu doa talik andre' ('he in that jacket inside') the verb omitted is 'went'. The omission of the verb (and occasionally the direct object) on the part of the children is very frequent as the examples included show, and is a major problem in the production of correct Italian written work.

The adjective of quantity, 'keči', which means 'how much' and 'how many' may be separated from the noun it modifies 'kečiame puta nakane?' ('how many we times passed by!' and 'keči gaje love menge dene!' ('How much the Gaje money gave us!').

The children tend to use Rom syntax when writing in Italian, especially as regards the placement of adjectives and adverbs which normally follow the nouns and verbs in Italian. 'You with me never play' and 'Behind jumped one on him' are typical examples. In addition the children frequently omit the verb and other linking devices such as conjunctions. In the sentence 'The Rom slowly the pistol out' the child omitted the verb 'took'. In proper Italian (or English) the two verbs in the sentence 'The man jumped, jumped.' would be separated by a conjunction.

Other serious problems are caused by tense sequence. In Rom Sloveni, as has already been mentioned, tense sequence is not the same as in written languages and switches from past to present, often within the same sentence, are used to achieve particular purposes within the Sloveni narrative tradition. These criteria in the use of verb tenses are applied by the children when writing in Italian. For example, 'Ancor quel gatto 'disturboso'' (the word 'disturboso' is not possible in Italian) che si flegato tutto e si vuole liberare ma non poteva liberarsi' ('And still that peaky cat that tied himself all up and he wants to free himself but he couldn't free himself'). In addition, 'ti' in Romanes, which corresponds to 'che' in Italian and 'that' in English and is non-omissible, takes the present tense even when the main verb is in the past. For example: 'Oi na jangha ti hilo mulo' ('She didn't know that he is dead') and 'Oni mislinde ti hili matčha' ('They thought that is a fish').

Other problems regard lexis. A relatively minor problem is the misuse of vocabulary due to translating Romanes idiomatic expressions directly into Italian. For instance, the Rom say 'I drank a pill' instead of 'I took a pill' as is said in Italian or English. In Romanes, which is a language with a limited lexis, one verb often expresses a range of meanings in different circumstances. An example is the verb 'meki' - 'to let'. From time to time, with and without the reflexive pronoun 'pe', 'meki' can mean 'allow', 'release', 'streak' (run very fast), 'lose control', etc. The children often use the corresponding verb in Italian with some of the meanings it has in Romanes, but which are not possible in Italian. In addition, the Rom Sloveni dialect normally does not use the definite article, and the children tend to consider it as a part of the word, and write it as one word.

A more serious problem is caused by malapropisms of Italian words. Romanes, and especially the Rom Sloveni dialect, typically absorbs words from the Gaje language into its lexis which are then Romanised by Romanes morphemes. This dialect is particularly rich in morphemes, and the habit of incorporating Slavic and Italian loan words, which can be conjugated or declined or otherwise changed by Romanes morphemes is a sign of the vigour of the language. Many times the words are then adapted and simplified according to the Romanes phonetic system. They then become characteristic of particular family groups, and even of a group of Rom in a whole area. Amongst the Rom Sloveni belonging to the Hudorovich clan in the cities (at least) of Piove di Sacco, Verona, and Udine, the Italian word 'doccia' (shower) is pronounced 'goccia', the word 'dondola' is pronounced 'gondola' and the word 'vomitare' (vomit) is pronounced 'gomitare (elbow)'. These are but a few of extremely numerous examples. The children then insist that the word as it is used in the Rom group is 'right' and refuse the standard Italian pronunciation and spelling. A solution to this problem is accepting the Rom variant as 'correct in Romanes' and proposing the standard Italian pronunciation and spelling as 'correct in Italian'.

Another problem in metathesis. This phenomenon is extremely frequent in the Rom Sloveni dialect, and many words are indifferently pronounced in one way or another. For example one can say 'gajendar' or 'gajendra' absolutely interchangeably, and often in the same breath a person will pronounce the word twice in two different ways. Since there is no written code of reference, there is not the unequivocal defining standard the Gaje expect, and metathesis is not a discriminating criterion. When the children speak Italian, they have the same casual approach towards the inversion of letters, both when speaking and writing. To them the difference between say 'platea' and 'paltea' is insignificant.

ROM SLOVENI NARRATIVE TRADITION

In contrast to other Rom groups which have an oral literature represented by stories, songs, poems and so forth, there is no corpus of codified myths of tales and no tradition of fables or any sort of fictional narrative amongst the Rom Sloveni. Nevertheless, there is an oral tradition amongst the Rom Sloveni which is governed by precise norms and conventions and which plays a fundamental role in the transmission of the cultural values and historic memory of the group. The purpose of narration amongst the Rom Sloveni is didactic - it aims to transmit the experiences and attitudes of the group and to influence the behaviour of the listener rather than simply to amuse or entertain. The prime and indeed the only criterion for the subject matter of a story is that what is told must be 'the truth'. From listening to the true stories of the lives of other Rom one learns how to live. Therefore, anyone who tells lies could hold enormous responsibility for the wrong choices made by whoever believes him, and in general, the habit of telling lies is associated with the Gaje. Any story which does not propose to tell the truth is seen by the Rom as an attempt to deceive or mislead, a fact which leads them to consider our narrative fiction as 'lies' or at the most magnanimous, as 'jokes'. Any story which resembles a fable or folk-tale is greeted with scorn and the comment 'he probably read it in the newspaper' is an unequivocal declaration of mendacity. In fact, those Rom who know how to read are often regarded with suspicion as it is felt that knowing how to read makes one vulnerable to the 'lies' of the Gaje. The implications for the children's attitude towards the 'narration' offered by the Gaje society are profound.

The Rom guarantee the truth of their stories in two ways. The first is the habit of accompanying them with a ritualistic oath affirming the truthfulness of what is about to be told, usually 'Ti muli Monia mri' ('That my Monia dead may be', Monia being the name of the narrator's youngest child) or 'Sa mre mule' ('All my dead ones') or 'Te khalavu ti meru' ('May I die if I am lying'). Besides swearing on his children or dead ones, the narrator guarantees the truthfulness of what he is telling in another important way: there is a very close identity between the narrator and his tale. One generally relates only one's own personal experiences, for, as the Rom say, 'kon jani kon hine' - 'who was there knows'. One may also relate stories told by one's parents whose stories are, so to speak, 'inherited' by their children. The narrator then is also usually the main character of the story and his honour speaks for its truthfulness. As the close identity of the story with its narrator is a guarantee of truthfulness, the quality of realism typical of Western literary tradition is irrelevant. Thus we find in 'Gaji Porini' [Appendix A] that the snake weighs two hundred pounds, is as big as a caravan, and runs after the protagonist 'as fast as a man'. Often the stories are openly contradictory. The number of bandits in 'Mro Dat' [Appendix A] varies from ten to twenty in various parts of the story. Many of the stories are about demons and ghosts and other mythical events such as women who suckle snakes or leeches being prescribed by doctors in Milan - all recounted as being the personal experience of the narrator.

Since narration takes place within the family group and the narrator is usually the father or grandfather, narration is associated with a strong bond of affection between the teller and the listener. The attitude of the listener towards the story is that of a total suspension of the critical faculties. The Rom often transfer their attitudes towards narration to television which tends to be viewed as a little window onto a world where events are seen as they unfold. Their concept of narration as testimony predisposes them to the acritical acceptance of everything seen in television, which to some extent has appropriated the role of 'narrator'. Often the Rom react to television characters are if they were real people, naming their children in their honour for example. On the other hand the realisation that what is seen in TV is not the literal truth causes them to lose all interest. Children believe that the stories they listen to on television really happen, including cartoons and science fiction fantasies.

The purpose of the stories is to point out danger and offer solutions and the 'lesson' is expressly and often extensively pointed out. Besides giving advice on how dangers can be avoided the stories also illustrate the qualities a Rom needs to succeed. Note that (as in Gaji Porini) the Rom expects no divine intervention on his behalf and accepts full responsibility for his own fate. 'It was God's will that the woman had with her a large jacket' but she had to be sufficiently intelligent to know how to use it. The story underscores the fact that it was not good fortune alone (or divine intervention) that enabled the woman to escape, but her own intelligence. Thus intelligence is the virtue the Rom admire and not courage or strength. Nowhere in the stories is there any evidence of a desire to dominate nature or circumstance by courage or strength. Courage, in the sense of overcoming or hiding fear is not a factor in their moral vision. The aim of the Rom is not to prevail over nature but to survive in it. Note for example in 'Mro Dat' all the efforts of the Rom are dedicated to excogitating a system whereby he can escape and it is this ability which saves him. Violence is not an option. The Rom never considered the possibility of killing the bandit.

The stylistic or linguistic characteristics of Rom Sloveni narration are at the service of its didactic function. They serve three essential purposes: to enhance memory; to solicit the identification between the listener and the fact narrated; to transmit the 'moral' or 'lesson' of the story. To this end the structural aspects, such as repetition are associated with grammatical aspects, in particular the use of verb tenses and point of view, and with stylistic aspects such as hyperbole to re-create the story in the mind of the listener. Ten-year-old children who refer to what 'we' did during the war, or different people who believe they have lived the same experience are a measure of the success of these narrative techniques. The stylistic characteristics of Rom Sloveni narration are quite distinctive and recur throughout. Significantly, work produced by school children writing in Italian reflects in grammar and style (if such a distinction is possible) the criterion of Rom Sloveni narration.

One way to enhance memory is to heighten the emotional impact on the listener by exaggeration. The use of hyperbole especially in regard to the most frightening or dangerous aspects of the story is a typical narrative technique. Thus in 'Gaji Porini' the snake encountered was as big as a caravan. Often it is the fear of the protagonist which is exaggerated. The clever Gaji was so frightened by her experience that she had to go to hospital. Besides danger or fear, any striking characteristic crucial to the point of the story is liable to exaggeration. In 'Mro Dat' we are told that the Rom travelled 200kms on foot to go to the market, when in actual fact the distance between Kocevia and Ljubliana is 60km. In the same way he is described as running 'as fast as a car'. Exaggeration is a stylistic technique which is frequently found in the writing of Rom Sloveni school children. One eight-year old boy describing how his father fainted after being badly bitten by a horse says 'he lay on the ground for two hours.' The following passage was written in Italian by a ten-year old boy who had been instructed to write a summary of a description of the earthquake in Udine (in which none of the details he mentioned occurred): 'And the trees flew up in the air and the cars turned over and the houses fell down and some people fell down and died of fright and the tiles from the roofs fell on the people's heads and the houses flew into a thousand pieces and all the people ran away on the roads.'

A further boost to memory is provided by repetition. In its simplest form, repetition means merely repeating a key word, such as the following passage from Mro Dat where in a total of 27 words, the word 'pani' occurs 11 times: 'Onda gelo paniaha, paninza. Onda paniaha, paniaha. Hine iek pani - ti ghav! Iek panuri hine, ka pe paniaha. Pani, tikni pani hine. Paniaha pirle Rom, paniaha'. Besides aiding memory, repetition here also serves to draw out the action and thus underscore the distance the Rom walked in the stream. Sometimes repetition is used to create certain dramatic effects. Notice, for example, in Gaji Porini: 'It leapt and leapt and leapt. It leapt after her, as fast as a man it leapt after her! It rose up as it leapt, it is already grabbing her, it grabs her!' Here repetition is used in conjunction with the imperfect tense to slow up the action (which by its nature is a rapid one) and thus charge the emotion of fear with a particular intensity, the verbal equivalent of slow-motion photography which is often used for the same purpose. Other times repetition is used to introduce a new element in the story, as in this example from 'Mro Dat': 'He went to the market, the Rom, he sold all his horses, now the Rom is coming back, on foot'. Repetition is another stylistic device which finds its way into the writing of school children: 'everybody dove in the water Rodolfo dove in and also Titeri and Anton and also Pepe dove in and also Noni and everybody dove in and all the people watched and pushed the horse out of the water and afterwards the tow-truck arrived and finally the horse was saved.'

The narrative tradition presents a number of characteristics whose function is to solicit identification between the listener and the story through reference to place or person. Definition of the location where the events described took place is always surprisingly precise. Such precision about place is due to the fact that all the villages and towns mentioned would be familiar to the listener, and thus a means of establishing contact with him. Often the narrator takes pains to remind the listener of this link. In 'Mro Dat' for example the narrator describes the Rom's journey in terms of places that are familiar to the listener. 'Do you know where Kocevia is? You have been to Ljubliana'. If the reference to person and place is precise, the reference to time is remarkably vague. While the stories are meticulously defined with regard to location and characters, almost nothing is said about time. If at all, time is usually defined in terms of the protagonist's age. Exceptionally time can be defined by some external event, such as those stories set in the war, but in the vast majority however, no mention is made of the time in which the event occurred, such as 'Mro Dat'. The reason for such imprecision is that the aim of narration is to establish a link between the listener and the story. The function of time deixis is therefore to emphasise the continuity between the past and the present, not demarcate the past. The narrator strives to link the story to the listener in whatever way possible. For this reason, comparisons are drawn from the environment at hand. The physical setting at the moment of telling is a stage upon which the narrator lays the scene, selecting his props from the background around him. In 'Gaji Porini' the snake is as big as the narrator's caravan.

By far the most startling characteristic of Rom Sloveni narration however is the use of changes in verb tense and point of view to plunge the listener into the story as one of the protagonists. An example is found in Mro Dat: 'They all flew down on the road and ran after you, Boom! Boom! In this case, the purpose of including the reader is to heighten the emotion of fear by involving the reader in the protagonist's flight. Sometimes a story can be told entirely from the second person point of view: 'You are my brother and I am your brother. I have a daughter and one day you married my daughter, you my brother. That cannot be among relatives, right? I didn't want you to marry my daughter for shame in the eyes of the other Rom. Son one day I took a knife and I came to where you were and I stabbed you with the knife and you died. Then I was afraid that the other Rom would kill me and I felt a pain in my heart and I fell down dead.' The following example was written by a 10-year old Rom Sloveni girl explaining the results of a research project her class had carried out on smoking: 'The survey that we carried out showed that nowadays young people, men and women smoke. A lot of boys and girls begin smoking because they feel more grown-up with a cigarette in their hand; others out of curiosity or as a way to pass the time; because I felt more adult; because I let myself be talked into it; because I saw others smoking; because I wanted to be like the others; because I saw people smoking on TV.'

Both pronoun references and verb tenses are used for functions other than simply indicating time or grammatical subject. Verb tenses send specific signals to the listener about point of view, and the role of certain elements in the narration. In narration each tense serves a specific function. Generally speaking, the imperfect tense is used for descriptions and background information while the past tense signals the plot sequence. The present tense is used to create certain special effects, highlighting the particularly dramatic moments of the story. For instance, let us observe the beginning of 'Mro Dat', which begins by explaining that the Rom had to travel a very long way through the forests to go to Ljubliana to buy horses, with a prevalence of the imperfect tense which is the usual tense for habits in the past, and thus for background information. 'He went, how shall I tell you Jane, so far to buy horses? Look, you know where Kocevi is? You have been to Kocevia. From Kocevia past Lipici, further, as far as that, outside Ljubliana. Far he went to buy horses, far. He [has/had] a pistol always in his boot. He goes in the forests. There are forests there, you have seen those forests. Fear grips you even now when you go.' The present tense here is used in conjunction with the imperfect to describe a habit. The introduction of the present in association with the imperfect, to convey habit implies a time continuity and blurs the distinction between past and present. Next we have the beginning of the story itself, signalled by a verb in the present tense which is immediately repeated in the past, followed by the first elements of the 'plot'. 'He goes - he went to the market. [He had] seven or eight horses. They saw that my father went on the other road. They were bandits, Croatian bandits, Gaje bandits. See now the Rom going up the mountain to the market. He went to the market the Rom, he sold all his horses. He sold all his horses, now the Rom is coming back, on foot.' From the verbs in the past tense we learn the following essential elements of the story: The narrator's father went to the market with seven or eight horses. Some Gaje thieves saw him going to the market. At this point the story takes a step back to re-tell what has already been told, but this time with a different and far more dramatic perspective, underscored by the use of the present tense: 'See now the Rom going up the mountain to the market.' We now know what he does not yet know, that thieves are lying in wait for him. We are watching him as he goes, waiting for the moment when they will assault him. The story then resumes the past tense to relate the next essential element of the plot: that the Rom went to the market and sold all his horses (and thus has money). The next sentence, charged with dramatic significance, is again in the present tense: 'Now the Rom is coming back, on foot.' The climax however is delayed by the injection of a comment by the narrator which explains why the Rom travelled so far, and points out how dangerous such a journey was. The story resumes thus: 'The Rom is coming down. The thieves recognised him. Those of whom some [went] down the road, one up the road. One jumps on him from behind!' Notice how the background information, the fact that the bandits recognised him and set out to ambush him is given in the past tense while the moments of highest dramatic intensity, such as the 'close-up' of the Rom walking to the market after we have learned that the bandits are watching him, and the moment when the bandit assaults the Rom are given in the present.

Another example is in 'Gaji Porini'. This story begins with a statement of the first element of the plot, in the past tense, before any background information has been given. 'This is something they tell in Yugoslavia. That a Gaji - where we were there were many of those old roads - went to work.' The next sentence contains background information and is appropriately in the imperfect tense with one in the present tense both of which describe habits, thus associating the time of the story with the present. 'So on an old road they go to the fields. And then that Gaji sees that snake. When she saw that snake on the road, he is sleeping, big, like that wagon!' Note the change in tense of the verb hiki (to see) which in the first instance is in the present tense which underscores the fear. In the second instance however, the verb 'to see' is part of the background information for the fact that the snake was sleeping in the road.

As in the case of other elements of style, children reflect these same criterion in the choice of verb tenses in compositions written at school. The following example was written by a ten-year old boy after three years attendance at school: 'A cat one time was playing with a thick string of yarn. That naughty cat has tied himself all up and he is biting the string! And now that cat is still doing bad things and the ball of yarn has got smaller and smaller. Still that naughty cat who has tied himself all up and he wants to free himself but he couldn't free himself. He is so stupid that he has tied himself all up.' This composition exemplifies (thought certainly not with the subtlety of the stories quoted above) the same basic pattern: the scene is set in the past; the tense then changes to the present for the most dramatic or eventful moments; the story ends by summing up the 'moral'.

A variety of stories have been used in the classroom, from stories of adventures with horses, to glimpses of daily life in the past, such as how to catch and cook a hedgehog, to stories such as snake stories that express the moral outlook of the Rom, to stories of the experiences of the Rom during the war, both in Yugoslavia and in the concentration camp in Italy. The reaction of all the children, both Gaje and Rom, was of great enthusiasm, and much importance was given to the fact that the stories are actually true. The material was extremely motivating for the Rom children, and writing exercises based on these stories were always willingly accepted, something that is not always the case. Although the time which is given over to Romanes is far too little, it has resulted in an improvement in the usage of Italian especially on the part of those children who show the greatest interference between Italian and Romanes. The children have acquired the notion of the relativity of language codes, (something they did not possess before) and now realise that some things which may be appropriate in one language are not necessarily appropriate in another. They have also been taught that many words which they know in Italian have Romanes correspondents, and they have been encouraged to discover these words whenever possible by asking their parents and grandparents. The Rom group, who found themselves involved in the education their children were receiving at school, reacted favourably (otherwise this experience would never have been possible) and largely thanks to this experience, began taking an interest in the school. One father has come to the school as an 'expert' to teach the Rom group. In general the Rom consider their language as a defence mechanism and thus something to be kept secret amongst themselves. The school was thus something to be kept secret amongst themselves. The school was, however, excluded from this attitude because of the atmosphere of trust and collaboration that was established between the Rom and the school. This in turn is mainly due to the attitude of interest and respect which the school, represented to them by the teacher for Gypsy children in Piove di Sacco, Luigina Dario, accorded their way of life. Appendix A gives translations of two Romani texts and Appendix B shows how they were used in the classroom.

APPENDIX A

The Rom comes down the mountain. The bandits recognised him, and half of them went down the road a bit, and one thief waited up the road. One jumps on him from behind. Wait! 'Take', he says 'your money out.' The Rom says, 'Iím a poor man', he says. Listen, listen how they knew! 'look' he says, 'Iím a poor man. I don't have' he says, 'anything'.

'What did you do,' he says, 'with the horses that today you were leading? Seven or eight horses that you had today?'

'Those,' he says, 'were not mine. 'You have seen,' he says 'that I am here on foot. Those were not my horses' he says 'I was just accompanying them for one who gave me a little money,' he says, 'just a few dinars.'

'No,' he says. 'They were your horses. We know you.'

They won't let him go, and they are going to kill him. 'Give over the money or you're dead!' The Rom slowly took the gun out. Listen! Listen! 'Hey,' he says, 'What's this?' The Rom took the gun and told the robber: 'Go on,' he says, 'On foot. Start running in front of me.' The Rom at his feet: Boom! Boom! He jumped and jumped. The Rom shot at his feet, the Rom keeps shooting him from behind, always from behind the Rom keeps shooting. He had a lot of bullets, the Rom had more than plenty with him. But there, Aiiiii, all of them flew down on the road and ran after you! They: Boom! Boom! The bandits shot at him with guns. Always our Rom have been fast on foot! Who could catch my father? Not even a car could have caught him! The Rom was so fast, he ran like a horse! Ten thieves after him, the Rom, who was yet a Rom! If he hadn't done that, they would have killed him there!

There was a mill down in the valley. He crossed the mountain, he didn't go by the road. He threw himself down on his stomach in the bushes, in the bushes, and there he came to where the mill was. There he hid. Wait! Then he went in the stream, in the stream. Then in the stream, in the stream, there was a little stream as far as the town. There was a little stream there, and he went with the stream. A stream, it was a little stream. The Rom walked in the water, in the water. Then they see him run down the mountain to the road. Listen! They saw him and they had already begun shooting with their guns! They go down and they see the Rom in the tavern. He began ringing at the tavern, the Gaje knew him. 'Tone', they say in Slovenian. The Gaje opened, and the whole town rang the bells, as an alarm! It was a large town. There was an alarm, and all the Gaje came with their guns. All outside with the Rom, they go up to where the bandits are shooting at them. Along comes a poor Gajo on a wagon, coming down the mountain from where the Rom my father had come from, all cut up. He had been sleeping in his wagon, travelling with his horse. God granted that the horse shied and ran away. The horse was clever, it ran straight along the road, it was where all the precipices were. The horse ran straight along the road, it saw where all the precipices were. The horse ran straight along the road. But the thieves had cut him, he was all cut up. If it had been my father... Instead they had caught that other Gajo back there, and he had been all cut up, out of anger. So the Gaje all went back, and the thieves were nowhere to be found. Then they all rang the bells that they ring for the markets, when they bring horses and cows. Those Gaje were clever, you know? They did it on purpose so the thieves would think of money and come down to hear, and then they would stop them. But no, the Gaje heard the bandits shooting up on the big mountain.

So the Rom escaped. But the poor Gajo was all cut up and bleeding on his wagon. With knives, how do I know how they wounded him? Or with a gun in his feet, that Gajo was left behind. The Croatians were dangerous! They would cut you all up! My father was fast, if not he would have been killed. All the Rom knew this story in the whole world. In the whole world, all the Rom know this story!

A Clever Gaji
This is something they tell in Yugoslavia, that a Gaji - where were there were many - went to work on those old roads. Many women worked, and they went to the fields on those old roads. Thus the Gaji saw the snake. When she saw it on the road it was sleeping, as big as that wheel! Listen! It was God's will that the Gaji had with her one of those big jackets. The Gaji was clever. If it had been another woman in her place the snake would have eaten her! The Gaji took off running, she passed the snake, and he was after her like that! He leapt and he leapt, he leap after her! As fast as a man the snake leapt after her. He rose up as he jumped, he is already touching her, he is grabbing her! The clever woman took off her jacket and threw it down. And the snake went inside the jacket because he thought the Gaji was inside it. Thus the Gaji was able to escape. She was dead of fright and she went to the hospital

Did you hear? The Gaji was clever and she threw down her jacket and the snake thought that she was inside, right? He went inside the jacket and he tore it up. The woman saw him tearing up her jacket. She was a clever woman and she escaped. I heard that in Yugoslavia, my poor old mother told it to me. That is the truth, all the truth is.

APPENDIX B

Example of the use of Rom text
The text, 'Mor Dat i Cora Hravati', to which the children attributed the title of 'A Rom of Quality', was used in a 5th class, and in a Romanes language group, in the following manner:

For the Rom children the objectives were as follows:

1. To be able to read and understand the text written in both Italian and Romanes. Romanes was transcribed according t the Italian phonetic system, even though this does not always correspond to the orthography used by scholarly journals, for two reasons: the first was that one of the purposes of the use of Romanes was to consolidate the reading and writing skills in Italian; the second was that from time to time certain captions in Romanes were used in the whole class group.
2. To be able to translate a text from Romanes into Italian and vice-versa.
3. To learn facts regarding the history of the family and group.
4. To learn to write new vocabulary items correctly in both Italian and Romanes.
5. To point out the necessity in Italian of a sentence formed of two elements: subject and predicate.

The sequence of the exploitation of the text, available in both Italian and Romanes versions, was as follows:

1. Work as begun in the whole class. The story was introduced, and the geographical location (Yugoslavia, between Kocevia and Ljubliana) and the time (in the 1920s, were pinpointed.
2. The story was read to the class in the Italian version by the teacher.
3. A questionnaire containing about 15 comprehension questions was distributed to the class and filled out individually by each child. The questionnaires were corrected collectively, which began the discussion of the story, and of its particular characteristics.
4. The narrative structure of the story was analysed. The stylistic features such as tense switching and exaggeration were explained in the context of an oral literature. Discussion and exemplification of these characteristics. Reconstruction of the principle episodes of the story.
5. The children each chose one episode of the story to illustrate with a drawing

Choice of a title for the story chosen by a class discussion and voting.
In the Rom group the work proceeded as follows:

1. The story was read in Romanes, and unfamiliar words were identified and discussed. Contrasting opinions were listened to. It was decided to verify the meanings of the unfamiliar words with parents and grandparents. Words to verify and translate were given as homework.
2. The drawings produced in the class were re-ordered according to the sequence of the story.
3. Each child in turn chose and read a caption from the story in Romanes to apply each drawing and translated it into Italian.
4. The sentences in Romanes were confronted with the translations suggested by the children, and if necessary a more appropriate form in Italian was sought, each child working individually under the supervision of the teacher.
5. Analysis of the grammar point to be focused on. In this lesson the attention of the children was drawn to an analysis of the subject-predicate unit in the simplest captions. Cards were made up continuing subjects and predicates in both languages. The children were asked to combine subject cards with predicate cards to make sentences: iek Gajoro + avi = a por Gajo comes; gra + prasle = the horse ran. These were compared to certain sentences in the text where the verbs were missing, and the children were asked to count the words in both versions and identify the missing element in the Romanes version. It was observed that in Italian a sentence always contains a subject and a verb, whereas in Romanes the verb is sometimes omitted.
6. The children were asked to write a brief summary of some episodes of the story in Italian.

Examples of the comparison of some significant sentences:

Romanes:
1. Rom poloke, pudini avri. (4 words) [The Rom slowly the gun out]
Child's translation:
1. Rom piano pistola fuori. (4 words) [Rom slowly pistol out]
Teacher's translation:
1. Il Rom piano piano tira fuori la pistola (8 words) [The Rom very slowly pulls out the pistol]
Romanes:
2. Rom leske nu pre: Bum, Bum! ov skucia skucinja. (9 words) [Rom him in the feet: boom, boom! He jumped, jumped!
Child's translation:
2. Rom a lui nei piedi: Bum, Bum! Lui saltava saltava. (10 words) [Rom at him in the feet, Bum, Bum! He jumped, jumped.

Teacher's translation:
2. Il Rom gli sparava ai piedi: Bum, bum! Lui saltava e saltava. (12 words) [The Rom shot him in the feet: Bom, Bom! He jumped and jumped.

The translations were compared and the missing words were identified. These turned out to be the articles and the verbs. In addition the translation of leske involved a preposition and thus added one more word.

Romanes:
3. An peni lore avri. (4 words) [Take, he says, money out]

Child's translation:
3. Dammi dice i soldi fuori. [Give me he says the money out]

Teacher's translation:
3. Il ladro minaccia: 'Tira fuori i soldi'. [The thief threatens: 'Take out your money'.

In this last case the point under consideration was the correct way to signal direct speech in Italian and contrasting it to 'peni' in Romanes.

A different grammar point is chosen to work on from each text, in general only one per text, and never more than two. In 'Mro Dat i ˇCora Hravati' the grammar point under consideration was the minimum sentence (the omission of verbs in Romanes).

The teachers who carried out this work were Luigina Dario, auxiliary teacher for Gypsy children and the fifth grade class teacher, Guiseppina Zara.

REFERENCES

Karpati M. (1982) 'i Rom e la Scuola Italiana', *Lacio Drom*, 18, pp.28-30

Kenrick D. and Grattan P. (1972) *Destiny of the Gypsies*. Heineman, London

Soravia G. (1970) *Dialetti Degli Zingari Italiani*. Pacini, Pisa

Strukelj P. (1980) *Romi na Slovenskem*. Cankarjeva Zalozba, lubljana

Uhlik R. (1955) *Romane Chibace*. Nashe Kniga, Sarajevo

Zanatta A. (1984) 'Esperienze e proposte di una didattica per gli Zingari nell'ambito dei nuoui programmi'. Conference paper, Opera Nomadi Conference, Rieti, 18-23 June

Zatta J.D. (1983) 'Il Racconoto di Rave', *Lacio Drom*, 1, pp.24-28

Adult Literacy Work with Sinti Gypsies in Bremen, West Germany

Ulrich Müller and György Szabo

About 300 Sinti live in Bremen. The Sinti are the oldest-established Gypsy group in Germany. Most of the adults are illiterate. The older people could not learn to read because of the persecution during the Nazi era, the younger because they have been disadvantaged at school or as a result of the travelling life of their parents. Between 1978 and 1983, the 'Bremer Volkhochschule', a municipal institution for adult education in Bremen, ran a literacy campaign for them.

The social and economic situation of the Sinti in Bremen is not very different from the situation of Travelling people in other European countries. Poverty and strict social control by police and administration set the boundaries of their life.

The Sinti live in a society in which the ability to read and write is presupposed as matter-of-course, so the aim of the literacy programme had to be the teaching of the standard language. When it started the Sinti reported how terrifying they found even the simplest enterprises such as shopping, consulting a doctor or calling on authorities, and how even selling door-to-door is difficult if one cannot read and write. Especially painful are the consequences of illiteracy while seeking a job. Many of the Sinti had lost employment when it was revealed that they were illiterate.

At the beginning also nearly all the trainees were fearful about their ability to acquire the standard language. Some had failed several times before to learn to read and write as a child, juvenile or adult.

At the beginning of the course nearly all the participants could read the separate letters of the alphabet. The relearning of the alphabet according to the phonic method provoked uneasiness. The relation between meaningless sounds and abstract symbols was very difficult for the Sinti in class to understand, possibly because they base their orientation on concrete objects. In order, however, to orientate themselves in a society in which writing regulates every action, many compensations had been found which tended to impede the learning process. For example, they might learn texts rapidly by heart or look at the shape of a word and then guess, or pay attention to the teacher's lip movements rather than synthesise the separate letters.

The texts created during this period were primarily designed to teach reading technique. But, given that literacy implies a conscious approach to the world, texts had to be created which enabled the Sinti not only to describe their experiences, but to become aware of them through the class. Such a programme had to be developed by Dr. Christel Manske, drawing on the experience of Paolo Freire in Latin-America (Freire, 1977). His concepts presume that the conscious apprehension of the world is only possible if there is a dialogue between equals in the course. The predominant language, and even more the predominant standard language always break the unity of the experiences of suppressed people and their comprehension in society. From this point of view illiteracy is not only the inability to read or write, but, above all, a lack of consciousness of one's relationship to one's own society, history and social position. Therefore the course also had the aim of giving the participants the courage to develop their own view on important social problems, to learn to formulate these views in the standard language and to agree upon an adequate viewpoint.

Our literacy programme starts with the question: 'What is a man ?'

'The question was vividly discussed. The discussion reflected the long persecution of the Gypsies:

> A man is a slave. A man is an animal forced to work. A man is nothing but dirt. A man is a poor devil.

But it also reflected experiences within the extended family:

> A man does not want to be alone, wants a family, wants love, that's only human....

We asked one Sinti 'Why is a man a poor devil?' He answered:

> Either I'm a poor devil and go on the dole or I try to get some money and am sent to gaol. I haven't had an education, none of us sitting here have, calling door-to-door doesn't lead anywhere, has no future, you're not even considered a human being. What can I say, what a man is, if you're poor you aren't a human being but if you're rich, no matter how bad you are, no matter how you've made your money, nobody asks you anything, well, then you are somebody.

The group agreed upon the following text:

What is a man?
A man is poor.
A man is rich.
Why?
Why is a man poor?
Why is a man rich?

The words 'what', 'a', 'poor', and 'rich', were read with the help of plastic letters which each participant had. The words 'is', 'why', and 'man' were marked with different colour pens and were memorised mainly from their shape as the vowels they contain do not correspond to the way the entire word is pronounced.

Already on the first evening all trainees were able to read the text fluently. But on the second evening it appeared that almost nobody could co-ordinate the letter and the corresponding sound. Nearly everybody knew the text by heart, having read it once. Therefore exercises had to be developed which questioned the class's existing 'knowledge' in various forms.

The experience of the first two years of the project led to the creation of a text collection called the *Bremer Sinti Fibel* which has aroused widespread interest (Manske, 1984).

The subjective difficulties of the Sinti trainees can be summarised as follows:

A. Readiness to get down to the laborious work of learning to read and write is hindered by the massive economic problems of the trainees. Literacy does not automatically lead to an improvement of the economic situation. The experience of being able to read and write, without having any use for it in daily life, was frustrating and impeded the learning process.
B. Literacy is bound to lead to an extension of social experience and to consequent transformations of consciousness. During the course some trainees came to recognise that they had lived up to that time with a completely insufficient knowledge of social circumstances and with largely inadequate conceptions and strategies of action as to their social survival. This engendered massive learning obstacles which increased with progressive knowledge. In some cases one could practically speak of their being afraid of knowledge: 'Before, we were happy, we didn't know anything. Now we are frightened.' This fear and the concurrent recognition of the necessity of education created a dilemma for .some trainees.
C. A massive fear of failure was problematic for some trainees. These fears were increased by the group situation. For this reason separate groups for men and women were established, since men were particularly afraid of failing in front of women, which created such stress in mixed groups that learning became almost impossible.

It appears that the best results in literacy programmes are obtained in small group or individual lessons. But that does not imply that literacy programmes can totally do without larger group sessions, which give additional possibilities for communication by avoiding some of the stress associated with individual performance.

A literacy programme organised over a longer period of time is probably not as effective as a crash course of intensive work. The experience of residential courses in a changed environment arranged during the project confirmed this view.

What bearing do the above described experiences have on the fundamental questions which must be raised in this book:

Adult Literacy Work with Sinti Gypsies in Bremen, West Germany

1. Is there any necessity to preserve Romanes in terms of literacy?
2. If so, is it not more effective to teach Sinti and Roma Gypsies reading and writing in their mother-tongue?
3. Supposing there were to be agreement to this among Gypsies, would it not mean the standardisation of a language which is very rich in dialects?
4. What would be the effects of written Romanes on social structure and social behaviour of this ethnic minority?
5. How can Gypsies take part in these discussions and ensure that their participation is decisive?

Our position on the first four questions has to be determined by looking at the last question. It is inadmissible to look upon this issue merely from a linguistic point of view. Any possible solution of these questions must include social and psychological aspects, but first of all the equalisation of this harassed ethnic minority with the majority in any society. It seems to us, for instance, to be useless to create dictionaries of Romanes purely for the sake of science or in the interests of researchers if there is no correlation of purpose or interaction between the scientists and the mother-tongue users.

Language is one of the most important components of identity. In order to save Sinti and Roma as an ethnic minority in a pluralistic society all who are concerned must make sure that Romanes prevails in a fast-changing world.

REFERENCES

Freire P. (1977) *Erziehtung als Praxis der Freiheit*. Reinbek, Hamburg

Manske C. (1984) *Sinti-Fibel - Alphabetisierung, von Erwachsenen..* Extra-buch Verlag, Frankfurt am Main

Bilingual Education Among the Inga (Quechuan) People of South West Colombia

Stephen H. Levinsohn

Some 15,000 Ingas, speaking five dialects of Quechua, live in the mountains and jungles of the Putumayo region, usually interspersed with 'whites' (native Spanish speakers). Their degree of bilingualism with Spanish varies from near-zero to almost 100 per cent, according to their proximity to major roads (compare Table One, below). Until recently all were educated only in Spanish, the official national language of Colombia.

Table One
Selected Primary Schools Attended by Inga Children, 1984

Location (status)	Accessible by	% Inga	No. of bi-lingual years	1st year intake	No. of 1st year classes	1st year Spanish fluency*
Highland						
Santiago (urban)	Major Road	30	1	45	2	3
San Andrés (rural)	Minor Road	60	2	41	2	2.5
Cascajo (rural)	Minor Road	80	-	30	1	2.5
Aponte (urban)	Minor Road	60	-	50	1	4+
Lowland						
Yunguillo (rural)	Path	100	2+	45	1	0/0.5
Osococha (rural)	Path	100	1	12	1	0/0.5
Guayuyacu (rural)	River	100	1	12	1	2
San Miguel	Minor Road	50	-	30	1	4+

*Spanish fluency is measured on a scale 0-5.
Note: Some figures are approximate. The author has not visited Yunguillo or Osococha.

Bilingual Education Among People of South West Colombia

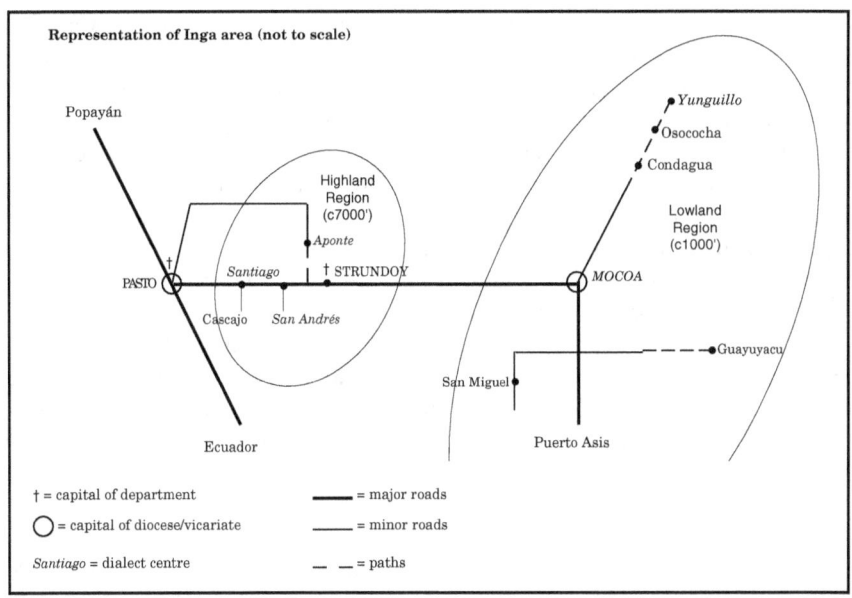

Historically two groups of Inga can be identified (Levinsohn 1991). First, there are the Ingas who today live and pertain to the towns of Santiago and Aponte. They are probably descendants of the baggage carriers who accompanied Sebastián de Belalcázar on his journey north from Quito, Ecuador in the 1530s in search of 'El Dorado'. The Aponte group was sent from Santiago before 1700, by the then governor of the region Carlos Tamoabioy, to defend the northern frontier of the area occupied by the Ingas from colonists moving in from the north, Aponte being situated about twelve hours walk over the mountains from Santiago, in the department of Nariño.

The second group of Ingas probably originated in the lowland jungle area near the present regional capital, Mocoa. Today they are divided into the speakers of three dialects: (1) Yunguillo and (2) Guayuyacu plus San Miguel, both in the lowlands, and (3) San Andrés, in the highlands. This last group, whose dialect centre is only two miles from Santiago, has detailed oral traditions of their journey from the lowlands. Although so close to Santiago, ethnocentricity and friction between the two communities have preserved the dialect differences characteristic of the people of San Andrés.

Thanks to the state and the Roman Catholic church, nearly all the villages in the Colombian countryside have a primary school, where instruction has traditionally been in Spanish. In the Inga area Franciscan nuns and Marist brothers established day and boarding schools for girls and boys in Santiago in about 1900. The Marists also opened a school in San Andrés in the early 1900s, which closed after fifteen years; the Madre Laura order of nuns established another primary school there in 1953. Secondary education has been available in the area since 1968.

Originally, all the schools in the region were run by the Roman Catholic church, though some were taken over by the state in 1976. The schools mentioned in this paper, however, with the exception of Cascajo, are still run by the Roman Catholic church, under contract from the government.

Formerly teachers with Inga children in their classes forbade them to speak their own language and caned them for doing so. Because, however, Inga children generally were not fluent in Spanish, few progressed beyond the third year of primary education. By the mid-1970s only half a dozen Ingas were teachers, 'normalistas' who had successfully completed their secondary education plus a year of teacher-training.

One of these teachers started to use Inga to explain to her classes the meaning of terms and concepts in Spanish. She estimates that, as a result, the number of children who had to repeat first year dropped from 70% to 30%. Her first teaching post was in Cascajo, but she was later moved to Yunguillo, where most of the children starting school were monolingual in Inga. There she was able to convince other Inga teachers of the value of using their mother tongue as a means of instruction.

In 1978 the Colombian government passed Decree 1142 of the Ministry of Education, which gave all linguistic minorities the right to education in their mother tongue. In the following year the Roman Catholic authorities in the Putumayo region introduced bilingual education in one of its schools among the neighbouring Camsá people, and indicated its desire to do the same among the Ingas.

Various partial studies on the Inga language were made in the 1950s and 1960s (for example, Caudmont 1953-61). As a result, when the writer took up residence in San Andrés in 1968 and began the phonological and grammatical analysis of the language, rapid progress was possible. By 1970, an initial orthography was being tried out based on Spanish, which, with minor modifications, has stood the test of time. The main mismatches between Inga and Spanish are in the area of the vowels (five in Spanish, three in Inga) and of the *r* (Spanish distinguishes *r* from *rr*; Inga does not, though different dialects realise the phoneme in different ways).

From 1970 booklets were produced in the San Andrés dialect and later the Santiago one, in order to stimulate interest in reading Inga. Most of these booklets contain short folktales, which were recorded on tape, then edited with an Inga speaker and reproduced in written form. They are sold at subsidised prices and are very popular. By 1978, some 20 titles were available, covering health, traditions, history and translations of Scripture portions, plus a dictionary and pedagogical grammar of the language. These titles were used, to a limited extent, by teachers in the schools of San Andrés and Santiago.

During the school year 1980-81 individual Ingas from highland dialect groups worked over a draft of a first primer, which was duplicated for use in the San Andrés school during the 1981-82 school year. The model used was that taught to the 'normalista' teachers, that is, key words plus a global approach, so that anyone who had learnt to teach reading in Spanish could employ the same method for Inga.

1982 saw the first primer revised and introduced in the Santiago school. A second year textbook on the Inga language was also produced, based on the set curriculum for Spanish, introducing basic grammatical and orthographic features. This was used in the San Andrés school. 1982 also saw the first of a series of five-day workshops accredited by the Ministry of Education, which Inga teachers from the Lowland region attended. In l982 these teachers adapted the first year primer to their dialect and culture. After using it during the 1982-83 school year, they extensively revised it. They then adapted and revised the second year Inga language textbook, adding text material and questions for comprehension. Finally in l984 they developed a first year 'Social Sciences' textbook, based on the new curriculum which had just been issued by the Ministry of Education. In 1983 an accredited workshop for Highland Inga teachers also revised and expanded their first and second year materials.

The Inga language is used, then, in the first year courses in which reading and writing are taught, for Social Sciences and to explain Spanish terms and concepts in other subjects. Teachers have in Inga a basic reading primer, and a Social Science textbook, focusing on features not covered in the standard textbooks in Spanish. They can also make oral use of second and third year materials. In the second and third years, part of the language course and some aspects of Social Sciences are taught in Inga. To support this work teachers have, besides the language course itself, Inga reading booklets (mainly on traditions and folklore, histories of the different Inga communities and of the Inca Empire, booklets on local flora and fauna, and materials for church use).

A research project directed by Professor Luis G. Galeano L. at the University of Nariño has also analysed errors in spoken Spanish committed by Inga children entering and in school. It is hoped to develop material for teaching Spanish as a second language to Ingas.

Logistical problems still arise, however. Except in Yunguillo and Osococha, 20-60 per cent of the children attending the schools are not Inga speakers. In some schools it is possible to have two first-year and two second-year classes, one for children whose mother tongue is Inga, and the other for those for whom it is Spanish. In others, the number of pupils is too small.

One or two teachers are trying to use both languages in the classroom. Few teachers whose mother tongue is Spanish, however, know any Inga.

Teacher training does not include orientation concerning the peculiar needs of linguistic minorities. As a result most teachers do not understand the problems being experienced by Inga children who are educated in Spanish. Even in schools in which bilingual education has been introduced, achievement still tends to be measured, even in the first year, in terms of the student's ability in Spanish. To combat this, Professor Galeano is organising accredited courses for teachers of Inga children. With only one three week course held up to 1985, and that course limited to twenty participants, changes of attitudes are bound to be slow.

Parental expectation measures scholastic success in terms of the child's ability in Spanish. In addition, peer group pressure creates an atmosphere in which some Inga children avoid speaking Inga in public.

Differing situations require differing approaches to bilingual education. It is not possible to instruct teachers to take a single approach to the teaching of Inga children. Inga children entering some schools have poor control of Spanish and there teaching reading and writing in the mother tongue is most desirable. In others they enter school fairly bilingual, and parental expectations and peer pressure may make it better to teach reading and writing first in Spanish. In others again, although the children understand Inga, they do not speak it, and the desire of the community is that the teacher create interest in reading in the mother tongue, once the skill has been acquired in Spanish.

REFERENCES

Caudmont J. (1953) 'Los fonemas del inga', *Revista Colombiana de Antropología,* I, pp.361-89, Bogotá

Caudmont J. (1954) *Cartilla de alfabetización inga-castellano.* Edición preliminar, Instituto Colombiano de Antropología, Bogotá

Caudmont J. (l961a) 'Estructura morfológica del inga' in Townsend, A.W.C. (ed.) *Vigésimo Quinto Aniversario del Instituto Lingüístico de Verano*, pp.401-412, Mexico

Caudmont J. (1961b) 'Materiales para el estudio lexicográfico de la lengua inga', *Divulgaciones Etnológicas,* III, pp.165-68, Barranquilla

Levinsohn S.H. (1991) 'Variations in Tense-Aspect Markers between Inga (Quechuan) Dialects' in M.R. Key (ed.) *Language Change in South American Indian Languages*. University of Pennsylvania, Philadelphia, pp.145-165

The Development of a Multi-Lingual Education Policy in Sierra Leone

Freddie Jones

Sierra Leone has just about 3.7 million people, according to the census of 1985. About twenty languages are spoken in the country, if we include English (the official language, the language of external communication and currently the only language of formal education), Arabic (the country is predominantly Muslim), and French, which is taught in many secondary schools and is also spoken by a few people who have active contact with neighbouring Guinea, but possibly do not speak a Guinean vernacular (Wyse 1991).

Let us define a speaker's 'mother-tongue' as the 'indigenous language in which the speaker demonstrates the highest proficiency'. The two mother-tongues that are together spoken by over half the population of Sierra Leone are Themne and Mende, each with just over 30%. Limba comes third with about 9%. In addition to their mother-tongue status, Themne and Mende are also widely spoken Lingua Franca languages in the North, and East and South respectively. As a mother-tongue, Krio, an English-based creole language, is spoken by about 2% of the population, mainly in the Western area, and is at the same time the most widely spoken second language in Sierra Leone. As Fyle (1976, p.44) notes, Krio 'serves as the language of the middle and lower reaches of officialdom, of business and industry and of some (in and) out- of-school education. It is the most important language of politics as well as the language invariably used when Sierra Leoneans of different language backgrounds meet informally at whatever level and for whatever purpose'.

Non-Sierra-Leoneans often ask why Krio has not been declared the official or co-official (with English) language, as has happened to Swahili in Tanzania and Kenya in East Africa, or Tok Pisin in Papua-New Guinea. Although, historically, relations between the Krios and the rest of the population of Sierra Leone have not been the most cordial possible, intermarriage, migration and other social circumstances have considerably improved the situation in recent times. Nonetheless, in my experience, while many Sierra Leoneans of other ethnic groups are quite happy to use the language at any time, the mere suggestion that Krio should be used as an or the official language raises quite a few eyebrows of disdain. Some reasons for this seem to be the fact that Krios only form 2% of the population, and the beliefs, still persisting in some quarters, that the language, like the people, is not indigenous to the country, and that it is a trade language which is little more than a corruption of English, and which cannot adequately express the cultures of Sierra Leone.

While most native speakers (and some other users) of Krio are, at least to some extent, literate in English, they are not literate in Krio, and most native speakers of other Sierra Leonean languages are literate neither in English nor their mother-tongues. A few only are literate in English, French, and to some extent, Arabic. It has been suggested that if the Arabic script were to be adopted for writing Krio, the literacy rate in the country as a whole (now probably 10-12%) would immediately be more than doubled (Fyle, 1976). This suggestion does not seem to have enjoyed the blessing of the authorities. A less optimistic school of thought argues that Sierra Leonean Muslims only rote-learn Koranic Arabic, and would be happy to leave Arabic for religious matters. In the absence of research findings, this is all really conjectural.

Some interested linguists and Islamic religious scholars such as Dr. A.K. Turay, former Head of the sub-department of Linguistics at Fourah Bay College, and Mr. M.T. Bangura, a lecturer in Islamic Studies at Milton Margai Teachers' College, have, however, actually devised an orthography based on the Arabic script to facilitate the acquisition of literacy in some of the native languages. In contradiction to the sceptics it has been claimed that some Fulahs and Mandingoes have been using the Arabic script to write their own languages for years, and that most of the 65-70% of Sierra Leoneans who are Muslims do, from their Koranic studies, know the values of Arabic symbols, and that this Arabic-based script has been successfully used to teach illiterates their own languages at experimental workshops.

In the 1980s, however, before war overtook the country the authorities responsible for education in Sierra Leone seemed more interested in using the Roman script for literacy purposes.

The earliest attempts to use the indigenous languages as vehicles of literacy were made by the British missionaries, after Sierra Leone had become a British colony in 1808, with the express intention of propagating the gospel through these languages. Later these languages were also used as media of instruction in mission schools. By 1961, when Sierra Leone became independent, the Bible had been translated into Limba, Mende and Themne at least, but English remained the language of upward social mobility. It is even claimed that a knowledge of it, particularly during earlier days, bestowed on people immunity from 'arbitrary arrests, payment of tax and local dues, and fines for infringement on certain customs and cultural offences' (Gbla 1984). Because of the status of the language, and for other reasons of expediency, to ensure the success of missionary work, a gradual recourse to the use of English in the mission schools was inevitable. The use of the mother tongues was relegated to the teaching of illiterate adult converts.

Ironically, after the attainment of independence, interest in the use of the indigenous languages declined further, although neighbouring former British territories like Ghana were encouraging and developing the use of their vernaculars, not only as vehicles of education but as subjects of study in their own right. Now some of them are major GCE O- and A-level and university subjects. Nonetheless, individual Sierra Leonean and non-Sierra-Leonean scholars have been concerned enough to undertake active research into some of the languages of the country.

A renascence of interest began in 1977, with the appointment of a new Minister of Education, who made definite plans to reintroduce the mother tongues into the schools as languages of education and as discrete subjects of study.

In 1978 and 1979, workshops were held, teaching materials produced and tested, and teachers were trained to teach Limba, Mende and Themne in pilot schools in areas where these languages were predominantly spoken. In September 1979 the first 26 classes were started and facts about nature, and the environment, and short stories and simple grammar and vocabulary were taught.

At the end of the first year a review of the project reported that it had been received with enthusiasm by the chiefs, tribal councillors and the public. Although one cannot draw statistically significant conclusions, some of the pupils in these pilot schools did better than their counterparts in the other schools.

On 23 October 1979, a National Planning Committee composed of professional teachers, representing the different tribes of the country, was appointed by the Minister of Education 'to advise his ministry on the co-ordination, centralisation and enhancement of the Indigenous Language Education Programme' (Gbla 1984). It was commissioned to study existing orthographies used by organisations engaged in literacy work, to reconcile their differences, and recommend a standard orthography for Mende, Limba and Themne. It was also empowered to form sub- committees to carry out a linguistic survey of the country, to produce materials for text books and other teaching aids for the pilot schools, and to recruit and train teachers and technicians for various aspects of the programme.

Orthographies, not only for the afore-mentioned languages, but also for Kono and Krio were standardised at a workshop held at the Ministry of Education Conference Room between April 24 and 28, 1984. They are semi-phonemic and based on the Roman script.

Seminars and workshops had still to be conducted in different parts of the country for the recruitment, training and retraining of teachers and technicians in the use of the new orthographies, and the implementation of other aspects of the programme. Workshops were held for the production of material for text books and other teaching aids. The officials of the Ministry, in collaboration with the Lutheran Bible Society in Sierra Leone produced Limba, Temne and Mende Readers I-IV respectively. UNICEF provided funds for a writers' workshop/seminar (4-6 January 1984) to produce materials for the printing of Krio Primers for the proposed Krio pilot schools to be chosen from the greater Freetown and Rural Areas of the Western Area of Sierra Leone. Krio Primers I and II and the Teachers' Companions were produced for them for the 1984/5 school year. All of these primers are being revised to reflect the newly standardised orthographies.

GOVERNMENT POLICY

In 1979 an official statement from the Ministry of Education declared:

> ...the language best known and understood by the child on his entry to school is the most effective medium of instruction in the preliminary stages of his school education, and government has therefore decided to use the child's mother-tongue as the medium of instruction in Classes I-III.

As an initial measure, in the areas where these languages are predominant, Themne, Mende, Limba and Krio were introduced in this role as soon as possible, while English was taught only as a subject. From Class IV onwards, the position was reversed, with English taking over as the medium of instruction and the indigenous languages as subjects to be taught up to GCE O-level.

The government sanctioned the use of English for secondary and tertiary education, for official communication and for written correspondence. It also approved of the use of Krio for country-wide inter-tribal communication, as well as the lingua franca role of Themne in the North and some rural parts of the Western Area, and Mende in the South and East. It is also the government's policy that the daily national news as well as government statements and public notices should continue to be broadcast in English, Mende, Themne, Limba and Krio on the national radio and television services and that English should continue to be used for broadcasting the international news and for all state functions.

In keeping with its desire to preserve the country's 'tribal and local community identities,' the government planned to introduce the teaching of the minor languages as subjects in primary schools in the areas where they are spoken, so that their native speakers would be literate in them.

To support its policy, the government vowed to encourage intensive research into all the country's languages at university level. A Department of Linguistics and Sierra Leonean languages at the University was soon to be autonomous, and it was hoped that it would undertake, as a matter of urgency, the production of grammars, dictionaries and other written material, and record folklore of the various tribes in their languages. It could be asked to provide short intensive courses for teachers of these languages at school level.

Regarding adult education, a functional literacy project, initiated by the Ministry of Education in collaboration with The Canadian University Service Overseas (CUSO) has also been going since 1979. The first set of teachers were trained to introduce literacy in the indigenous languages. Some of its earliest students have replaced a few of the teachers and were reported to be proving more effective, since they are more highly motivated. The content of the courses concentrated on:

The Development of a Multi-Lingual Education Policy in Sierra Leone

1. training local farmers in modern farming methods
2. environmental health education, and
3. general education for community living, e.g. writing letters.

The primers written so far were two on agriculture, two on health and two on general education and were in Mende and Themne.

The Ministry official in charge of this project reported that the response has been very encouraging. He hoped that these adults would ultimately be able to use the skills they acquired in learning through their languages to learn English and Arabic (as most of them, are Muslims) and that, if they master the Arabic script, they would be able to use it to write their languages. The project also benefited from help given by the German Adult Education Project in Sierra Leone, the Sierra Leone Adult Education Association and the People's Education Association.

What of the future for Krio in particular, the mother-tongue of this writer? The processes of collection of material, and translation of basic educational material hitherto available only in English, must continue. Without useful, interesting supporting literature at all levels of the learner's reading ability, the whole purpose of achieving practical utilitarian literacy would be defeated. I am planning to work on a pedagogical grammar of Krio that will highlight comparisons and contrasts with English grammar.

There is a need for a Krio-English/English-Krio dictionary simpler than that of Fyle and Jones (1980), and also for a multi- lingual dictionary of Krio-Mende-Themne-Limba to help facilitate multilingual literacy. While a Krio-English dictionary might facilitate the learning of Krio and English, if we intend to spread multilingual literacy, so that individuals are literate both in the mother-tongues and in the country's main lingua franca, then a multilingual dictionary of this kind is essential.

These projects are ambitious and will take years to complete. Many formidable difficulties lie in the way. Chief among these are the difficulty of sustaining the interest of financial sponsors and the difficulty of convincing the conservative public about the role the mother-tongue could play in education in the face of the powerful presence of English. As Dalby (1981) notes:

> African languages will never play their proper role in the life of the country unless they can be seen to facilitate upward mobility and the availability of equal opportunities for the whole population.

My answer to the first problem (that of money) is that for too long the lack of financial sponsorship has been used as an excuse for doing nothing. I believe that, if the work can be done, the money will be found to bring it to the light of day in the form of print. To the second problem I say that what is important is for the people to be made to realise that their languages can be made to complement rather than replace English in the business of nation building and development, and that literacy in whatever language is better than illiteracy.

REFERENCES

Dalby D. (1981) *National Languages in Education.* Paris, UNESCO Restricted Report on Sierra Leone

Fyle C. (1976) 'The Use of the Mother Tongue in Education in Sierra Leone' in Bamgbose A. (ed.) *Mother Tongue Education - The West African Experience.* Paris, UNESCO

Fyle C. and Jones E.D. (1980) *Krio English Dictionary.* Oxford, Oxford University Press

Gbla J.K. (1984) *Past, Present and Future of Mother-Tongue Education.* Co-ordinator's Report, Freetown, Sierra Leone, Pilot Schools Programme

Wyse A.J.G. (1991) *The Krio of Sierra Leone.* Howard University Press, New York

Caribbean Creole: The Politics of Resistance

G L Brandt

This paper will distinguish three forms of Creole: the term 'Caribbean Creole' will be used to refer to Creole as it was and is spoken in the Caribbean; 'British Caribbean Creole' will refer to the form of Creole now spoken in England: 'British Youth Caribbean Creole' will refer to the particular form of the Creole which is spoken by British Black young people.

The term 'British Caribbean Creole?' poses a number of questions, both about the phenomenon itself and the phrase used to describe it. In the 1980s debates on these issues moved into the centre of educational, linguistic and academic as well as community concern. The debates centre on the following issues:

1. What is the best descriptive term to use? Creole? Black English? Or some other alternative?
2. What is the socio-historical context of the language?
3. What is the socio-historical scope of the language? What are its strengths and limitations? Is it indeed a language?
4. How is this language used in contemporary British society?
5. What are its implications for schools, education and other institutions in society.

The term dominant in current usage among British (mainly White) linguists and sociolinguists is the term 'Black English'. This term has crept into English usage mainly through the work of certain American linguists such as Labov (1966). Labov was a forerunner in articulating a case for the 'logic' of non-standard English, later described more precisely as 'Black English'. Thus, Black people who spoke 'standard English' were seen as speaking 'White English' as opposed to the 'Black English' spoken by middle-class Whites or Blacks, in that content was not dictated by unnecessary verbiage. Along with the growing general assertion of many linguists that all languages are equally good, this school affirmed that the language spoken by the majority of Black working class, inner city people was not deficient but different.

The borrowing, however, of the term 'Black English' can be seen as bringing with it a range of problems and issues which are still controversial even in the American context. In the British context the problems are compounded in that, despite similarities, the socio-cultural and linguistic backgrounds of American Blacks and British Blacks differ. Notwithstanding this, British sociolinguists have tended to adopt the term 'Black English' as the apparent basis of their acceptance of notions of equality, which can validate the language forms used by oppressed Blacks.

Initially this term seemed to present a useful and accurate alternative to the previous terms used to describe the language(s) of Caribbean Blacks in this country. This term suggested a considerable shift from previous notions of 'bad English' or 'dialect' (meaning a second-class form when compared to 'Standard English'). Even the term 'Creole', like 'pidgin', had, and still has in the case of the latter, a negative quality to it.

The term 'Creole' is, nonetheless, used technically by linguists as a general term to denote a variety of languages that have evolved through pidginisation in a range of countries. It is important to note that despite many common syntactic and structural features and even shared lexical items, these Creoles remain distinct and discrete languages.

'Creole' has now been re-adopted by Caribbean Blacks as a positive description not given by White non-Creole speakers, but by themselves. Therefore, the adoption of the form is itself an act both of resistance, and assertion out of the simple technical usage of linguists. I shall follow this usage, first to look at the socio-historical background to British Caribbean Creole, which will of necessity mean looking at Caribbean Creole, and secondly at the interaction between language and social policy and education, and finally at the oppositional interface between the use of Black Youth Caribbean Creole and the discourse of schooling.

PATTERNS OF DEVELOPMENT IN CARIBBEAN CREOLE: HISTORICAL AND ETHNOGRAPHIC CONSIDERATIONS

In sociolinguistic discourse the distinction between pidginisation and creolisation tends to be made at the level of development, the range and scope of usage, and the question as to whether the language is the mother tongue of any of the speakers. A pidgin is seen as a contact language, auxiliary to the native languages of its speakers. Hall (1966) argues that:

> For a language to be a true pidgin, two conditions must be met: it's grammatical structure and its vocabulary must be sharply reduced ... and also the resultant language must be native to more than those who speak it.

Hall summarises the distinction between a pidgin and a Creole by stating that 'a Creole language arises when a pidgin becomes the native language of a speech community'. He asserts that creolisation is simply one facet of the broader process of 'nativisation', in which a language is taken over by a group of speakers who previously used another language, so that the new language becomes the native language of the group. Todd (1981) summarises the positions adopted previously by both Hall and DeCamp in this way:

> A Creole arises when a pidgin becomes the mother tongue of a speech community. The simple structure that characterised the pidgin is

carried over into the Creole, but since Creole, as a mother tongue, must be capable of expressing the whole range of human experience, the lexicon is expanded and frequently a more elaborate syntactic system evolves.

This phenomenon, Todd declares is sociological rather than merely linguistic.

Debates over the nature and origin of Creoles have centred on issues such as whether Creoles are indeed languages in their own right, whether they are monogenetic or polygenetic, whether they are comparable with 'standard' languages in their complexity, lexicon, and ability to express abstract thoughts and feelings. What should be the major element in these discussions is at best marginal and at worst negated, that is, the social context of the dynamics of the original creation and regeneration of Creole.

Theories about the origins of Creoles can be placed into two large general categories: monogenetic and polygenetic theories. Monogenetic theories suggest that most 'Atlantic' pidgins and Creoles derive from a common 'genetic' ancestor, while polygenetic theories suggest that the genesis, development and regeneration each pidgin and Creole must be considered as independent. There is of course much variation of perspective within these broad categories. Hall (1966), Cassidy (1961), Valdman (1964), Taylor (1956), De Camp (1971) and Bickerton (1983) contain references to many earlier contributions.

Some of these contributions are only examples of the ways in which racist bias can influence the discussion of languages without a written tradition. But after many years of discussion on whether Creoles are indeed languages at all, or simply broken, bastardised versions of the related dominant language, linguists and sociologists have moved on somewhat.

Todd (1981) tends to the polygenesis school of thought. She argues that:

> ...the syntactic structures of the Creoles are those of the languages that were originally in contact, and though many pidgin features clearly reflect the usages of the contact languages, other features are unique to the pidgin.

Her analysis, asserting the existence of some self-generated features in Creoles, requires us to interpret the development of any language terms of its independent internal dynamic. This paper seeks to link the social context within which Caribbean Creole was created to its regeneration within urban metropolitan settings such as London, especially as it relates to young speakers for whom it may or may not be the first language or the language of the home.

HISTORY AND DEVELOPMENT OF CARIBBEAN CREOLE

Many languages came into contact in the 'New World', even before one takes African languages into account. In Guyana, for example, there was Dutch, French, English, Carib, Mucushi, Wapishana, and Wai Wai, to name but a few.

Slave society, however, was institutionalised after the virtual annihilation of the Indians and the introduction of African slaves. Within this rigid structure was created the language we now refer to as Caribbean Creole.

It is important to note that, contrary to the continued focus by linguists on the 'vertical' relationship between English and the African languages, there needs to be an analysis that examines the 'horizontal' language relations, to provide a more adequate understanding of why the White settlers were in fact trying to learn Creole which the slaves who did not share a common language had developed primarily for communication among themselves.

The closed, hierarchical structure of slave society meant that relationships between slaves and masters were fixed and largely instrumental with a downward bias. Thus limited interaction was necessary or desirable, since the 'masters' were not interested in more than rudimentary exchange, and as the slaves were seen as chattels, they were not expected to do very much responding. When relationships were extended they were usually in the form of brutal rape or sexual servicing.

The slaves, on the other hand, having been brought together from different language groups, and having been intentionally tribally and linguistically separated, needed to create a common language, first as a lingua franca, and second as a language of resistance. This resistance was both symbolic as well as interactional: hence the need for the white 'masters and mistresses' to learn the Creole of the slaves. Caribbean Creole did not simply, if at all, develop from the pidgin used between 'master' and slave, nor was it a substratum development, but a rapidly evolving independent language exclusive to the slaves. The fact that the lexical items were largely European is balanced by the fact that these items were not simple adoptions, but adaptations with profound syntactic and semantic differences.

Each new slave became, ultimately at least, tri-lingual. The first language was the original mother-tongue; the second the African pidgin-becoming-Creole, created for horizontal communication with the people that mattered most to them, members of their underclass. The third language was the pidgin spoken with the white oppressors. It would, therefore, seem that any monogenetic theory which attributed Caribbean Creole simply to a universal and exported Portuguese pidgin, generated and spread by seamen, could be tremendously patronising to Blacks, racist, and a misconstruction of the historical facts.

The dynamic of Creole development within slave society was based on the need of the slaves to communicate with their own underclass, not with the oppressors. In relation to the latter, the interest of the slaves, to understand what the slave 'owners' were saying, would have been more likely to foster an understanding of English than foster Creole. The ultimate liberation of slaves rested not simply with resistance but also to some extent with the degree of infiltration and subversion that could be achieved.

There were specific and appreciable differences between the structures of the 'vertical' and 'horizontal' Creoles. First, socio-sexual relations among the slaves were full, involving courtship, dowry negotiations, marriage or pair-bonding and cultural celebrations and rites at births and deaths, and entertainments and recreation. By contrast, white-black relations were profoundly limited. In addition, it was in the interest of the slaves to have an exclusive language with which to identify, and exclude the oppressor. In advanced and post-slave society, Creole was profoundly influenced by the language of the runaway slaves or maroons, who had maintained even more of their original African languages.

Although, however, there is a clear analytical distinction between 'vertical' and 'horizontal' Creole, many speakers could probably be placed at various points on a broader Creole continuum with varying degrees of mutual intelligibility. This continuum was then evaluated by the dominant British in terms of the proximity of points on it to English. This evaluation subsequently became a parameter as well as an indicator of social status in post-slave society.

The house-slave/field-slave division could be seen as the embryo of this social and linguistic reality. The house-slaves would make use of multilingual skills to their own advantage, using English and 'vertical' Creole with the White 'masters', while maintaining 'horizontal' Creole as a means of communication, identification and solidarity with the field-slaves. For the house-slaves, knowledge of English became an additional tool of resistance, especially for those who went beyond orality to acquire literacy in English.

By the abolition of slavery there had developed a high degree of mutual intelligibility between 'vertical' and 'horizontal' Creole. For some speakers this meant a convergence, although there were also communities in which there was a clear bias in one direction or the other. The addition of indentured labourers speaking other languages such as Hindi or Madeiran Portuguese led to a further enriching of the lexicon of Caribbean Creole.

The abolition of slavery did not, of course, dissolve the hegemony of White rule and a European value-system. The cloak of 'freedom' acted as a legitimating tool for the negation of Caribbean as 'poor' or 'broken' English. The language policy of colonial society was of the colonies being 'English-speaking', even though the majority of the population would have been largely Creole-speaking, with varying degrees of proficiency in the English language. This undervaluing of Creole was compounded in the education system and was more or less a prerequisite for upward mobility. Yet, in apparent contradiction to this, Creole was at the same time not only respectable among its speakers, but had a monopoly on certain cultural and domestic functions such as wakes, Quech Quechs (in Guyana), comic entertainments, jokes and storytelling. Although up and coming local politicians would not make their political appeals totally in Creole, it was a necessary ingredient of any speech.

This is the backdrop to the attitudes and linguistic usage of emigrating Caribbeans, and also to the attitudes and tendencies of policy-makers in Britain.

LANGUAGE AND SOCIAL POLICY IN BRITAIN:
BRITISH YOUTH CARIBBEAN CREOLE AND EDUCATION

Post-war West Indian immigrants arrived in Britain with a varied command of Creole and English. Some were clearly bilingual; others were on a continuum between standard English and Creole. In addition there were West Indians from colonies such as Dominica and St Lucia who spoke a French-related Creole. It did not take long for Caribbean Creole to adapt itself to a British Caribbean Creole with a distinct 'daughter' language, British Youth Caribbean Creole. The question raised of education is: what is the significance and relevance for policy-makers and classroom practitioners of British Caribbean Creole within the educational and language policy debates of the 1980s.

There is now a welcome and growing trend, encouraged by the European Union, to provide for the teaching of mother-tongues in British schools. This has not, however, so far involved Creole, which was not considered seriously in the major DES-funded Linguistic Minorities Project (1983). There is a language hierarchy in England, with English, French and German at the top and the Black languages at the bottom. At the very nadir are those languages without a written tradition.

The current move towards an anti-racist position in educational theory demands that educationalists at all levels must understand the multi-faceted nature of British racism. The linguistic strand is not the least of these facets in importance, in that it is the channel through which knowledge is mediated and transmitted, the major tool of communication, and consequently an important lever of repression, and, by the same token, of resistance. Language forms, like all other socio-cultural phenomena in a racist society are stratified in relations of power and dominance. Therefore, in examining oppositional discourses and Black resistance to racism, it is important to examine the use of language.

Progressive education advocates starting from the child's own experience, language and culture when constructing the learning experience. The question in relation to British Caribbean Creole (especially in the Secondary School) is: Is there an implicit tension between the political purpose and the educational objective? Does the incorporation of British Caribbean Creole into educational practice pose a threat to the strength and quality of Black youth resistance to racism in the British educational system as well as the wider society?

The table on the next page presents a model of the shifting perspectives on the status and scope of Caribbean Creole within social and language policy, and the ways in which these have been translated into practice for Afro-Caribbean Blacks.

The emphases within this model are by no means isolated within particular period, but also represent a range of coexistent, philosophical positions, both within education and the wider community, currently influencing individuals, institutions and society at large. The phases are not self-contained, nor did they begin only when the West Indian immigrants first came to these shores. They are woven into the structure and history of racism in Britain, which is based on the inter-related and overlapping systems exploitation: imperialism, capitalism and racialism.

Imperialism was both ideological and economic. Coupled with the ideological notion of 'natural' military and maritime superiority was the economic intention exploiting third world countries for the benefit of Europe. In return the colonised later received the dubious privilege of the status of 'British subjects'. This appellation later proved to have less of a trade-in value than it seemed at first.

Shifting Perspectives in Education and Language Policy and Practice in Relation to Afro-Caribbean Blacks

Phase and ideological base Features	Post-War Immigration Assimilation	Recolonisation Integration	Neocolonisation Pluralism	Anti-racism Equality & Justice
Status of speakers	Subjects 2nd Class	Immigrant, Culturally deficient 2nd Class	Immi-Brit, Culturally different 2nd Class	Racially dominated (Equality as goal)
Description and status of language	Broken/poor English	\multicolumn{2}{Dialect, Non-Standard English, Black English, London Jamaican etc.}	Creole (British Caribbean Creole)
Under-pinning philosophy	Racial domination by assimilation Deficit	Racial domination via: Tokenism (unacceptable), Difference	Accommodation (acceptable), Opposition	Resistance
Pedagogy	Correction Remedial	Correction Adaptive	Specialised use, Creative writing Progressive	The radical solution Assertive

Racialism provided a basis for the legitimisation of the exploitation of Blacks by Whites. In the job advertisements, the invitation that went out to the Caribbean colonies was with the explicit intention to exploit an old relationship in a new way (cf. Sivanandan 1982). With the economic boom that came after World War II there was a restructurisation of the organisational arrangements of exploitation. A great influx was encouraged to come from the 'British colonies' to take part in labour-intensive production in the 'motherland'.

The great mass of people coming into this country in the '50s and '60s found they had a special place reserved for them in the social/racial division of labour - at the bottom. In addition they had brought with them a heritage of second-class citizenship, and cultural and social subjection, and, despite their designation as 'British citizens', a connotation of 'alienness'. These elements combined to form a more sophisticated form of racism based on a network of racialism, imperialism, capitalism, xenophobia and marginalisation both at the institutional and the personal level. Therefore the alienation of Blacks in the 1950s and early 1960s went hand in hand with an educational policy of 'sink or swim', paying no special attention to the needs of Caribbean immigrants. The language of these immigrants was clearly seen as 'poor' or 'broken' English, which was not too much of a problem while they (the immigrants) could understand the basic instructions of the factory or transport service - basic communication was all that was necessary.

In the 1950s and 1960s state policy moved on towards a notion of assimilation, which was predicated upon a liberal racism which implied that Black people may not be equal to White people, but if they are assimilated, they will not be problems. The focus at this point was already largely cultural: Black people were expected to be assimilated into the fabric of a supposedly monolithic British culture and in all but colour, become White.

During this phase Creole was seen as a bastardised form of English, spoken by people who had come into contact with English in their native countries and had failed to learn it properly. West Indian children in schools were seen as poor speakers of English, and the appropriate pedagogy was seen as one of 'correction'. There was a concomitant devaluation of Creole and an assault on the dignity of its speakers.

Nonetheless, even for those Black People who, as it were, accepted the principle of becoming 'White', the going proved rough. They were discriminated against in employment, housing, and social benefits. Colour, alas, proved to have a continuing importance belying the predictions of the assimilationist thesis. Black people were the victims of both verbal and physical attacks. The policy of assimilation was therefore seen to be inadequate in meeting the needs of Black people or even of keeping the peace.

The policy of integration attempted an alternative route to the maintenance and protection of the social order. Instead of Black individuals being expected to get lost in the social fabric or perish, the presence of the Black community was acknowledged, with a call to it to make an effort to integrate. During this phase Creole began to be given a nominal increase in status. It was now to be seen not as merely broken English, but as a dialect of English like Cockney, or Geordie. Since, however, working class language, like regional dialects, had low status anyway, Black Creole speakers' position was still firmly at the bottom of the social and linguistic hierarchy. The deficit model as a justification of domination was replaced by the tokenism of 'unacceptable difference'. The pedagogic approach to Creole did not change from being corrective, but did make a slight shift in emphasis from a 'remedial' approach to an adjustive one.

It must be emphasised again that these phases are not self-contained or discrete. In 1983 Honey was still propounding the 'handicap' of 'non-standard English speakers', including, of course, Creole speakers.

The premise of the next phase, cultural pluralism is that there are a range of cultures in society which are in themselves homogeneous and have shared interests. These cultures interact with each other by negotiation over points of potential conflict in order to come to a consensus. The state is seen as a neutral arbiter on behalf of the injured party and against the guilty party. Thus class, and indeed race, could be seen as epiphenomenal to the interests of these competing cultural groups.

Yet, throughout the 1970s, cultural pluralism was being articulated in terms of race, which was presented as almost synonymous with culture, conflating the other two main pluralist formulations, 'multi-ethnicity' and 'multi-racialism'. The dominance of culture as a focus has been premised on the idea that it is all-embracing, that the various races of people living in Britain are also ethnic groups, and that each of these ethnic/racial groups has an identifiable culture, representative of the whole group. Thus, in order to bring about positive change, it is argued, only simply needs to promote cultural exchange and understanding. Cultural difference, therefore, becomes the focus of attention as opposed to the real issues of power, domination and oppression - in short, racism.

In relation to Creole this shift is realised in a 'progressive' approach to Creole. There is a nominal acceptance of British Caribbean Creole but mainly for specialised use in creative writing and the like. This means a partial validation of British Caribbean Creole within the discourse of schooling.

BRITISH YOUTH CARIBBEAN CREOLE AND ANTI-RACIST EDUCATION

Mullard (1983) argued that anti-racism has always been a part, or even the essence of Black struggle. We may, therefore, consider the phases so far adumbrated as the mechanisms by which the structures of racism attempt to maintain the racial status quo and the power relations between Black and White.

Anti-racism, however, has recently become more widely acceptable as ideology and as educational principle. The fact that it is being taken on so slowly and so reluctantly is an indication of its oppositional nature. As Mullard argues, compared with the other policies, anti-racist education depends on Black definitions rather than White ones, and is not a device of the oppressors, but an indication of the struggle and resistance of the oppressed. The goal is social and racial justice.

This is the climate within which British Caribbean Creole is emerging as an important issue, indicative of the self-assertion of Black Caribbean peoples. This renewed stand is also partly a response to growing state repression signalled by various events such as the increased and increasing police powers and further refinements of the discriminatory immigration laws. Black youth has become the ready and visible target. But, unlike their parents, they are not simply concerned about fighting for acceptance, but are also fighting for equality and justice. The question then posed for anti-racist pedagogy is: what does the anti-racist teacher do about British Caribbean Creole, or, more precisely, British Youth Caribbean Creole?

Whatever analysis one makes of the linguistic differences between these varieties, the most important function of the use of Creole by Black young people is that of resistance, both symbolic and interactive. This function is independent of other uses of British Youth Caribbean Culture such as to exclude non-speakers etc. As long ago as 1976 the Select Committee on Race relations and Immigration reported:

> It is often pointed out to us that sometimes during their early teens, at secondary school many West Indian pupils who up till then have used the language of the neighbourhood, begin to use Creole dialect ... its use is a deliberate and psychological protest, an assertion identity.

This is an accurate observation, even if one may question the analysis.

The writer's own fieldwork suggests that, like their ancestors, Black young people do in fact use their Creole oppositionally. There are a number of other uses, but the dominant use is for resistance. This is so, whether in the formality of the school, the semi-formality or informality of the youth club, or when 'hanging out'. This use of Creole is not restricted to youths, but is marked and more noticeable since, in the main, the language in which they principally function is English.

At one level there is, therefore, a strong case to be made for the incorporation of Caribbean Creole, as the first language of young Black people of Caribbean origin, into the discourse of schooling. This argument would be based on the fundamental educational principle that the teacher should start from the pupil's own experience. This experience should be validated, legitimated, and incorporated into the learning situation as 'really useful knowledge', in harmony with the principle of moving from the known to the unknown, from the specific to the general, from the particular to the universal. This is also in accord with current linguistic thinking, that it is beneficial to children to become proficient in their mother-tongues if they are later to acquire a second or third language.

When one views Creole in this context, however, given the foregoing discussion a fundamental tension arises, especially if one is to accept that schooling also has a repressive function to maintain and reproduce the social, racial and sexual status quo. Thus what could on one hand be interpreted as a progressive and educationally sound thing to do, could prove to be a disservice to Black youth and a retrograde step in co-opting, through schooling, the language that had been used as a tool and symbol of resistance.

REFERENCES

Bickerton D. (1983) 'Creole Languages', *Scientific American*, July, p.108

Cassidy F.G. (1961) *Jamaica Talk: Three Hundred Years of the English Language in Jamaica*. Macmillan, London

DeCamp D. (1971) 'The Study of Pidgin and Creole Languages' in Hymes D. (ed.) *Pidginization and Creolization of Languages*. Cambridge University Press, Cambridge

Hall R. (1966) *Pidgin and Creole Languages*. Cornell University Press, Ithaca

Honey J. (1983) *The Language Trap: Race, Class and the 'Standard English' Issue in British Schools*. National Council for Educational Standards, London

Labov W. (1966) *Social Stratification of English in New York City*. Centre for Applied Linguistics, Washington DC

Linguistic Minorities Project (1983) *Linguistic Minorities in England - A Report for the DES*. University of London Institute of Education, London

Mullard C. (1983) 'Anti-Racist Education: A Theoretical Basis', *Journal of the National Association for Multicultural Education*

Select Committee on Race Relations and Immigration (1976) *Enquiry into the West Indian Community*. HMSO, London

Sivanandan A. (1982) *A Different Hunger*. Pluto Press, London

Taylor D. (1956) 'Language Contacts in the West Indies', *Word*, 12, pp.173-79

Todd L. (1981) *Pidgins and Creoles*. Routledge and Kegan Paul, London

Valdman A. (1964) 'Du Creole à Francais en Haiti', *Linguistics*, 8, p.84

CONCLUSION

Conclusion: What Is To Be Done?

Sponsored by the old Greater London Council, work on this book began in the golden afterglow of the progressivism of the 1960s and the 1970s when we still believed that Thatcher's reactionary policies were a mere interruption of the path toward that mutual understanding of peoples which would simply dissolve the pathologies of racism and ethnic inequalities. Disillusion was to follow - but worse than that - even the resultant hard-won realism about the effects of racism in education appeared to evaporate under a new Labour Government in 1997. They picked up with enthusiasm the anti-racist rhetoric which John Major had forced on a reluctant Conservative administration; but the new government showed even less respect for the value of cultural difference than the old; in practice the operation of their 'Standards Fund' has come to look more and more like the deficit philosophy, which operated even before the ideological victory of multiculturalism, as described by Brandt in this volume.

In 1984, at the Woolwich conference, on the initiative of the 'Shaktee' Brent Asian collective, the following resolutions were passed without dissent:

1. *That all education authorities, local authorities and county councils:*
   a) adopt a policy of multi-lingualism and multi-literacy for staff, students and administrators. Such a policy should be not only be implemented in schools, but throughout all authorities and their many departments.
   b) adopt a comprehensive policy on anti-racist education, which should be rigorously implemented and constantly monitored.
2. *That more authentic Romani speakers from different groups should be represented at future workshops and language sessions at which recommendations about orthography and standardization of Romanes are made.*
3. *That more serious consideration should be given to the linguistic and educational needs of children in pre-school educational facilities.*
4. *That Caribbean Creole languages should be accorded the status of minority languages within the United Kingdom.*
5. *That, in order to ensure that academic research is not used against the interests of those researched, individuals embarking on researching Caribbean Creoles should:*
   a) have close consultation with members of the Black communities concerned;
   b) provide those members with clearly defined aims and objectives and make explicit the purpose and consequent utility of such research to the researched;

c) indicate in any educational research how the findings could be implemented effectively in the classroom.
6. That the term Creole be used to refer to the languages of Caribbean peoples.
7. That more research is needed into the African 'roots' of Caribbean Creoles.

These resolutions exemplified multilingual idealism, pointing forward to an anti-racist approach that it was hoped would move far beyond the vapid multiculturalism of the day. Those who framed them did not realise that their anti-racist rhetoric could be appropriated for a resurgent monoculturalism which would perpetuate the inequalities that have come to be known as institutional racism in Britain, while in other countries resentment at the wrongs done to 'one's own people' has boiled over into full-blooded ethnic cleansing.

For a while the ideas of this book seemed to make some progress against the tide. In Britain, the term 'Creole' gained some currency (Dalphinis 1986a). In the former Yugoslavia in 1986 the government threw its weight behind the creation of a Romani literary language at a conference in the beautiful winter Olympic city of Sarajevo (Shipka 1989). We hoped this policy would have a ripple effect on other governments in the region; instead, as Sarajevo burned, it became the multicultural figleaf of Serbia's moral bankruptcy, and surviving Roma have been forced out of Bosnia and Kosovo, just as half a century earlier they were murderously ethnically cleansed from Croatia by the Nazi-sponsored Ustashe, who, incredibly, are now again part of the Croatian government. Indeed Romani asylum-seekers from the violent racist nationalism spreading throughout Eastern Europe have come to constitute the newest demonised immigrant scapegoats in Western Europe and North America.

In Sierra Leone too, the optimism portrayed in Freddie Jones' paper in this volume has been washed away by a tide of war. What remains of the work he details? We wish we could say.

In Britain many teachers felt that the Swann Report *Education for All*, (1985) marked a genuine move toward anti-racism. They were not entirely wrong. The Committee of Inquiry into the Education of Children from Ethnic Minority Groups was set up by the Callaghan government in 1979 under the chairmanship of Anthony Rampton on the assumption that children from ethnic minorities needed some special help in order that their performance in schools should catch up with those of the British. The committee's enquiries, however, even after Mrs Thatcher had replace Mr Rampton by the altogether more amenable Lord Swann, failed to sustain the thesis that the supposed lack of success was due to some deficit in the ethnic minority children. Indeed, they found no evidence that there was a real failure in general by Black and Asian pupils to achieve the same averages as others; the slightly lower than average achievements by Afro-Caribbean pupils would have been entirely accounted for by the social class profile of this section of the immigrant population, had the Thatcher government permitted its statisticians to make social class comparisons.

Conclusion

Let us be clear about this: the best informed analysis of the statistics of the Swann Report, so far from demonstrating the deficit both Callaghan and Thatcher assumed to exist, suggests that, comparing like with like, within each income-group of parents, children from New Commonwealth Immigrant communities were probably getting slightly better results in school than white children (Acton 1986). That did not mean, however, that there was no racism in schools. The Swann report cited horrendous statements by teachers, as well as pupils to show that ethnic minority achievement occurred in spite of the attitudes in schools - which were often worse in small towns than large cities. And, of course, getting good GCSEs and A-levels was no guarantee that Black children would be given an equal chance with other British children in the labour market. The Swann Report therefore declared against the idea of instituting special educational programmes for ethnic minorities; the problem was not the ethnic minorities themselves, but racism, and what was therefore required was an inclusive, anti-racist 'Education for All' - the slogan adopted as the eventual title of the Report.

So far, so good. The problem, however, is to determine the content of anti-racism. It is easy enough to say what anti-racism is against; it requires a great deal more hard painstaking curriculum development to give it something to be for. The Swann Report is a huge 871-page text compiled on three sometimes contradictory levels. The lowest level of the structure consists of appendices which comprise original research reports by academics, some of which are truly scholarly. The main part of the edifice is the carefully constructed body of the report, which was adjusted by the committee to be acceptable to all of them, and contains a number of vaguenesses, ambiguities and gaps. The most public and visible section of the whole thing, however, was the summary by Lord Swann, which, although he endorses the overall anti-racist message, shows that the poor man clearly failed to understand many of the statistics of his own report, most notably on the subject of IQ tests.

Acton (1986) argued therefore that its inadequacies made the Swann Report profoundly damaging to the project of multilingualism. Despite its self-proclaimed anti-racism it continued to use confused racist categories to classify ethnic groups. Although the main conclusion of the report was that we ought to improve schools to bring out the best in all their pupils by changing the attitudes of 'the majority', the ethnic character of this 'majority' was never defined, and this is perhaps the key to the linguistic mystification in the report. The chief actor on the British ethnic scene was never mentioned. The English ethnic group, so powerful and widespread, is invisible. There was only one reference to the existence of a specific English culture, when the word 'Anglo-centric' is used on p.760. Replacing the English where some named reference to the majority is inescapable was an imperialist concept invented in the 18th century, 'the British'. This was used with a systematic ambiguity. We all have rights because we are all British and not foreigners. Some of us are Welsh British, some of us are Pakistani British - and on the other hand some of us are just British and normal.

'English' thus appeared in the report only as the name of a language, which was thus given some spurious universality. Making English the sole language of instruction was thus seen not in its true light as the privileging of the literary and administrative standard of an ethnic group numbering 30-35 million against the languages of the other 20 million, but rather as the impartial property of everyone, a supposed 'unifying factor'! So, despite some fine words about the importance of modern language teaching, the monolingualism of the English (many of whom fail even to master their own literary standard) was implicitly seen as normal, rather than the pathological product of bad language teaching.

Revealingly, the report asserted (p.388) that 'English as a Second Language Teaching' (E2L) must not be confused with 'Teaching English as a Foreign Language' (EFL) since E2L must teach 'the national language of this country to children who will subsequently have to function in this language throughout their educational experience and their adult lives.' Of course E2L must be effective - but what a terrible judgment on foreign language teaching! Clearly the writers do not believe that foreign language teaching can ever lead to a functional knowledge of a language - which makes their bland assurances elsewhere about the need for Asian languages to come into the modern languages curriculum rather worthless.

Given the prejudices in the report, its opposition even to bilingual education was inevitable. In its monolingual blindness, it saw functional mastery of other languages to the point where they can become languages of instruction as detracting from rather than adding to the mastery of English. What then of Wales, where despite the action of the spiritual ancestors of Swann in keeping Welsh out of schools for decades, it is now an established reality, with Welsh bilingual children actually doing better than average at English? Not the same thing at all, said the report, because Welsh is a *national* language 'of the country and as such lies at the heart of its culture and traditions'. Presumably British Punjabi culture is to have a transplanted English heart. Or perhaps the Welsh are honorary foreigners.

Despite Swann's assertion that evidence from most ethnic groups, that separate community language classes, such as Saturday schools, though marvellous meeting places, were not very effective at teaching languages, the report welcomed LEA support for them (in utter contrast to its anti-separatist position on E2L) but it did not welcome those languages into the primary school except as things for pupils to be 'aware of'. The report claimed this would be seen as 'respect' for the language by ethnic minority pupils. It said it was unconvinced by evidence that bilingual education or mother-tongue maintenance assists the usage of English. It did not say why it was unconvinced, except of course that such evidence would make its prejudices untenable.

On the other hand, it was fine, said the report, for 'community languages' to be included in the modern languages curriculum of secondary schools (but we've seen how little it thought of the capabilities of that). It did not stop to ask the obvious question, how it is that pupils who have been told 'English only' throughout their primary school career, and perhaps have had their own language or 'dialect' repressed, are going to react to being told at the age of 12 that it is after all a good and sensible idea to learn some other language? Is it surprising that so few of them do ?

'Britain', the non-ethnic state, was invested with an idealised, imaginary history. For example, Lord Swann wrote 'Over the centuries Britain has evolved durable institutions and traditions, embodying a humane and tolerant philosophy. These have been taken as models by many nations, and they were, I believe, an important attraction to many of the ethnic minority citizens who came to this country.'

How can one react dispassionately to such rubbish? To which centuries out of the last five of our glorious history is he referring ? In the first two Britain had laws of genocide and expulsion or slavery against Gypsies, Jews and Blacks; and as these fell into abeyance, she embarked on a systematic campaign of conquest, rapine and exploitation against the peoples of a quarter of the globe, even claiming to wipe out one nation, the Tasmanians, completely. Gypsies continue to be hunted from one roadside to the next. 'Humane and tolerant philosophy!' Such words are an insult in a text which purports to deal seriously with the conditions of Gypsies and Black people in Britain.

In the face of such a resolute incapacity for self-criticism, it is perhaps not surprising that linguistic minority politics have shrunk from challenging the dominant ideology head-on. Nonetheless the inability of the English to speak other languages remains a problem in the real world. The last Conservative government reacted by instituting its policy of specialist language secondary schools. The first of these, the Anglo-European school in Ingatestone, Essex, remains a comprehensive, but gives all its pupils the chance to learn more languages and travel widely. It has welcomed many ethnic minorities, including Gypsies. It remains, however, a lone outpost of multi-lingualism in a sea of ethnocentrism, a wonderful experiment that diverts attention from the philistinism elsewhere.

The word 'bilingualism' remains dominant. As we noted in our preface, even those professionals who were actually at our conference have had to adopt a policy of broadening the use of the word 'bilingualism' rather than abandoning it. For example, 'within the terminology of the Inner London Education Authority and Haringey, 'bilingualism' means regularly to use more than one language, without reference to the level of fluency.' (Dalphinis 1987). This new approach challenged the view of bilingualism as a kind of mental handicap, as the colonising nations thought in the 1930s, and asserted that it is a positive resource which enhances intellectual development. This was backed by empirical research (Dulay, Burt and Krashen 1982, Hakuta 1986), and had an effect, within a general context of policy against discrimination by race, class or gender, on the policy of at least some Local Education Authorities with substantial numbers of pupils who have a home language other than English. In the 1990s, in some circles at least, it has become the conventional wisdom (Edwards and Alladina 1991).

Thus, for example, in the 'Education Service Policy Statement on Bilingualism' (1985, cited in Dalphinis 1987) of the London Borough of Haringey (in which the Linguistic Minorities project identified the presence of

87 languages in 1981), we find both 'bilingualism' as an emphasis on the needs of those whose home language is not English and 'multilingualism', an emphasis on the need for everyone for more than one language:

> ' As Haringey is a multilingual borough, all members of the community should be able to perceive that every level of the Education Service recognizes the importance and value of the languages spoken within borough boundaries.
>
> All educational establishments must seek to ensure that no pupil/member of the community is placed at a disadvantage or denied access to services or opportunities through disregard of his/her language background and that all aspects of provision reflect the needs of a linguistically diverse population.
>
> The Education Service must play its part in assisting all members of the community to maintain and develop their knowledge of written/oral fluency in the languages of their home and community and wherever possible this should involve specialist teaching.
>
> Members of the community must be given the opportunity to develop their awareness of other languages and to become fluent in more than one language.......'

Professional linguists normally write for each other in a very dry and unornamented style; it is interesting to see how they are forced into prolixity when they try to sell their ideas in the market place of politics. In this case a deft use of the leaden jargon of educational theory has been used to facilitate a slide from a policy whose origins lie in the perception of 'immigrants' as an 'educational problem' to a policy of linguistic broadening for everyone.

It is important to realise, however, that the opposite may occur. Beauchamp (1985) shows that although the arguments for bilingual education are couched in terms of 'fundamentally redressing political and economic power between the haves and have-nots', the reality is 'that the minority group learns the dominant's group's language of economic and political power within the society.'

The development of 'Communicative Language Theory' (Dalphinis 1986b) provided a possible intellectual underpinning for institutional moves in education from strategies of 'containment of the problem of bilingualism' to positive and transformative strategies aiming at the interactive use of language. These moves began sometimes to take place in the late 1980s and early 1990s as part of the overall anti-racist and anti-sexist strategy in schools and Further Education Colleges. Dalphinis (1987) urged teachers to understand the way in which the racist bias of English is codified for the bilingual student by vocabulary items (like *black*mail), by dismissive attitudes to foreign languages, and the mocking of the accents of second language speakers of English. Space had to be created for pupils and students to identify racism and its legacies and to develop coping strategies, to initiate from their own standpoint discussions of cultural and language differences. Teachers should both make sure that their own use of English is clear and seize every opportunity to let students bring their own language into the institution, as for example by posters or the translation of advertisements.

Some institutions began to create their own programmes and timetables for change after reviewing teaching materials to ensure they reflected our multi-ethnic society in illustrations and in exemplification. They identified needs for new materials, curriculum development, in-service training and changes needed in examination syllabi; but although both education authorities and commercial publishers have begun to produce such materials, it proved a slow, resource-hungry business.

A group of students in the Further Education (and sometimes the school) system for whom this is particularly important are refugees. Their experience can be even more discouraging if not handled from a positive perception of the bilingual student. Those who have escaped war, famine and political conflict are often traumatised by their experiences. Learning of the new language and environment must take place within a positive perception of the refugee students' own store of experience and learning in their own language. Negative views of their language will only reinforce the kinds of human experience the refugee has fled from.

Until 1989 the 'Iron Curtain' curtailed the number of refugees in Western Europe, while the 'Cold War' legitimated the status of the few who left Eastern Europe. Since then, however, the restraint on racist violence that was placed by the former state socialist governments has progressively disappeared, leading to substantial outflows of refugees, especially Roma, or Gypsies. Conservative ministers, led by Michael Howard, himself the son of refugees, fulminated against these new arrivals, whom they accused, in the defiance of the evidence, of being just 'economic refugees'. Mere fulmination, however, was hardly going to keep out those fleeing East European skinhead violence and robbery, or who had seen their children kicked out of school just for being dark-skinned. A Labour Government came in, but the new Home Secretary, Jack Straw, backed up by a junior minister, Mike O'Brien who openly urged racial discrimination against Roma, and implemented even more punitive measures against asylum-seekers, interning the adult men, and leaving their families congregated together in relatively deprived areas, where specialist liaison teachers with ethnic minorities and Gypsies were left to arrange education for the families with precious little by way of extra resources.

The new government proclaimed its new policy of 'inclusion'; but balanced it with a robust policy of exclusion against those, whether workshy scroungers, rowdy youths, troublesome tenants or 'bogus' asylum-seekers who were to be seen as sabotaging the new social contract. The emphasis was to be on obligations as well as rights; and nowhere would the obligation be pressed more than the obligation to gain training or education for the labour market - which would enable minorities, whether ethnic groups or single parents to be reincluded in society. The patient work that had been built up since the Swann

Report in bringing minority cultures into schools was dismissed as inadequate because of the continuing inequality of ethnic groups in the labour market. Going right back to the assumptions of the Callaghan government, the Blair government assumed the answer to this was to raise the standards of ethnic minority achievement in school, and renamed the grant-aid for ethnic minority education, the 'Standards Fund'.

The 'deficit theory' was back with a vengeance. The new policy was not about bringing minority cultures into the curriculum - that had already supposedly been done in the new, ever more inflexible national curriculum, the government's gold standard which could not be improved upon (except of course in the private schools exempt from it to which the rich and powerful continued to send their children.). The new policy was about the ethnic minorities themselves shaping up and raising their standards. Ethnic minorities had to come into the mainstream - and therefore, instead of funds going to multicultural teams who would help schools to welcome ethnic minorities, the money should go to schools themselves, through devolved budgets, to make sure members of ethnic minorities raised their attendances and examination results. Meanwhile there has been a steady drizzle of redundancy of multicultural specialists, many from ethnic minorities themselves.

The new policy of the government, backed up by OFSTED, was partly fuelled by its misreading of the Swann Report, following Swann himself, as demonstrating 'ethnic minority under-achievement'. Taking this as a fact, OFSTED set out to look at low-attaining ethnic minority pupils to see why they were doing so badly. It never thought to do the opposite, to seek out high-attaining ethnic minority pupils and ask what they might be doing right. The final report (OFSTED 1999) showed how the OFSTED 'research' had selected in a wholly non-random way just 48 schools, mainly in poor, deprived areas, with around double the national average getting free school meals. They then found - what a surprise! - that Bangladeshi, Gypsy and Black Caribbean in those of these schools that had bothered to keep records that OFSTED itself characterises as 'fragmentary', were doing less well than the average. They did not target other ethnic groups whose achievement they presumed to be satisfactory. In fact they did not risk examining any statistics which might contradict their thesis.

Such research does not of course tell us anything about ethnicity, because like was not compared with like. All it tells us is that children in economically deprived areas tend to do less well in school than the average. Such a failure to understand the nature of statistical reasoning is depressing. This report contained no new statistics of its own, and yet, disgracefully, it was spun by government spin doctors and so widely reported in the press as evidence of worsening *general* ethnic minority under-achievement in schools.

The depressing emphasis on the normalisation of ethnic communities is perhaps at its most acute in considering Traveller children. An earlier report, (OFSTED 1996), although admitting 'significant and unexplained underachievement' declared that 'the advancements made in the provision of Traveller children are significant and demonstrate the success of the central funding programme.' The 1999 report, however, ignores the fact that Traveller children had made 30 years of progress since the 1960s when the community had been 90% illiterate (Liégeois, 1998, pp.74-5). It simply identifies 'Gypsy Traveller pupils' as 'the group most at risk in the education system', and states that 'at the point of transfer to secondary schools, Gypsy Traveller attainment is well below school and national averages' and posits that 'raising the expectations of Gypsy Traveller pupils among secondary school teachers is probably the most urgent priority' in the context of school initiatives to raise attainment.'

Following this, during the summer of 1999, the Department for Education and Employment made two decisions. Again ignoring the accumulated expertise of teachers, it placed a six-month contract with researchers to look at Traveller under-attainment (again ignoring the study of Traveller achievers). And in the 1999 Standards Fund Circular (16/99), it amalgamated the previously separately administered grant aid for Traveller education (reducing its level from 65% to 57% of expenditure along the way) with that for other ethnic minorities, recommending that, like them, as much of the grant be devolved to schools as possible. In other words, instead of grant-aid being made to Traveller Education Services and other multicultural specialists to undertake practical programmes for ethnic minorities, for which they have to report each year, in future schools will receive the money just for having ethnic minorities on their rolls. And those who study the Romani language remain as marginalised in academic life as Gypsies in society (c.f. Grant 1998).

All of this is being done in the name of a proclaimed anti-racism which allegedly will not tolerate differences of outcome for different ethnic groups. One must however, question the government's understanding of what, exactly racism is. The Labour party has certainly pursued vigorous ethnic minority politics, which has resulted in its taking the majority of ethnic minority votes, and most ethnic minority MPs belonging to them. The watchword of this politics has been the term 'institutional racism' a concept lifted from the anti-racist critique of multiculturalism during the 1980s. The 1980s analysis of 'institutional racism' pointed out that mere respect for cultural difference did nothing to counter disadvantage or inequality of power and wealth. The fact there were no rules saying Black people could not become barristers or judges did not negate the fact than only a tiny minority could afford the training, or make their way through the personal networks. Equal opportunities exist only when the rules are put in place to stop the people at the top helping their own friends unfairly, and when having the right name, the right language, the right accent, the right gender, the right school background do not put you two steps ahead of the rest. This can only truly happen, however, when there is a redistribution of resources which enables the poor to catch up.

The Labour government, despite eschewing redistribution of wealth, has continued to proclaim its opposition to 'institutional racism'. For example, it has strongly endorsed the conclusion of the Macpherson report that the failure of the investigation of the murder of Stephen Lawrence can be attributed to institutional racism in the Metropolitan Police Force. This is a rather strange analysis. We would not deny for one moment that institutional racism exists in the Met: there is too much testimony from Black and Asian police officers to doubt it, but the failure to catch Stephen Lawrence's murderers is down to the assumption of the investigators that the murder must be related to Black drug-trading, with the consequent abusive treatment of Black witnesses and failure to collect evidence about the most obvious suspects. Such actions are not really *institutional* racism: they are plain old-fashioned *individual* racism on the part of the officers involved (albeit possibly compounded by general incompetence and maybe even corruption.) To speak of institutional racism as though it primarily referred to 'canteen culture' and the psychopathology or discriminatory actions of individual police officers - or fire officers, or teachers or foremen at Fords - has actually served to divert attention from the structural factors identified by the academic analysis of institutional racism, of which language and its use remain of the utmost significance. Ethnic identity at work is established and contested through language (Day 1998) yet OFSTED and the DfEE assume that ethnic inequality at work could be cured by better school attendance and examination results.

In fact, if we look at the three particular ethnic minorities targeted by the 1999 OFSTED Report, the Bangladeshi, Gypsy and Black Caribbean communities, we can observe that each contains a majority of speakers of stigmatised languages without an established written tradition: Sylheti, Anglo-Romani, and Jamaican, all of which are still treated as 'broken languages' or 'dialects' by speakers of literary dialects such as Bengali, standard English, or even the new Romani literateurs of Eastern Europe.

Without recognising, without even mentioning, these languages, the 1999 OFSTED Report declares 'teaching pupils to become literate in English should be given the highest priority'. Presumably, after the Standards Fund Circular has been implemented, this will be even more likely than at present to be attempted by monolingual English teachers with no training in linguistics. The likely cause of problems faced by these communities in schools is thus presented as though it were the solution.

To sum up, although it was widely bruited as doing so, the 1999 OFSTED Report presents no evidence whatever that there is any general problem of ethnic minority underachievement in schools. All it suggests is that schools in poor areas do less well. Ethnic minorities are not actually to blame for this. Their problem is individual and institutional racism. So far from mounting an attack on institutional racism, this OFSTED Report, and the DfEE policies that have followed in its wake are prime examples of it. The need for speakers of disadvantaged and oppressed languages to organise, to carry out their own intellectual groundwork, and face down their oppressors is as urgent as ever.

Conclusion

REFERENCES

Acton T. (1986) 'Reacting to Swann' in *The Swann Report and Travellers, Report of an ACERT/NGEC Conference*. University of London Institute of Education, London

Ager D.E. (1997) *Language Policy in Britain and France: The Processes of Policy*. Cassell, London

Antaki C. and Widdicombe S. (1998) *Identities in Talk*. Sage, London

Beauchamp E.R. (1985) *Bilingual Education Policy: An International Perspective*. Phi Delta Kappa Educational Foundation, Bloomington Indiana

Dalphinis M. (1986a) 'French Creoles in the Caribbean and Britain' in Sutcliffe and Wong

Dalphinis M. (1986b) 'Language and Communication: Problems and Resolutions of the Creole Question within the British Education System' in Saakana and Pearce

Dalphinis M (1987) 'Bilingualism, Dialect and Equal Opportunities in Education', *Language Issues (The Journal of the National Association for Teaching English as a Second Language to Adults)*, 1(3).

Day D. (1998) 'Being Ascribed and Resisting: Ethnic Group Membership at Work' in Antaki and Widdicombe

Dulay H.C., Burt M., and Krashen S. (1982) *Language Two*. Oxford University Press, Oxford

Edwards V. and Alladina S. (eds.) (1991) *Multilingualism in the British Isles*. Longman, London and New York

Grant A.P. (1998) 'On the Marginalisation of Romani Linguistics in Britain and America, 1920 -1945'. Paper to the 4th International Conference on Romani Sociolinguistics, University of Manchester, September.

Hakuta K. (1986) *Mirror of Language: The Debate on Bilingualism*. Harper and Rowe, New York

Liégeois, J-P. (1998) *School Provision for Ethnic Minorities: the Gypsy Paradigm*. 2nd Edition. University of Hertfordshire Press, Hatfield

OFSTED (1996) *The Education of Travelling Children*. OFSTED, London

OFSTED (1999) *Raising the Attainment of Ethnic Minority Pupils: School and Local Education Authority Responses*. OFSTED, London

Saakana A.S, and Pearse A. (eds.) (1986) *Towards the Decolonisation of the British Educational System*. Frontline/Karnak, London

Shipka M. (1989) *Medunarodni Nauchni Skup - Jezik i Kultura Romani - International Symposium on Romani Language and Culture*. Institut za Prouchavanje Nacionalnih Odnos, Sarajevo

Smithers R. (1999) 'Woodhead Falls a Fraction Short', *The Guardian*, Friday 15 October, p.2

Sutcliff D. and Wong A. (1986) *The Language of the Black Experience*. Basil Blackwell, Oxford

Swann Lord, Chairman, (l985) *Education for All The Report of the Committee of Inquiry into the Education of Children from Ethnic Minority Groups*. HMSO Cmd 9453, London

Notes on Contributors

Dr. Thomas Acton is Professor of Romani Studies, Greenwich University. He has written or edited several books on or for Gypsies. He ran the first Gypsy Council caravan summer school for Gypsy children in East London in 1967.

Safder Alladina moved from work as an Advisor for Multicultural Education, Berkshire to academic research in Europe and North America.

Alice Binchy took a PhD in 1994 on the Irish Travellers and their language at Somerville College, Oxford and is researching on racism against Travellers and refugees in Tallaght, Dublin.

Godfrey Brandt has worked at London University Institute of Education, the Arts Council, and the Commonwealth Institute.

Jessica Burke was a Research Officer, Institute of Education, University of London and Chair of the Caribbean Communications Project.

Yvonne Colleymore was the founder of Arawidi Books, which specialises in texts for Caribbean children. She was a member of the Rampton/Swann Committee, a founder of the Caribbean Communications Project and has published several books on Home Economics and Nutrition. She has taught in both schools and colleges.

Hugh Dale is a Senior Lecturer in Sociology, Brixton College, and one of the founders of the Caribbean Communications Project.

Dr. Morgan Dalphinis is Executive Manager, Academic Development, City College, Birmingham. He has worked as an Inspector, Senior Inspector and Chief Inspector in Haringey, Southwark and Hackney LEAs and has also taught in schools, Adult Education and Further Education and lectured at the University of Maiduguri, Nigeria. He has published both academic studies on Creole languages and poetry in St. Lucian Patwa.

Hubert Devonish is a lecturer in Linguistics and English, University of the West Indies. He is heavily involved in the attempt to create a literary Creole in Guyana.

Ivy Devonish is a teacher in London, and was a tutor with the Caribbean Communications Project.

Notes on Contributors

Dr. Paul Ellingworth is Translation Consultant, United Bible Societies and an honorary Professor at The University of Aberdeen.

Dr. Victor Friedman is a full Professor of Slavic Languages, University of Chicago.

Dr. Ian Hancock is a full Professor of Linguistics, University of Texas at Austin and is joint delegate from the World Romani Congress to the United Nations. He has published many papers and books on Creole languages and on Gypsies.

Herbert Heuss works for the Prajktbüro zur Förderung von Roma-Initiativen, Eppelheim, West Germany.

Dr. Frederick Jones moved from the University of Sierra Leone to the Technische Universität, Berlin, where he lectured on Creole languages. Currently he is Head of English and Communications at St Augustine's College, Raleigh, North Carolina.

Dr. Donald Kenrick worked in Adult and Community Education, Hackney. He has written or edited several books on Gypsies and Languages.

Dr. Ron Kephart gained his PhD in Anthropology from the University of Florida, and works in the area of anthropological linguistics. He has assisted in the preparation of Creole educational materials in Carriacou.

Phyllis Knight was the Project Co-ordinator for the Caribbean Communications Project.

Dr. Stephen Levinsohn is an International Linguistics Consultant with the Summer Institute of Linguistics, and has worked on Inga mother-tongue teaching programme in primary schools in Colombia.

Jane Mace works in the Centre for Continuing Education and Development, South Bank University.

Evangelos Marselos worked in Adult Education with Gypsies in Athens before gaining a state research grant to prepare a dictionary of Romanes as a doctoral dissertation.

Ulrich Müller works in Adult Education, Bremen, West Germany.

Hasina Nowaz used to be a teacher at the Centre for Bilingualism, London Borough of Haringey, who was seconded to work on the EEC Mother-Tongue Project on materials in Bengali.

Dr. Marion Papenbrok has carried out research on the role of Cultural Centres for Gypsies, West Germany.

Eva Pongracz lectures in Art Education, University of Pécs, Hungary.

Dr. Maria Roussou was a Lecturer in Cypriot Studies, University of Birmingham with special interests in oral history and sociolinguistics. She was formerly a teacher and seconded to work on the EEC Mother-Tongue Project on materials in Greek.

Dr. Mark Sebba has moved from research at York University to freelance film and video production, and from that to teach Linguistics at the University of Lancaster

György Szabo works in Adult Education in Bremen, West Germany.

Dr. Laszlo Szego, a Romani intellectual, worked in the State Publishing house in Budapest, Hungary. He has edited anthologies of papers on Gypsies.

Dr. Elemer Várnagy has been involved for many years in the education of Boyash children. He has been Professor of Romani Studies at Zsámbek High School since 1994. Previously he was for many years a lecturer in education at the University of Pécs.

Dr. John C. Wells is a Lecturer in Phonetics, University College, University of London.

Eglon Whittingham has been a teacher and teacher-trainer in Jamaica. He now works as a lecturer and researcher for Caribbean House and Southlands College.

Dimila Yekwai was a lecturer at the Industrial Language Training Centre, Finsbury Park, North London and was formerly in publishing.

Jane Dick Zatta is a teacher, who has devoted a great deal of time to assisting the Slovene Rom in Italy develop educational materials in their own Romanes for use in schools; she is now Professor, Department of English Language and Literature, Southern Illinois University.

A DISCLAIMER

None of the opinions expressed in this book should be taken to represent the policies or views of any of the past or present, or indeed future, employers of any of the writers or editors.

www.ingramcontent.com/pod-product-compliance
Lightning Source LLC
Chambersburg PA
CBHW070650120526
44590CB00013BA/906